SOME CLASSIC CONTRIBUTIONS TO PROFESSIONAL MANAGING

Volume II

HISTORICAL PERSPECTIVES

ACKNOWLEDGMENTS

The General Electric Company wishes to express its thanks to the following persons, institutions and publishing companies for permission to reproduce the material used in this book:

AMERICAN MANAGEMENT ASSOCIATION,
New York, New York;

AMERICAN SOCIETY OF MECHANICAL ENGINEERS,
New York, New York;

AMOS TUCK SCHOOL OF ADMINISTRATION AND FINANCE,
Dartmouth College, Hanover, New Hampshire;

LAWRENCE A. APPLEY;

EFFICIENCY SOCIETY,
New York, New York;

INSTITUTE OF MANAGEMENT SCIENCES,
Philadelphia, Pennsylvania;

LILLIAN GILBRETH;

HARPER AND BROS. PUBLISHING COMPANY,
New York, New York;

MRS. HARRY ARTHUR HOPF;

RICHARD D. IRWIN, INC. PUBLISHING COMPANY,
Homewood, Illinois;

LIONEL NAUM;

ERWIN H. SCHELL;

HAROLD F. SMIDDY;

LYNDALL URWICK.

CONTENTS

VOLUME II: HISTORICAL PERSPECTIVES

CONTENTS

The Present State of the Art of Industrial Management*

1912

This first "Management Progress Report" was presented by a committee of which James M. Dodge was chairman and L. P. Alford, secretary. It was the forerunner of similar reports each ten years since 1912.

It presents what was being done, the views of the advocates and opponents of Scientific Management and the important emphases. These include not only techniques of production, but also of human relations.

The minority report stresses the art of Managing as being more important than the science.

Excerpts appropriate to the subject have been made from the Discussions which followed the presentation of this and the subsequent reports included in this volume.

* "The Present State of the Art of Industrial Management," Majority Report of Sub-Committee on Administration. Presented at the Annual Meeting 1912, of The American Society of Mechanical Engineers. No. 1378, *Transactions*, Vol. 34, 1912. Permission to excerpt by courtesy of the Society.

THE PRESENT STATE OF THE ART OF INDUSTRIAL MANAGEMENT

MAJORITY REPORT OF SUB-COMMITTEE ON ADMINISTRATION

DURING THE PAST FEW YEARS a number of striking phenomena, in connection with industrial management, must have become evident even to the most superficial observer. The more important are:

a. The widespread, popular interest in the subject which had its rise in a statement made before the Interstate Commerce Commission, in a hearing on the matter of proposed advances in freight rates by carriers. An attorney for the shippers stated on November 21, 1910, that it was estimated that by the application of newly discovered principles of management "in the railroad operation of this country an economy of $1,000,000 a day is possible," and further that these principles can be applied with equal success "in every form of business activity." This popular interest is shown by the great number of articles published in the daily papers and popular magazines, mediums that give but scant attention to technical subjects, except of the most striking nature.

b. The suddenly intensified interest in the subject on the part of employers and business executives in many lines of activity, shown by lectures, addresses, professional papers and reports presented to their associations.

c. The opposition of labor unions to the newer methods of management, shown by statements of labor leaders, in a few instances by strikes, and by an attempt to prohibit by law the use of some of these methods in Government shops.

d. Governmental recognition of the matter shown by the appointment of a special committee of the House of Representatives to investigate systems of management in Government arsenals and shops, which reported in March 1912; by the appointment of a civilian board by the Secretary of the Navy to investigate management in the navy yards, which reported in July 1911; and by Senate bill S 6172, now in committee, which is intended to prohibit time study and the payment of premiums or bonus on Government work.

e. The rapidity with which literature on the subject has accumulated. One directory of books on business management lists 500 titles, and states that 75 per cent of them have been written within five years.

f. The formation of two societies having as an aim the furtherance of the application of the principles of management.

g. The separation of persons interested in the matter into two camps, one of enthusiastic advocates, the other of vigorous opponents of what is called the new element in management.

h. The unquestionable proof of the advance that can be made in unskilled work, as shoveling material, and in ancient trades, as bricklaying, by the application of the principles of management. This is the most striking phenomenon of all.

The Principles of Manufacture

2. Before defining the element in the art of management that has given rise to these phenomena, it is necessary to review briefly the beginnings of modern industry. This gives a historical setting from which the present can be more truly judged.

3. Modern industry is stated by some writers to have begun in 1738 when John Wyatt brought out a spinning machine. Others place the period as between 1750 and 1800, when the power loom and steam engine came into being.

4. Early British economists held that the application of the principle of *division of labor* was the basis of manufacture. From Adam Smith's *Wealth of Nations*, 1776, we quote:

> This great increase of the quantity of work which, in consequence of the division of labor, the same number of people are capable of performing, is owing to three different circumstances; first, to the increase of dexterity in every particular workman; secondly, to the saving of the time which is commonly lost in passing from one species of work to another; and lastly, to the invention of a great number of machines which facilitate and abridge labor, and enable one man to do the work of many.

5. Charles Babbage, the great British mathematician and mechanician, believed that from the above-quoted statement the most important principle was omitted. This omission he supplied as follows in his *Economy of Machinery and Manufacture*, 1832:

> That the master manufacturer, by dividing the work to be executed into different processes, each requiring different degrees of skill and force, can purchase exactly that precise quantity of both which is necessary for each process; whereas, if the whole work were executed by one workman, that person must possess sufficient skill to perform the most difficult, and sufficient strength to execute the most laborious, of the operations into which the art is divided.

6. It appears, however, that another principle is the basic one in the rise of industry. It is the *transference of skill*. The transference of skill from the inventor or designer to the power-driven mechanism brought about the industrial revolution from handicraft to manufacture. It will be necessary to refer to this principle frequently throughout this report, in showing the meaning and position of management in industry.

7. No better single illustration of the application of this principle can be found than in the invention of the lathe slide rest by Henry Maudsley in 1794. The simple, easily controlled mechanical movements of the slide rest were substituted for the skillful human control of hand tools. So complete has been this transference of skill that today hand tooling is a vanished art in American machine shops. Very few lathe hands can chase a thread with hand tools, yet all can cut good threads on an engine lathe, thanks to the slide rest. After the traditional skill of a trade, or the special, peculiar skill of a designer or inventor, has been transferred to a machine, an operator with little or no previously acquired skill can learn to handle it and turn off the product.

8. An example of the extent to which this transference of skill is carried today is presented by the shoemaking industry. The United Shoe Machinery Company builds some 400 machines used in shoe manufacture. These are so highly organized that the greater part of shoe-shop operatives are unskilled except in a single readily mastered detail of the work. The skill in shoemaking is now in the mechanical equipment of the shops. This transference is a development of the past 50 years.

9. James Nasmyth, a British engineer, inventor of the steam hammer, had this to say in 1851 of the application of this principle in his own works:

> The characteristic feature of our modern mechanical improvements, is the introduction of self-acting tool machinery. What every mechanical workman has now to do, and what every boy can do, is not to work himself, but to superintend the beautiful labor of the machine. The whole class of workmen that depend exclusively on their skill is now done away with.

10. Methods of analyzing and recording operations were early developed. Adam Smith records the divisions of the work of manufacturing pins, listing 11 operations. Charles Babbage gives a table from a French investigator, showing the number of operations, time for each, cost of each, and expense of tools and material for making pins in France in 1760. He gives a similar table for English manufacture in his day (see Appendix No. 1, Table 2, from *Economy of Machinery and Manufacture*, 1832).

11. He further comments on the use of the watch to time operations. We quote from his instructions to one making such observations and using a skeleton form that he recommends:

> In filling up the answers which require numbers, some care should be taken:
> for instance, if the observer stands with his watch in his hand before a person

heading a pin, the workman will almost certainly increase his speed, and the estimate will be too large. . . . The number of operations performed in a given time may be frequently ascertained when the workman is quite unconscious that any person is observing him. Thus the sound made by the motion of a loom may enable the observer to count the number of strokes per minute, even though he is outside the building in which it is contained.

12. M. Coulomb, the noted French physicist (1736–1806), who had great experience in making such observations, cautions those who may repeat his experiments against being deceived by such circumstances. We translate a single quotation:

> I pray (says he) those who wish to repeat them (the experiments) if they have not time to measure the results after several days of work, to observe the workmen at various times during the day without their knowing that they are being watched. We cannot be too well warned of the danger of self-deception in computing either the speed or the effective time of work through an observation of a few minutes.

13. Thus we see the application of the principle of *transference of skill* at the basis of the development of the industry, and an early appreciation of the value of the detailed study of operations in making that transference more complete. But the machine was the viewpoint. It was looked upon as the producing unit. Combined and contrasted with this was a lack of knowledge of scientific principles and their sure application. Charles Babbage treats of this forcefully. We quote:

> There is perhaps no trade or profession existing in which there is so much quackery, so much ignorance of the scientific principles, and of the history of their own art, with respect to its resources and extent, as is to be met with amongst mechanical projectors.

14. In the same vein he emphasizes the need of accurate drawings as if having in mind the poor quality of the work from the average draftsman of his day:

> It can never be too strongly impressed upon the minds of those who are devising new machines (says he) that to make the most perfect drawings of every part tends essentially both to success of the trial, and to economy in arriving at the result.

15. He further points out that there is another important factor in successful industry, in addition to machinery. We read that "in order to succeed in a manufacture, it is necessary not merely to possess good machinery, but that the domestic economy of the factory should be most carefully regulated."

16. These quotations foreshadow modern methods of thinking out the work in advance and transferring this thought to the workmen. The subsequent development has had the effect of advancing still further the division of labor, and beginning the division of thought. The drafting room presents the first example of the trend, in its collection of engineering data, in its prediction of results and the formation of staff organization.

17. But from the period of the last quotation almost to the present there has been no change in the basic principles discovered and applied in industry. There has been nothing but an extension of those already known. The place of greatest advance has been in the drawing room. The art of machine design has been greatly developed. The last half of the last century saw a tremendous increase in inventions, a tremendous furtherance of the application of transference of skill to machines and tools. The skeleton of an industrial organization of this period, one that was too large for a single executive to manage, consisted of a designing department and a production department, each with a head responsible to the manager.

18. The first of these, the one that was the means of embodying skill in the machinery and tools of production, was highly developed and organized. Experiment, research and detailed study were constantly resorted to, to aid in reaching the desired result. The work was highly specialized and the employees highly paid. Not infrequently the manager or chief executive devoted much of his own time to this part of the business.

19. The production department presented a contrasting condition. The workmen were given the tools and machines designed in the drawing room and using their own unaided skill were expected to produce work of the desired quality and quantity. Except in rare instances, no effort was made to transfer the skill of the management to the production department and the employees, or to undertake the division of executive thought. Very little consideration was given to the workmen as a producing unit.

Features of the Change

20. Within the past twenty or twenty-five years, certain changes have taken place in the attitude of many production managers toward the problems that they face and the forces and means that they control. An increasing amount of attention is being given to the worker. An early evidence was the development of profit-sharing, premium and bonus systems to reward increased effort and output. There followed welfare work, industrial betterment movements, the adoption of safeguards and regulations to minimize industrial accidents, the substitution of the principle of accident compensation for employers' liability and an improvement in the physical surroundings and conditions of factories. All of these tendencies have been fostered and to a great extent initiated by employers.

21. Another tendency, less pronounced in character, has as its object the improvement of the personal relations between employee and employee and between employee and employer. It is an effort to establish the best of factory working conditions in those things not physical in nature, to develop and maintain a shop atmosphere free from all harassing and hindering influences. It is an attempt to make use of the results of experimental psychology, in improving working conditions.

22. But the most important change and one that comprehends the others, is in the mental attitude toward the problems of production. The tendency is toward an atti-

tude of questioning, of research, of careful investigation of everything affecting the problems in hand, of seeking for exact knowledge and then shaping action on the discovered facts. It has developed the use of time study and motion study as instruments for investigation, the planning department as an agency to put into practice the conclusions drawn from the results of research, and methods of wage payment which stimulate coöperation.

23. All of these changes have affected the production department much more than the designing department. The effect is to extend the principle of transference of skill to production, so that it completely embraces every activity in manufacture. The skill of the management is consciously transferred to all of the operations of the factory. This extension is expressed by these phrases: the drawing room is the planning department of design, and the planning department is the drawing room of production.

Nature of the Committee's Investigation

24. To obtain information on present conditions your committee wrote to the recognized experts, to executives of plants in many lines of industry, to students of industrial problems, and has had many interviews with men in these various fields. The response to our requests has been in the main most generous. We are deeply indebted to the information thus received for a large portion of the following sections of this report.

25. Throughout the following pages there is a plentiful use of illustrative quotations. Many of these are taken from correspondence resulting from our investigations. Others are from the mass of literature mentioned in Paragraph 1e.

26. On some points diametrically opposed views have been expressed. In such cases we have presented both. In no case has credit been given for these views or quotations, as the information was solicited in confidence.

Definition of the New Element in the Art of Management

27. Requests for a definition of the new element in the art of management brought forth a difference of opinion as to its existence. The opposed view is given in the following quotations:

> I am not aware that a *new* element in the art of management has been discovered———

> There have been no new discoveries in scientific management of industrial institutions. Common-sense men have used common-sense methods always. The term "scientific management" is a catch-word which assumes that industrial institutions have not been scientifically managed—which is not the case. My experience and the experience of my friends has been that there has been no new element injected into the art of management.

243

In the writer's opinion there is very little that is new about it (the art of management). There is hardly any part of it that has not been practised by managers for the past 100 years. The trouble is there are not enough managers with sufficient initiative to set the system moving properly.

————the problem presented is not the adoption of something entirely new; but rather the extension to every detail of our work of something which we have already tried.

28. Turning now to the other side of the question, from a large number of definitions of this new element we select the following as very nearly conveying, taken together, the complete conception as our investigation has disclosed it:

The best designation of the new element I believe to be "scientific management." This term already has been adopted quite generally and although frequently misused, carries with it the fundamental idea that the management of labor is a process requiring thorough analytical treatment and involving scientific as opposed to "rule of thumb" methods.

The writer ventures to define the new element briefly, but broadly, as: The critical observation, accurate description, analysis and classification of all industrial and business phenomena of a recurring nature, including all forms of coöperative human effort and the systematic application of the resulting records to secure the most economical and efficient production and regulation of future phenomena.

Stripped of technicalities, the method of the modern efficiency engineer is simply this: First, to analyze and study each piece of work before it is performed; second, to decide how it can be done with a minimum of wasted motion and energy; third, to instruct the workman so that he may do the work in the manner selected as most efficient.

The Taylor System is not a method of pay, a specific ruling of account books, not the use of high-speed steel. It is simply an honest, intelligent effort to arrive at the absolute control in every department, to let tabulated and unimpeachable fact take the place of individual opinion; to develop "team play" to its highest possibility.

As we conceive it, scientific management consists in the conscious application of the laws inherent in the practise of successful managers and the laws of science in general. It has been called management engineering, which seems more fully to cover its general scope than a science.

29. These quotations convey the ideas of a conscious effort to ascertain and study facts and systematically to apply them in instructing the workmen and in controlling every department of industry. Setting these against the underlying principle of the transference of skill, we conceive the prominent element in present-day industrial management to be: *The mental attitude that consciously applies the transference of skill to all the activities of industry.*

30. Here emphasis is placed upon the word *all* for, as shown in Pars. 17 and 18, the restricted application of this principle to machines and tools has been highly developed for a long period. But its conscious application in a broad way to the production departments, and particularly to the workmen, we believe has been made during the last quarter century.

Rise of This Mental Attitude

31. The rise of this change of attitude in regard to industrial management is shown in the papers on the subject in the *Transactions* of this Society. These are sixteen in number. The period covered is from 1886 to 1908. The practice upon which several were based extended over a number of years before the paper was presented. Papers on accounting have been excluded.

32. The first, No. 207, classifies *management of works* as a modern art having a vast amount of accumulated experience, points out that the executives must have "a practical knowledge of how to observe, record, analyze and compare essential facts in relation to . . . all . . . that enters into or affects the economy of production and the cost of the product," and makes a plea for the interchange of management data.

33. Eight following papers, Nos. 256, 341, 449, 596, 647, 928, 965 and 1012, deal with methods of wage payment, showing the increasing attention given to the workmen during this period. Of these methods the "premium plan" described in paper No. 449 has an extensive use today in machine shops. It probably ranks third, in extent of use, being exceeded by day work and piece work in the order named. Paper No. 647 outlines elementary rate fixing; that is, the minute study of each detail of each operation. From this, motion study and time study have grown. The "bonus system" of paper No. 928 also has an extensive use, probably ranking fourth.

34. Paper No. 1003, "Shop Management," is the first complete presentation of the subject. This paper with the subsequent writings of its author, stands as the only comprehensive outline of industrial management. Papers Nos. 1001, 1002, 1010, 1011 and 1115, are amplifications of certain features of No. 1003, based on the same practice.

35. Paper No. 1221 deals with the training of workmen, and outlines practical, tested methods of bringing about the all-important transference of skill.

Labor-Saving Management

36. Since these papers were presented, and during the development of popular interest in the subject, the term "scientific management" has been generally and loosely applied to the new system and methods. This is commonly taken to mean that there is a science rather than an art of management. A truer interpretation is that it means management using scientific methods, these being taken largely from the sciences of physics and psychology.

37. The expression "labor-saving management" better conveys the meaning of the movement. It has the further advantage of being easily and surely understood because of its strict analogy with the term "labor-saving machinery." It is no chance that puts these two terms labor-saving machinery and labor-saving management in conjunction, for the first is the past development and the second the present trend of industry, and they will be closely and inevitably associated in the successful manufacturing of the future. Throughout the following pages of this report the terms "industrial management" and "labor-saving management" are used, the first to denote the subject broadly, the second the newer attitude.

The Regulative Principles of Industrial Management

38. The lack of accurate thinking and clear expression in regard to management is nowhere better shown than in many of the statements of the so-called principles. These can be divided into two classes, personal characteristics of managers and mechanical means of applying. It is evident that neither can show us the way in which the activities of industry are to be regulated.

39. In our investigation preparing for this report, one correspondent writes as follows:

The regulative principles of management along scientific lines include four important elements:

a. Planning of the processes and operations in detail by a special department organized for this purpose.

b. Functional organization by which each man superintending the workman is responsible for a single line of effort. This is distinctly opposed to the older type of military organization, where every man in the management is given a combination of executive, legislative and judicial functions.

c. Training the worker so as to require him to do each job in what has been found to be the best method of operation.

d. Equable payment of the workers based on quantity and quality of output of each individual. This involves scientific analysis of each operation to determine the proper time that should be required for its accomplishment and also high payment for the worker who obtains the object sought.

40. Another correspondent finds the solution of problems of management in the observing and regulating of three classes of industrial phenomena:

a. The economic results of different arrangements and forms of materials and operations upon them, either to produce equipment or product. This covers the whole field of recorded experience from invention and design of product and tools down through the successive shop processes to ultimate finished product and its tests in service. It is the object of the scientific method to make the best of this experience, in its essential details, readily available for all concerned, and to see that it is actually absorbed and put in practice.

b. The economic results of varying executive methods for effectively directing human efforts as a whole in the use of the above experience. This covers the entire field of building up, coördinating and controlling the supervising organization of a plant with its statistical and recording systems.

c. The economic results of steps taken to raise the industrial efficiency of the individual worker in every grade of service. This covers the whole problem of labor reward, intensified ability, conserved energy and the general relations of employer and employee.

41. We have pointed out that the underlying principle, that is, cause in the widest sense, the application of which has built up modern industry, is the transference of skill. This basic principle is put into effect on the management side of all industrial activities, through three regulative principles which sum up the ideas in the above quotations, Pars. 39 and 40. These have been concisely stated

as [1]: (a) the systematic use of experience; (b) the economic control of effort; (c) the promotion of personal effectiveness.

42. The first includes the use, in all essential detail, of traditional knowledge, personal experience and the results of scientific study on the part of the executive force. It implies the accumulation and use of records and the setting up of standards.

43. The second includes the division and subsequent coördination of both executive and productive labor; the planning of single lines of effort, the setting of definite tasks and the comparison of results; and the effective training of the workers. It implies the previous acquisition of skill by the executives.

44. The third includes a definite allotment of responsibility and the adequate, stimulative encouragement and reward of both executive and productive labor; the development of contented workers, and the promotion of their physical and mental health. It implies the most thorough comprehension of the human being.

The Practice of Management

45. As labor-saving management springs from a change in mental attitude, the beginning of its practice should be with persons having final responsibility, the proprietors of closely-owned businesses, the directors of larger establishments, or the officials having charge of Government works. Before any changes are made, such men should clearly understand the viewpoint from which all of the managerial work is to be done, the principles that are to be applied, the general method of their application and the results expected.

46. A similar mental attitude must be fostered among all the members of the executive force and a period of training for them begun. This may include a redistribution of function and responsibility, and will include a detailed study of production by scientific methods. This is the period of division of thought, training of the management staff and setting up standards of performance. This must be carefully performed before there can be effective transference of skill to the workers in the production departments.

47. The usual conception of modern management is that it affects the workmen most of all, tending to stimulate them to turn out increased production to their possible hurt. This is wrong. If the principles outlined are followed, the executive, or non-producing, labor is the most affected. Its individuals are compelled to study, plan and direct. They must acquire knowledge and skill in order to transfer it. It is a system of management that forces the executives to manage.

48. This being so, the introduction of modern management in a plant must be made slowly. The causes of most so-called failures are principally two: a failure of the executives to acquire the vital mental attitude and too great haste in application. The latter seems to be the dominant one. Your committee feels compelled to emphasize the danger of attempting to hurry any change in methods of management. Each step of the work should be made permanent before the next is begun.

[1] *American Machinist*, vol. 36, p. 857, "The Principles of Management," by Church and Alford.

49. We have examined records of production which clearly show a lessening of individual output among workers who had been trained for some time and had achieved good results as soon as untrained workers were put with them, thus lessening their share of personal supervision. Later the original standard of production was again reached, but the results seemed to be directly proportional to the amount of skillful supervision, during a lengthy period of training.

50. After those who are to operate the new methods have acquired the necessary knowledge and established sufficient standards, the work of putting these into effect can be begun. This means the fixing of the best attainable working conditions and giving each worker definite tasks with an adequate reward to each one who attains to the standard set. This part of installing the methods must be accomplished with tact and patience, remembering that leadership and example are powerful aids in bringing about enthusiastic coöperation.

51. The training of the workers is essential in this part of the application. This must be far more than mere demonstration, the mere showing that a thing can be done. It must be patient teaching and help until the required degree of dexterity is acquired, that is, up to the habit stage. It is evident that such work cannot be hurried.

52. Such, broadly, are the three steps in the practice of management. It is now necessary to investigate the internal elements of permanence in such methods. If the proper mental attitude is once taken, we believe it will never be given up. This is substantiated by a few cases when early attempts to improve management were failures and the methods abandoned. Later, however, other attempts were made with substantial success. The mental attitude outlived the failure. Thus in a given industrial organization this feature would not be lost except by a loss of the executive staff.

53. The permanence of records of performance and standards needs only to be mentioned to be appreciated. Once set up in an industry, disaster is invited if they are disregarded.

54. To these is added a third in the nature of a spur from the working forces to the managing force. An adequate reward is one of the essentials. Whatever disturbs the mechanism of production interferes with the earning of the rewards. The workers at once object, pointing out the trouble and insisting that it be rectified. The management is spurred to keep all conditions up to the fixed standard. Examples of this action have been brought to the attention of your committee.

55. The practice as outlined, while built upon fixed standards and procedure, is by no means rigid and inflexible as has been alleged. The design and construction of labor-saving machinery is carried on with a multiplicity of different details. Labor-saving management should likewise use a variety of details suited to the requirements of different industries and plants. There can be nothing fixed in such human endeavor except the underlying principle. As a simple matter of fact we have found different methods, details and nomenclature in use in different plants. Many efforts have undergone marked change and development since first installed. Further, this idea of rigidity is repudiated by some of the foremost management experts.

56. In Par. 39 is emphasized the need of a scientific study of everything connected with production. The methods used are adapted from the research laboratory. But the purpose of their use is changed. The scientific investigator uses his laboratory to discover facts. Their discovery and declaration is his end and aim. The management investigator uses laboratory methods to discover facts for immediate use. The end and aim is utility. This is the test of industry. It is therefore unwise and in fact detrimental to carry investigations to an extreme. Enough facts must be observed to shape intelligent action. Persons having time study and motion study in charge should possess that rare, intuitive, human quality that causes its possessor to know when enough observations have been collected to form a sound working conclusion.

57. The position of the expert in the practice of management is more clearly seen as experience increases. The element of mystery has already departed. This is to be welcomed for it means the downfall of mere "systematizers." One of the unfortunate features of this great movement has been the rise of alleged experts who have been ready to promise extravagant results if they were allowed to systematize an industrial plant. The test which their work cannot meet is the one of permanence.

58. An industrial manager who has had signal success in directing large enterprises sums up the more undesirable characteristics of systematizing practice as:

a. The publication and quotation of statistics regarding gains made through the use of particular systems, without a frank statement of the degree of inefficiency of the plants before reorganization.
b. The failure to view the plant from the investor's standpoint rather than as a laboratory offering opportunities for interesting and expensive experience.
c. The failure to admit that every application of past solutions to unstudied new and different conditions *is* an experiment.
d. The waste of time and money on problems that will yield to scientific treatment, but which do not recur often enough to justify such a solution.
e. The undervaluing of effective leadership in management and consequent lack of permanency in results.
f. The overvalue of emasculated "system" leading to a curious non-responsibility on the part of any person for the total result.
g. The frequent assumption that the treatment of the problems of similar plants should be identical.
h. The failure to properly appraise in a growing concern the value of its internal asset of "goodwill."
i. The imperfect analysis and appreciation of the human factor in industry, with a consequent failure to reckon patiently with "habit" and "inertia" and a tendency to hasty "substitution," bringing about the breaking up of valuable organization.

59. The real expert concentrates on the facts of a given problem, and from a wide experience in analysis, coördination and practical responsibility works out a solution by scientific methods, suited to the material and human factors involved. The tendency is for him to do less of the detail work of installation, but to train and direct the persons who are permanently to manage. This is a true process of transference of skill.

Statistical Data

60. Your committee hoped to present statistics on the extent to which labor-saving management is in use. This could not be realized. Many industrial managers whom we have addressed have not honored us with their confidence in this direction. In fact, it seems as if a secretive stage is now with us. There are two reasons for withholding such information. The first is identical with the one that has developed "trade secrets" and secretiveness in regard to machines, tools and processes, the desire to keep things of value away from competitors. The second is a belief that in the minds of some persons a reflection is cast upon the ability of the executives of an industrial establishment if outside experts are employed. Frequently a system of management is referred to as the development of someone in the organization, although it was installed by a management expert, employed for the purpose.

61. Some idea of the variety of the industries in which labor-saving management is in use can be gained from Appendix No. 3,* which lists a total of 52.

Broad Results of Labor-Saving Management

62. In cases where the use of labor-saving management can be considered a success, the broad results have been: a reduced cost of product; greater promptness in delivery with the ability to set and meet dates of shipment; a greater output per worker per day with increased wages; and an improvement in the contentment of the workers. This last item is shown by the fewness of strikes under the new management, and in the refusal of those working under the changed conditions to join in a strike of their fellows in the same plant who were not working under the new methods. This last-mentioned situation has arisen a number of times. In one case an attempt was made to strike a room where about one-half of the operators were under the new conditions. These refused to go out; the rest went.

63. These results indicate certain advantages to both employer and employee. But it is charged that the movement has not yet entirely justified itself from the economic viewpoint, for it has not reduced the cost of product to the consumer. The implication is that its possibilities will not be realized until employers, employees and the public are alike benefited. With this view we are in most hearty accord. Labor-saving machinery has brought the comforts that we all enjoy today. Labor-saving management promises to extend those comforts. Where properly administered it is conserving labor and is thus contributing to the good of society at large, and although the benefit to the consumer may not yet be generally felt, it has already developed to a certain extent and will continue to develop as the natural result of increased production.

J. M. DODGE, *Chairman*	WILFRED LEWIS	
L. P. ALFORD, *Secretary*	W. L. LYALL	*Members*
D. M. BATES	W. B. TARDY	*Sub-Committee on*
H. A. EVANS	H. R. TOWNE	*Administration*

* Appendices to this A.S.M.E. *Report* are not included in this volume.

MINORITY REPORT OF SUB-COMMITTEE ON ADMINISTRATION

I am unable to sign the majority report in its entirety, much as I admire the thoroughness with which it has been prepared and its great interest. In its general tenor it distinctly implies the desirability of what is termed labor-saving management, involving the planning department, functional organization and the bonus system. Perhaps this statement is not strictly justified, but I cannot avoid the impression after reading the report most carefully. That the methods of management have undergone a great change in recent years I certainly agree. I would explain it by stating that in many respects the art of management is developing into a science. In common with most lines of work, the method of investigating facts has changed. Phenomena are analyzed, information is obtained accurately, the mental attitude of the manager is scientific rather than empirical. Things that used to be known generally by gradual experience are now known specifically by detailed observation. In the course of this development many new systems and ideas have been invented, time studies, motion study, payment systems, functional management, etc. Some are new, others partly new, others simply practices of many managers put into definite form. The science of management will classify these for us, perhaps even explain their advantages and limitations so that we may in time know which is preferable and when.

2. But the introduction of the use of these methods has been attended by claims as to the results that might be obtained by their use, and these claims have led to such absurd statements as that made before the Interstate Commerce Commission, which is referred to in the report. I feel most strongly that each of the suggestions that have been made to improve methods of management may have merit, but I do not feel that any one of them is a panacea for all our inefficiency. For instance, in certain classes of work, time studies are valuable; in others, they may be a waste of time. In certain classes of work I consider piece-work or bonus systems desirable; in others, I consider them inferior to day work. Functional management may be an improvement in certain industries; in others, I do not consider it suitable. In some cases the workman cannot be trained by the skilled executive; in others, he can train him with ease.

3. In general I feel that labor-saving management is not any particular system, but will always remain the art of selecting and applying the most appropriate methods furnished by the science of management, the science that records what these methods are and the results obtained from them. As you will see, I agree with your correspondent in his last paragraph, quoted under Par. 28; but his opinion is not really represented in the trend of the report.

H. H. VAUGHAN
Member, Sub-Committee on Administration

DISCUSSION

CHARLES B. GOING expressed the view that there was a lack of correspondence between the title and the substance of the majority report. His impression from reading the report was that, after an introductory attack upon the analysis of the elements of industrial management, it proceeded to argumentation on its own behalf and presented, not a survey of the present state of the art of industrial management as it exists in this country, but an interpretation of a theory of management as it exists in the convictions of the majority of the committee. He did not intend to depreciate the interest of the conclusions expressed by the majority of the committee, but only to point out that these do not constitute a report on "the state of the art of management," and that they give us no more than a fragmentary idea of the conditions under which this art is carried on in the United States today.

A most commendable stand is taken by the committee in using the term "scientific management" descriptively, and not in the titular sense, applicable only to the Taylor system, in which it has often been employed. Scientific management should mean, as the committee says (Par. 36), "management using scientific methods, these being taken largely from the sciences of physics and psychology." But even with this definition in mind, the committee appear to have limited their views too closely to questions of physics and to have given inadequate attention to the questions of psychology, which, in the estimate of many students of the subject, are really paramount in the art and practice of industrial management.

Scientific management, using the term now in its titular sense, offers one method of finding standard individuals. There are other methods, forming no part of the systematic ritual of this school, which are stated to be far more effectual in discovering and distributing standard individuals. There are policies or methods of much interest, designed to better the conditions of operation with the apparently large numbers of non-standard or sub-standard individuals by whom so much of the work of industry is now carried on. Quantitatively, these schools of thought and of practice are of much importance in the existing state of the art of industrial management. The Taylor system is but one factor. There is much valuable contribution to thought and practice outside of the list of publications published in the Society's *Transactions* and listed in Par. 66.

By leaving this apparently out of its consideration, and concentrating its attention upon a single factor instead of analyzing the entire equation, he thought the majority report of the committee was but another contribution to an already overburdened controversy, and that it had left the general survey not only unfinished, but scarcely even begun.

A. HAMILTON CHURCH. Of the two reports presented by the committee, the minority report raises the question as to whether the claims of certain groups of men to the possession of the key to all progress, have any measure of justification.

As it appears to me, the various schools of management have not presented to us any well-balanced theory of management capable of being developed in a hundred different ways according to special needs. On the contrary, it is as if they had presented to us a barrel of gunpowder, a telescope, and a magnetic compass and claimed these mechanisms to be the whole science of maritime warfare. Certain definite and concrete mechanisms such as planning departments, stop-watches, despatching boards, instruction cards of extraordinary complexity, and special methods of remunerating labor are interesting and useful, but do not make, either singly or combined, a science of management.

Moreover, the original claims, already generously broad, have been so expanded by some of the younger disciples that almost every modern method is claimed to be the direct outcome of the wisdom of one or another of the rival schools of scientific efficiency. It is because of this kind of thing that the minority report is important.

Turning to the majority report, we find that the prime underlying principle of management engineering is the transference of skill. This is an illuminative statement, and I venture to think, of great practical value. It is put very tersely in the sentence in Par. 8, "the skill in shoemaking is now in the mechanical equipment of the shop." That is a clear-cut picture of a change that is already complete, and it helps us to realize exactly what is meant by the transference of skill. It also helps us to understand why, in the engineering trades, there are such wide discrepancies in the amount of work turned out by individual operators. It is because, in these trades, the transference of skill is by no means so complete. For one thing, the capacity and range of the average machine tool is large, and to some extent indefinite. A considerable amount of skill is still vested in the worker. Still more, a remarkable amount of ignorance as to what the machine will or will not do is shared by the employer and the workman.

The report shows why this is bound to be so at the present stage. In the process of transfering hand skill to the mechanical fingers of the machine, the report emphasizes the fact that more attention has been devoted to designing it, than to the problem of using it afterwards.

The more I think over this problem, the more I am convinced that the true line of progress is the exhaustive study of machines, their capacities and limitations. I have held this opinion for many years, and the system of industrial accounting I have been advocating for the past decade was, I believe, the first step made towards bringing forward the machine to its true place as a factor of production. But I must confess that until this principle of the transference of skill was brought out so clearly by this report, I did not realize exactly why the machine tool was frequently so surprisingly ineffective under indifferent handling.

I will pass over the acceptance by the committee of the three regulative principles of management, *viz.*: (a) the systematic use of experience, (b) the economical control of effort, and (c) the promotion of personal effectiveness, which were worked out by Mr. Alford and myself, except to say that the credit for the formulation of these principles belongs in a larger degree to Mr. Alford than to me, and I will conclude my remarks by calling attention to a phrase used in Par. 51 of the report, *viz*.: "the habit stage."

All the mechanism of organization in the world is valueless beside the steadiness of production that comes from the establishment of good habit throughout a plant. I will go further, and say that the whole object and end of organization should be to create the right kind and degree of habit in every one of the persons engaged in production, from the president down to the shop sweeper.

It is not enough for the workman to be so instructed that he forms good habit. Every living link in the chain of production requires equally to be so trained that his acquired habit is harmonious with all the rest. The report has mentioned this aspect of the question where it insists that the executives and not the workman are the persons most important to be reached. Few people understand that the principal work of an expert organizer is not the designing of elaborate blanks and cards, but the fostering, with tireless patience, of correctly adjusted habit in each member of the staff.

As the new ideals of management engineering appear to me, and this view seems confirmed by the committee's report, they may be summed up in three sentences:

> Take nothing for granted.
> See that every effort is adapted to its purpose.
> Cultivate habit.

These sentences are, of course, merely practical derivatives of the three regulative principles referred to in the report. Each of them in turn implies other things which will readily suggest themselves. Thus, the possibility of cultivating correctly adjusted habit depends obviously upon proper mental and physical conditions for the living forces. It implies "lead" and not "drive."

It is an interesting question where the new spirit that we find abroad in industrial management has come from. To some extent, I think, it is part of a larger movement, the realization of a sense of social solidarity, of social responsibility of each for all, that is so marked a feature of the times. But it also arises, in part, from another cause. Scientific men tell us that the great difference between a savage race and a highly civilized one is that the former remains in a condition of natural innocence, and the latter has arrived at self-consciousness. This, I think, is the real state of affairs in regard to management engineering. We are passing from a stage at which there was a simple and unconscious following of tradition, into a stage of self-consciousness in which we are moved to subject our habits and our motives to severe self-scrutiny, and examine afresh every item of our daily practice. It is a very painful stage to have arrived at. Most of us are so content with our comfortable natural innocence that we do not like to part with it, but it is a process that once commenced, must continue.

The examination into new methods of remunerating labor, the adoption, with caution, of searching instruments of analysis, such as time study, the use of precise methods of accounting—these are not causes, but *consequences,* of this newly awakened self-consciousness. It is beginning to be recognized that production is an aggregate of infinitesimal separate acts, in each of which there are three main components. First, experience must be drawn on; secondly, the resulting effort must be intelligently adapted to the end in view; thirdly, this intelligent effort must become habitual. And to secure the successful performance of these acts, the living forces concerned must be maintained in the pink of condition, both mental and physical.

C. B. THOMPSON. A fact not to be ignored is that labor, organized and unorganized, has taken its stand, at least temporarily, in opposition to the development of scientific management. While many of the objections raised have been so unreasonable as to be abandoned almost from the start, there are three criticisms made by working men which persist in spite of explanation: In the first place, they seem to cherish an innate resentment against time study—"putting the stop-watch on them," as they express it. It "makes them nervous," "makes them speed up unduly while under inspection," "is simply another means of slave driving," "is used unfairly," "is un-American." They say also that the method of minute planning in advance and of specific instructions as to details, is destructive of the initiative which has been the backbone of American industrial progress. Further, they assert that the enhanced product due to these methods is not fairly divided between the management and the men; that an increase of 400 per cent in production, as in the classic case of Schmidt, the pigiron handler, has been accompanied by an increase of only 60 per cent in wages.

It is neither wise nor expedient to pass by these criticisms without comment. That they are all unmerited may perhaps be shown: for instance, it has been demonstrated that time study, carried on by one who is trained in the subject (and whose training is ethical as well as intellectual), is not unfair, nor is it used as a new method of driving, nor is it in any sense un-American. Time study has been carried on for decades in psychological laboratories for purely scientific purposes and with instruments even more refined than the despised stop-watch, but no one suggests that this use is open to criticism. When it is once clearly understood that time study in an industrial establishment, made under the proper conditions and by the proper persons, is aimed at similar scientific results, and that these results are then to be applied to work, subject to the mutual consent of employer and men, based on a conviction of their reliability and essential justice, these objections will disappear. But on the other hand, there is no doubt that time study can be and has been abused, and the working man has a right to be "shown."

Similarly in regard to the alleged destruction of initiative. Here the facts are clear. The machinist does not consider his initiative restrained when he is asked to do his work in accordance with the drawings supplied him by the drafting department. Systematic routing and planning of work and the development of a science by which it shall be done are, as the committee points out, analogous, for the production department, with the working drawing. We all believe in liberty, but we recognize, or are capable of being shown, that true liberty is liberty under law; that the artist is not in the least trammelled in his genius because he has been taught the laws under which he must use his materials; nor is the citizen any the less free because he, in common with all others, must conduct himself in accordance with the law of the land.

The problem of just distribution of the increased product is not capable of easy solution and demonstration, and much yet remains to be done in this field. No one has yet solved the problem of justice in distribution, and it does seem somewhat hyper-critical to allege against scientific management that it has not done what any other movement or individual thus far has not been able to do. Rather it should be given credit for having pointed out the industrial necessity of justice in distribution, and of having proposed steps in that direction. The solution of this problem is not to be looked for from engineers. When an engineer wanders into the field of economics, he is apt to make about the same diverting spectacle that the economist would who would undertake to expound the principles of machine design. Probably the wages question will be worked out in the future as it has been in the past by neither the engineer nor the economist, but by the daily struggle and adjustment known as the "higgling of the market." In this struggle the rights of the working men will have to be conserved and enforced by organization. Only by pooling their strength can they meet the superior strategic position of the employers.

The report of such a committee as this should not have overlooked the opportunity to begin or extend the campaign of education in these particulars. Something more than education is necessary, however. Labor unions are a potent and active force in present-day industry, and we should get their enthusiastic coöperation. They are the culmination of decades or centuries of development. In spite of their numerous mistakes and injustices they have, on the whole, justified their existence; and whether you agree that they have or not, they are a condition and not a theory that confronts us. It would seem to be the part of wisdom, therefore, not to take the tack of ignoring or combatting the doubts and questionings and opposition of the labor unions, but rather to persuade them of the advisability of acquainting themselves with the facts, of recognizing the inevitability of the march of labor-saving management, and to secure their active coöperation in its development. A proposal at this time to retain their positive help in the extension of scientific management may seem Utopian, but it is warranted by certain facts and precedents in the history of trade unions. They have already established their right to determine the lighting, heating and ventilating facilities of establishments in which their members work. There are cases on record in which they have required owners of old plants to scrap their obsolete machinery and install new and modern devices, in order that the owners themselves may make sufficient profit to pay adequate wages to their employees. *It is but one step, and a short one, in the extension of this principle to say to the owner that he must modernize his establishment in every detail, not because the working man is interested in the owner's personal profits, but because only such an establishment can pay the working man the wages which his standard of living demands.*

The objections of the working men are naturally grounded in their personal experience and interest. The criticisms of the "friends of labor," however, are in most cases disinterested; though it must be said that in too many cases they are based upon a faint acquaintance with the facts. So far as they are disinterested, they must be recognized and met. It is sheer folly to adopt the attitude of the "hard-headed businessman" and display a lofty contempt for the increasing interest in the welfare of the working men, which has been developing into a powerful force during the last century. "Hard-headed" is too often a mere euphemism for hard-hearted. Intelligent humanitarianism is not only legitimate but is one evidence of upward progress, and is neither to be ignored nor treated with contempt.

But businessmen have a right to ask the humanitarians that they be intelligent and informed. It is the business of businessmen to supply the information needed from the data which are usually at their exclusive disposal. When, for instance, it is alleged that scientific management is "dehumanizing," the charge should be met with the actual histories of men who have worked under this system. Many plants where it has been developed can show, on the part of their employees, an increase of leisure, of interest in their work, of knowledge and improvement in general character, and an enhancement of all-round welfare. Mr. Taylor, and especially Mr. Gantt, have not ignored this side of the subject; but, in proportion to the mass of data in their hands, their contributions have not been full enough. This committee must have had an opportunity to look into this side of the case; and it is to be regretted that they have not improved it more fully.

In a remarkable book, *Fatigue and Efficiency,* by Josephine Goldmark, published by the Russell Sage Foundation, a chapter is devoted to "The New Science of Management: Its Relation to Human Energies." In this chapter are pointed out the advantages of the new methods from the point of view of the working man. After enumerating the perversions to which scientific management may possibly be put, the author says:

> If the unscrupulous use of scientific management were all that could be charged against it, the system could defend itself easily enough. . . . More serious is the contention that the efficiency engineers themselves have failed to gauge fairly the tax of increased productivity upon the workers. . . . What we need as regards both men and women (and the only answer which will allay the suspicions aroused by scientific management) is more knowledge as to the ultimate physical adjustment of the workers to the heightened intensity of their tasks.

And lest this seem to have too philanthropic a sound, I hasten to add the word of a prominent manufacturer, William C. Redfield, of Brooklyn. He says: "Once for all, let it be said that no management is scientific or permanently profitable which either promotes or permits human overstrain, or which taxes the future of women and children." This reflects, I think accurately, the judgment of many thinking people. The problem of the health of employees is one which demands and must have adequate consideration. No one who knows scientific management at first hand can deny that it has been given such consideration by those who are entitled to class themselves as scientific managers. Edith Wyatt's investigation of the subject with reference to women workers, the results of which are described in Chap. 7 of the book by Clark and Wyatt, *Making Both Ends Meet,* is conclusive on this score (and incidentally is somewhat misrepresented in Miss Goldmark's discussion). Numerous instances of the effect of this work on the health of employees might have been collected by the committee and should be given.

I know of a case of a girl who asked to be put on a task 50 per cent greater than what she had theretofore performed. At the time she appeared to be in a sickly condition. The factory nurse was consulted as to the advisability of allowing her to undertake the task and gave her consent on the condition that the girl be allowed to go back to her ordinary work if at the end of a fair period it was evident that the task was too severe for her. After the expiration of four weeks the nurse reported (and it was already evident to the manager) that the girl was not only doing the task easily but had greatly improved in health. This in the nurse's opinion, was due partly to the improved condition under which the girl worked, to the better method she had been taught, to the higher wages she received, and to her increased contentment. This same girl shortly afterward asked for an increase of 33⅓ per cent more in her task, but this was refused.

In this report the committee emphasize the "transference of skill" as the basic feature of the new labor-saving management. Unfortunately, however, it appears that this term is used with two meanings. Throughout most of the report it seems to mean the accumulation of skill by the planning department and its transference from this department by actual instruction to the workmen just as machinery is said to be the transference of skill, according to the report, from the designer and draftsman to the machine. The idea intended to be conveyed is undoubtedly right, but the illustration chosen is unfortunate.

Transference of skill, when considered with reference to the industrial revolution and the introduction of machinery, might easily be interpreted to mean the transference of skill from the workman to the machine. What actually happened was that the machine brought to the aid of the workmen some of the vast forces of nature; and in addition, it superseded the skill of the hand worker. That this was a distinct loss to the hand worker who was unable to adjust himself to the new conditions is incontestable in the face of economic history; and the sad record of the change is a solemn warning to present-day managers to take every step possible to make the adjustment to new methods of management as easy and gradual as possible. The machine developed a new kind of skill on the part of the operator; but now it is a minute skill easily acquired and subject to sudden loss with the change in the design of the machine.

The old-fashioned, all-round workman has disappeared or is rapidly disappearing; and though his replacement by the modern, keen-eyed, high-strung, quick-moving specialist is not to be altogether deplored, it has had certain serious consequences. It has made the present-day operator narrower in his knowledge of industry and his skill less adaptable and elastic. It has also rendered obsolete the old methods of apprenticeship, and the present chaotic condition of this subject presents a striking illustration of the failure of managerial thought to bring about the necessary readjustments.

H. M. WILCOX wrote that he felt that through the unfortunate adoption of the term labor-saving management, the committee have allowed themselves to lose the perspective of the subject of scientific management as a whole. The definition of the word science is "knowledge duly arranged and systematized," and this so-called new element in industry is chiefly the arranging, systematizing and recording of principles evolved by the art of management, so that the term scientific management is the most logical to use. The term labor-saving appears to have detracted from other phases of scientific management.

ROBERT THURSTON KENT. Time study is the basis of all modern management. The provision of a machine to make time study should be as revolutionary in the art of time study as was the invention of the power loom in the art of weaving. Among other things it absolutely eliminates the human equation. It provides a method in which there is not only no possibility of error in measurement, but which furnishes at once a true statement of the time elapsed in the performance of any operation and a record and instruction card of the best method of doing a job.

In *The Psychology of Management* the following statement appears:

> Measurement is a most necessary adjunct to selecting the workers and the managers and assigning them to the proper functions and work. They cannot be selected to the greatest advantage and set to functionalized work until (*a*) the unit of measurement that will of itself tend to reduce costs has been determined; (*b*) methods of measurements have been determined; (*c*) measurement has been applied, and (*d*) standards for measurement have been derived.

It is obvious that micro-motion study at once presents a means of most economically determining and applying all these standards.

It was the writer's privilege to be present at many of the experiments which led to the development of micro-motion study and to observe how it was applied to the transference of skill and experience. Scientific management makes use of the best methods of all trades which can be transferred to the trade under consideration. The experiments under which micro-motion study was developed are an illustration of this point. The work involved was the assembling of braiding machines, obviously a machine shop proposition. The original method of assembly involved the bringing of the various pieces to the job in a box or boxes from which they were taken as required by the worker. Many unnecessary motions were used to transfer the individual pieces to the growing machine which were promptly revealed by the moving picture machine. A bench which would bring the top of the completed machine at a convenient level for the workman was built and the parts were arranged in an orderly manner in bins behind him, thus reducing the number of motions.

In other trades in which some of the experimenters had been engaged it had been found advisable to group the units composing a single assembly on a packet, arranging them in the order in which they were needed. This suggested a similar packet scheme for the parts of the braider. A horizontal packet was first made up and the motion picture machine revealed an irregularity and lack of rhythm in the movements of assembling which seriously cut down the efficiency of the workman. A change to a vertical packet and a standard height of portable assembly bench was thereby indicated. On this packet the various parts are hung on pegs in that exact position which micro-motion study has revealed as the most economical of motions both as regards time and length of travel. Micro-motion study revealed the deficiencies of previous methods and permitted the development of the final accepted methods in a small fraction of the time and expense which would have been necessary under conditions existing before its invention.

F. A. WALDRON. Literature on scientific management has dwelt largely with the labor problem, while the other elements which tend so much toward maintaining factory output have been to a large extent ignored. Scientific management in its highest sense can be likened to the proper functioning of the human body, in which each part carries its own portion of the load, does its own share of the work at the proper time and distributes energy in proper proportions to all parts of the human frame.

There has been more or less tendency in the management of industries to divorce the financial and sales organizations from the factory or shop management in such an arbitrary manner that the two act in a way indicating that each is working for itself regardless of the broader interests of the company of which each is a part. So long as the sales end can get orders to the factory and be duly credited, the fact as to whether this order contains enough specific information to complete it, is ignored, and it is left for the factory to make it out as best it can. A serious loss in volume of output may thus be caused. I can recall several instances in my experience where an output of from $50,000 to $100,000 worth of business was held awaiting detailed information on minor items before the order could be shipped. It is essential to keep the entire organization in balance. Do not overload sale and advertising departments if the factory cannot handle the work. Build up on a solid foundation surely and gradually. Educate not in the factory alone, but along the entire line.

Output. In the excitement of the moment, the quality of output should not be lost sight of. This cannot be maintained by the mere placing of tools, instructions and drawings in the hands of the workman. Men must be trained and it takes time and money to train them. Unless this training embodies the elements of thoroughness and completeness, they become half-rate and slip-shod men, looking for pay day and taking little if any interest in the work.

Ideal factory conditions rest almost entirely on one basic principle which is *constant volume of output.* It is not always possible to maintain this owing to conditions that may arise, such as orders, capital, and the proper supply of materials and help. Every green workman broken in means sacrifice in profits, quality and volume of output. As these weak spots develop, however, we should try to build them up in such a way as to make conditions tending towards constant volume of output, as nearly perfect as possible.

It is far better to work at a steady even gait for a year than to intensify the production to a point where all the work is done in six months and your factory is idle for the remaining six months.

The extent to which time study should be carried depends entirely on these conditions and the expense incurred by ultra-refinement could better be invested, oftentimes, in raw materials or finished stock of proper quality. It is the province of the industrial and efficiency engineer to help guide the manufacturer as to how far he should go into a question of this kind.

A factory with an undersold output is no place for a premium or bonus system. Accurate and simple accounting and routing are requisites here. With an oversold output, a premium, bonus or piece rate system, based on accurate time study, combined with accurate and simple accounting and routing are necessary to produce the maximum efficiency on the shop end, combined with a purchasing, inspection and stock department that can keep pace with a well developed shop organization.

Purchasing. The most effective coöperation between the factory and purchasing departments is as essential as time study or production engineering work. Of what avail is time study and intensified production if the materials the purchasing agent buys at the lowest price will not meet the requirements of the product in quality? Work will either be thrown away before it is assembled, or if sent out in the finished product, it will react on business. The only way is to buy to specifications and see that the material is on hand before it is needed and that the specifications are conformed to.

Low prices paid for materials are not necessarily exponents of a purchasing agent's efficiency. The man who can discriminate and buy the right thing at a fair price is the kind of man that lasts in this period of competition and exacting requirements.

Serious delays and expenses are often caused by incomplete or incorrect specifications for simple materials and supplies. This trouble can be obviated by a symbol or number system which ties all materials used in the factory to a standard specification which is definite and complete in its wording.

Engineering. A product improperly designed and well made cannot maintain its place in the market, and, conversely, a product properly designed and improperly made, cannot be sold. To design properly and to see that it is properly made, is the measure of efficiency of the engineering department.

Proper strength, lines, proportions, tolerations, inspection, instructions, manufacturing specifications, tool design and manufacturing, should be done in this department and done thoroughly. Time study and bonus system are thrown away if done on work that cannot be used, or hurts trade. Further, responsibility is more readily placed if this is done in the full sense and meaning of the word "complete."

The engineering department in the modern organization of high efficiency is the most important of all, as it is the fountain head from which all specifications are issued, designs made and quality of work determined.

Inspection. To insure proper materials being given to the workmen is the first and most important duty of the inspection department, followed by proper tools, condition of machines, jigs and fixtures for the reasonable performance of acceptable work. These functions are just as necessary to efficient work as time study or bonus system, for without these the intensified production would be lacking, owing to the fact that conditions for perfecting the work would not be constant and the failure to perfect such work would be beyond the workman's control.

After these requirements have been brought up to the proper standard of efficiency, this division can control the quality of the work as specified by the engineering division and is in a position to insist on its quality being maintained.

Maintenance. To do a full day's work, a man must have proper light, heat, power machines, tools and fixtures, etc., in proper working condition, and it is up to the management to see to it that he does. One of the most common troubles is the condition of belts, long ago recognized by Frederick W. Taylor and covered in his paper on "Shop Management."[2] His system with the belt, bench and scales in a factory using many belts is the best obtainable and shows direct results in volume of output and saving in belt bills.

Countershafts, main shafts, jack shafts, motors, machine repairs, should receive a systematic supervision to insure constant and efficient operation. It is true that time study develops these requirements, but these requirements should be attended to first or time study will in a way be wasted.

Accounting. To have reasonably accurate costs is both desirable and necessary, not only as a means of efficiency but also to eliminate unprofitable articles of manufacture and produce the more profitable ones. This system requires methods of factory accounting which interlock with routing system, time keeping, and stores, requiring a close coöperation with the stores, inspection and producing work of management.

Proper distribution of overhead charges, accurate time study and charges, accurate material charges, controlled from a central point in which all is charged against its proper account by the same mental interpretation is the only accurate way, combined with a symbol method, not too complicated, which places the burdens where they belong at the time the expense is incurred.

Stores. Raw and worked materials must be properly accounted for, and the truthful conduct of a stock room is important and necessary. Stores records should be

---

[2] *Transactions,* American Society of Mechanical Engineers. Vol. 24, p. 1337.

complete and show enough information to gauge efficiency without being so complicated and cumbersome as to require more time to tell the story than an inventory.

Maximums and minimums should be so proportioned as to allow a minimum amount of capital being tied up in fixtures, stock, raw materials and work in process as well as all materials spoiled or defective. A graveyard in a store in plain sight of all is a mighty object lesson to the management and workmen.

The broad or commercial interpretation of efficiency engineering, or scientific management, is profitable management, in which the final measure of success is the return on the investment. As this return is dependent on other than labor elements, it would seem but fair that we carefully and earnestly consider the fact that no man can do efficient work at a machine unless the conditions are made right for the performance of such work and that each function of the industrial organization requires as close, if not closer, attention on the part of the management as do the workman and the machine.

FREDERICK W. TAYLOR. The preparation of this report has evidently involved careful research, followed by a close analysis of the materials gathered in. The viewpoint from which the whole subject is examined is new and original. Most writers upon this subject have emphasized the necessity of reducing to a science the knowledge which in the past has been in the heads of the workmen. The change from rule of thumb to scientific knowledge has been largely dwelt upon, and its importance pointed out. The thought of the committee, however, centers mainly about transfering this knowledge to the workman after it has been acquired by the management; and from this viewpoint scientific management is very properly summarized as "the mental attitude that consciously applies the transference of skill to all of the activities of the industry."

The committee very properly call attention to the significance of the change in the mental attitude of both sides which takes place under scientific management. This would seem to be the most vital element in scientific management. It was, indeed, looked upon as of such importance that, during the hearings before the House Committee "to investigate the Taylor and other systems of management," man after man came from the shops which are being run under scientific management, to testify that the very essence of this system lies in the great mental change which comes both to the management and to the workmen. In fact, with but few exceptions, these men testified that without this complete mental revolution, scientific management could not exist.

This mental change is great and far-reaching. It means essentially a change from suspicious watchfulness and antagonism and frequently open enmity, between the two sides, to that of friendship, hearty good-will and coöperation. It means a change from the old belief that the interests of employer and employee are in many respects necessarily antagonistic, to the firm conviction that the true interests of the two are mutual.

This feature of scientific management is of such importance that it seems desirable to make one of the causes for the change in mental attitude a little more clear. The following illustration may help to do this:

Into the manufacture of any article there enter two items of expense, the cost of the materials of which it is composed, and the cost of what are commonly called "overhead expenses" or general expenses, such as the proper share of power, light, heat, salaries of officers, etc.

Now, if these two items of expense, cost of materials and general expense, be added together and their sum subtracted from the selling price of the article, we have what is called the "surplus." And it is over the division of this surplus between the company and the men that most of the labor troubles and disputes have come in the past. The men want as large a part of this surplus as possible in the form of wages, and the company as large a share as possible in the form of profits. And in the division of the surplus, under the older systems of management, both sides have come in many cases to look upon their interests as truly antagonistic.

A part of the great mental revolution that occurs under scientific management is the complete change in the viewpoint of both sides as to this surplus; from looking upon the *division* of the surplus as the important question, they both come to realize that if, instead of pulling apart and quarreling over it, they join together and both push hard in the same direction, they can make this surplus so large that there is no need to quarrel over its division, because each side can get a far larger sum than they had ever hoped to get in the past. And each side realizes that this result would have been entirely impossible without the hearty coöperation of the other. The workmen see clearly that without the constant help and guidance of those on the management side, they could not possibly earn their extra high wages, and the management see that without the true friendship of the workmen their efforts would be futile, and they are glad to have their workmen earn much higher wages than they can get elsewhere.

The introduction of scientific management is, so far as I know, the first large movement in industrial history in which a great increase in the output of workmen was at once accompanied by a large increase in the earnings of the workmen. The great increase in output resulting from the introduction of labor-saving machinery was not at once accompanied by much if any increase in the wages of operatives, and in many instances the introduction of labor-saving machinery resulted in paying lower wages to the operatives of these machines than had been received by similar hand workers before the introduction of machinery. The main profit was absorbed at first in almost all cases by the manufacturers, who introduced the new labor-saving machinery. In the end, of course, the operatives, along with all the rest of the world, have profited immensely through the introduction of labor-saving machinery.

One of the most notable features of scientific management, however, is that the group of men who have introduced it have insisted that the workmen coming under its principles should at once be paid from 30 per cent to 100 per cent higher wages than they could get elsewhere. This fact is not appreciated by the general public, and largely because the labor leaders, consistent in their fight against the introduction of any labor-saving device, have seen fit to misrepresent far and wide almost all of the good features of this system; and in doing this they have strenuously denied that the workmen coming under scientific management are paid higher wages than heretofore. Quotations such as the following, taken from the famous circular distributed by President O'Connell throughout the Machinists' Union, are typical of this misrepresentation by labor leaders:

> Wherever this system has been tried it has resulted either in labor trouble and failure to install the system, or it has destroyed the labor organization and reduced the men to virtual slavery and *low wages,* and has engendered such an air of suspicion among the men that each man regards every other man as a possible traitor and spy.
>
> The installation of the Taylor system throughout the country means one of two things—*i.e.,* either the machinists will succeed in destroying the usefulness of this system through resistance, or it will mean the wiping out of our trade and organization with the accompanying low wages, life-destroying hard work, long hours, and intolerable conditions generally.

In answer to this statement of O'Connell's, however, in the sworn testimony given before the House Committee to investigate the Taylor and other systems of management there was presented a schedule of the present wages in comparison with the past wages of all the workmen who had been more than 12 months in the employ of a company which was using scientific management. This statement showed that the workmen were then receiving on an average 73 per cent higher wages than when they first came under scientific management. The list of employees included all kinds, even the colored men who helped move the materials around the floor of the shop, and the sweepers, etc.

The testimony also showed that the company, after paying this 73 per cent increase in wages, found itself better off than it was under the older type of management. That fewer workmen were turning out three times the output formerly obtained and that the selling price of machines manufactured had been reduced 25 per cent.

It is object lessons of this sort which are rapidly convincing those who investigate scientific management that the interests of both sides are mutual, instead of antagonistic.

The historical portion of the report shows careful study, and is evidently the result of much research. In certain particulars, however, it is somewhat misleading; that portion of it, at least, which includes the quotations from Adam Smith, etc., and particularly Tables 1 and 2, given in the Appendix.

Although the fact is not specifically stated, still the general impression from reading this part of the report is that "time study," which is the foundation for "the transference of skill from the management to the men," was practically carried on in 1760 and in 1830, as it is now under scientific management. This is, however, far from the truth, and in the interest of historical accuracy it may be desirable to make a statement as to the beginning of "time study," although I realize that questions as to who started time study, and when it was started, are of very little consequence, the important questions being, what is time study? and, how shall we make it more useful?

Time study was begun in the machine shop of the Midvale Steel Company in 1881, and was used during the next two years sufficiently to prove its success. In 1883, Emlen Hare Miller was employed to devote his whole time to "time study," and he worked steadily at this job for two years, using blanks similar to that shown in Par. 367 of "Shop Management." [3] He was the first man to make "time study" his profession.

It is true that the form of Tables 1 and 2, given in the Appendix to the Committee's report, is similar to that of the blanks recording time study, but here the resemblance ceases. Each line in Table 2, for instance, gives statistics regarding the average of the entire work of an operative who works day in and day out, in running a machine engaged in the manufacture of pins. This table involves no study whatever of the movements of a man, nor of the time in which his movements *should* have been made. Mere statistics as to the time which a man takes to do a given piece of work do not constitute "time study." "Time study," as its name implies, involves a careful study of the time in which work *ought* to be done. In but very few cases is it the time in which the work actually was done.

Previous to the development of "time study" in the Midvale Steel Works, there have in all probability been many instances in which men have carefully studied and analyzed the movements of other men, and have timed them with watches. (No such instances have, however, come to my personal attention.) Any such former work was without doubt confined to isolated cases, and was of short duration; and (most important from the historical point of view) it did not lead to the development of a new trade, or, more properly, to a new scientific occupation, "the profession of time study."

Any former efforts of this kind would bear the same general relation to the time study done in the Midvale Steel Works that the many early attempts at flying bear to the work of the Wright brothers.

The Wright brothers started "man flying."

The Midvale Steel Works started the "profession of time study."

(I do not of course intimate that the two developments are of equal importance.)

Time study is the one element in scientific management beyond all others making possible the "transfer of skill from management to men." The nature of time study, however, is but imperfectly understood, and it is therefore important to define it clearly. "Time study" consists of two broad divisions, first, analytical work, and second, constructive work.

The analytical work of time study is as follows:

[3] F. W. Taylor, *Transactions*, American Society of Mechanical Engineers. Vol. 24, p. 1436.

a. Divide the work of a man performing any job into simple elementary movements.

b. Pick out all useless movements and discard them.

c. Study, one after another, just how each of several skilled workmen makes each elementary movement, and with the aid of a stop-watch select the quickest and best method of making each elementary movement known in the trade.

d. Describe, record and index each elementary movement, with its proper time, so that it can be quickly found.[4]

e. Study and record the percentage which must be added to the actual working time of a good workman to cover unavoidable delays, interruptions, and minor accidents, etc.

f. Study and record the percentage which must be added to cover the newness of a good workman to a job, the first few times that he does it. (This percentage is quite large on jobs made up of a large number of different elements composing a long sequence infrequently repeated. This factor grows smaller, however, as the work consists of a smaller number of different elements in a sequence that is more frequently repeated.)

g. Study and record the percentage of time that must be allowed for rest, and the intervals at which the rest must be taken, in order to offset physical fatigue.

The constructive work of time study is as follows:

h. Add together into various groups such combinations of elementary movements as are frequently used in the same sequence in the trade, and record and index these groups so that they can be readily found.

i. From these several records, it is comparatively easy to select the proper series of motions which should be used by a workman in making any particular article, and by summing the times of these movements, and adding proper percentage allowances, to find the proper time for almost any class of work.

k. The analysis of a piece of work into its elements almost always reveals the fact that many of the conditions surrounding and accompanying the work are defective; for instance, that improper tools are used, that the machines used in connection with it need perfecting, that the sanitary conditions are bad, etc. And knowledge so obtained leads frequently to constructive work of a high order, to the standardization of tools and conditions, to the invention of superior methods and machines.

It is unusual to make a study such as this of the elementary movements of the workmen in a trade. The instances in which this has been done are still rare [5]: And it

---

[4] Recording these movements so that they can be readily found is the most difficult element of time study. The writer threw away his first two years of time study because it was so poorly indexed that he was unable to find the elements when he needed them.

[5] Most of the men who have made what they call "time study" have been contented with getting the gross time of a whole cycle of operations necessary to do a particular piece of work, and at best they have thrown out the time when the workman was idle, or evidently purposely going slowly.

would seem that this must be due to a lack of appreciation of the great power which is given to the man who possesses a knowledge of the time value of these elements, and also to a lack of appreciation of the large variety of work to which these elements apply. How many men, for instance, know that a man who has received his education in "time study" through analyzing the elements of the movements of machinists engaged in manufacturing conveying and hoisting machinery, can go with this knowledge into another establishment manufacturing machinery not in the most remote degree resembling hoisting machinery, and there use this knowledge to fix accurate daily tasks for the machinists? Yet during the past year and more, a young man trained in time study in the Link-Belt Works in Philadelphia, has been setting the daily tasks in one of our arsenals manufacturing a large variety of war materials, including the great disappearing gun carriages used in our coast defence.

Surely, when the significance of such a fact as this is appreciated, companies employing machinists, even though they may be manufacturing radically different kinds of work, will join together in studying the rudimentary elements of the machinists' trade and then in publishing this knowledge so that it may be available for hundreds of companies, where now it is the private property of the few concerns who have had the patience and the courage to be pioneers in this field. It is the lack of published data regarding the time required to perform each one of the elementary operations in our various trades (more than any other element) that makes the introduction of scientific management such a slow process.

If we accept the committee's definition of the new management as the "transference of skill from the management to the men," it is evident that the management cannot transfer knowledge and skill until they themselves possess this knowledge, and up to this time each new company introducing scientific management has been obliged to obtain this rudimentary knowledge through their own analysis and study, a very slow and tedious process.

Seventeen years ago, I predicted, in a paper read before this Society,[6] that books would be published similar to our engineering handbooks, embodying a time study of all of the elementary operations occurring in our various trades; and, was then greatly laughed and sneered at for making this statement. Only one such book has as yet appeared, but I wish to repeat my prophecy with more emphasis even than before —that hundreds of books of this sort will be published in the future, and in the not far distant future. These books will make possible "the transference of knowledge and skill from the management to the workman" on a large scale throughout the country, and the introduction of scientific management will then indeed proceed at a rapid pace.

CARL G. BARTH. I am gratified with the report as an endorsement of the kind of work I am permanently engaged in; particularly as I find among the names of the members of the committee who have signed the majority report, that of a personal friend who only through this investigation has become a convert to scientific manage-

[6] "A Piece-Rate System," *Transactions,* American Society of Mechanical Engineers. Vol. 17, p. 856.

THE PRESENT STATE OF THE ART OF INDUSTRIAL MANAGEMENT

ment. I am unable to take as broad a view of the matter as the committee have attempted, as I am tied down too closely to the daily details and difficulties of the practical introduction of scientific management to devote much time to its broad historical and economic aspects. Part of the report, also, has a rather amusing side for those of us who now for several years past have been working with some success in this field, in that it is virtually a declaration to the effect that the committee have assured themselves that there really is such a thing as "scientific management," and that it does accomplish some of the things, at least, which its exponents allege that it does. It reminds me of the farmer who came to town in the early days of the automobile to assure himself that there really was such a thing as a horseless wagon not requiring tracks to run on, and that it actually did carry people around in the streets without running wild and upsetting everything in its way, except when in the hands of a driver possessing more ambition than experience and sense of responsibility.

As regards the minority report, I see no good reason for its coming into being, as it contains nothing that I cannot agree to, and to my mind nothing that it recommends conflicts with the majority report.

It merely asserts that there are places in which, and conditions under which, the introduction of scientific management would not be a paying proposition; a matter that I do not believe anybody will dispute. In fact, experience has long ago taught me that there is hardly an establishment in which there is not some department or corner of the works which is not better left almost untouched by the new order of things, except in the matter of having its relations to the rest of the works properly dovetailed into this.

To take the automobile for a second illustration, I have never heard of anybody recommending its use to the extent of declaring that walking is no longer a profitable and sensible method of locomotion, to be eventually given up entirely; though we also know that some automobile enthusiasts do use the automobile at times and in places where walking would be more appropriate.

As regards the attempt of the committee, and others, to give a more appropriate name to what we all now pretty well understand by scientific management, I like to state that I have until recently preferred to refer to what I am trying to do, as the "Taylor system of management"; and that Mr. Taylor himself was the first one to discourage me in thus using his personal name in that connection, and to suggest substituting therefor the term scientific management. However, as I am not only not ashamed of, but on the other hand exceedingly proud of, being accused of being Mr. Taylor's most orthodox disciple, I have stuck to the former until recently; though since numerous imitators have invented a number of substitute names, so far as I can see to no practical purpose, I have become more favorably inclined to the use of the term scientific management. Accordingly, I now refer to myself as an exponent of the "Taylor system of scientific management," and feel that in doing so I have just about the whole thing.

In his discussion Mr. Gillette tries to point out that Mr. Taylor and his disciples have not covered the whole field and mentions as an example, cost and accounting as a matter to which they have paid no attention. However, the mere fact that Mr. Taylor has not written on every subject of his activities, must not be taken as a proof that he has neglected any important matter connected with the management of an industrial institution. The fact is that Mr. Taylor's disciples also owe him a great debt for the cost and accounting system he has handed over to them, one which for completeness and flexibility stands absolutely unequalled even today, in spite of the great attention this subject has recently received.

Mr. Church also mentions that the study of machines is a matter thus neglected. However, this is also a subject which Mr. Taylor gave serious attention over 25 years ago, or about the same time that he first took up the study of the art of cutting metals, and this has played one of the most important roles in the subsequent work done by myself in the perfection of some of Mr. Taylor's methods.

Again, one speaker suggested that there should be a special purchasing agent for buying labor, as if that too were a brand new idea, whereas Mr. Taylor has also pointed out the desirability of that, and as long ago as 1895 gave us an example of it in a man employed by some Western company at a salary of $5,000 a year, who had the buying of labor down to a fine art.

Mr. Gantt has told us about the disastrous results of changing to piecework from his bonus system of paying, in a plant systematized by himself, and I fear that what he said might have been misleading to some of the audience.

There is no question that piecework based on careful time study is the best and most just form of contract between employer and employee, and though I have not introduced Mr. Taylor's differential piece rates for some years past, I still believe that system is the best suggested to date. However, it is so difficult to get employers to wait until all such standards have been provided, and such time-study men have been trained, as are absolutely essential for the introduction of a piece-rate system, that we are usually forced by circumstances to beg the question and to resort to the expedient of a bonus or premium system.

These systems have the advantage of any piece-rate system, and particularly the differential, in that they may be established and give some satisfaction to both parties concerned, long before it would be possible to make a success of a piece-rate system.

However, there is no doubt in my mind, that the differential piece-rate system conceived and used by Mr. Taylor some 30 years ago, is the ideal of all the schemes suggested to date for paying workers in any other way than by straight day wages.

Regarding the use of a moving picture machine for motion and time studies, it looks to me to be practically the same thing as was offered to the Watertown Arsenal at the time we took up that part of the work there. I do not remember the inventor's name, only that he was connected with the Navy or with one of the navy yards in one capacity or another. While the scheme was interesting, it was declined after a conference between the commanding officer Mr. Merrick, and myself, particularly on the opinion expressed by Mr. Merrick, who is one of the most experienced time-study men in the country, and because of the anticipated great expense both of procuring and operating such a machine. Perhaps this was a mistake, for no doubt the machine can be successfully used for motion study, and hence for the elimination of useless motions, but I am still open to conviction regarding the use of any machinery of this kind in connection with time study. The two main difficulties in time study are: first, to judge when a worker is working at a proper rate and to make proper allowances when he is not; second, to make proper allowances for necessary rests, etc.; and I do not see how any kind of machinery can help us in these difficulties.

HUGO DIEMER. The report of the committee indicates that in their opinion there is no system of management any more than there is a system of music, chemistry or education.

The committee are to be commended for a strong effort put forth to get at the fundamentals. It should be borne in mind, however, that it is possible to go to extremes in our search for basic principles. For instance, we might consider that the basic principle of mathematics is measurement. If we contented ourselves with this bald statement, we would not explain the scope and objects of the science of mathematics as fully as if we extended our definition somewhat.

I believe we should not content ourselves with saying that the principle of division of labor is the basis of manufacturing. If we add to this statement a further one that the principle of division of labor gives rise to such matters as organization, control, specialization and functionalization, we are adding to our definition the sort of matter which we would consider it necessary to add to our definition of the basic principle of mathematics.

Attention is called by the committee to the fact that early writers foreshadowed the planning department, also that motion and time study are not even nineteenth century products, but that they were known and practiced at the opening of the manufacturing era in the eighteenth century.

The relationship of these isolated cases to the modern science of management is not much more definite than Jules Verne's prediction of the submarine and the aeroplane to the modern perfection and utilization of these ideas. Even in King Solomon's time we had pretty well regulated subdivision of labor, also the eight-hour day with Saturday half holiday and pay checks.

There is no present-day science that was not foreshadowed by disconnected parts in earlier centuries. For this reason I would change the definition which the committee have given for the second basic principle, which they designate as the transference of skill. The committee illustrate as examples of this principle the transference of the skill of the inventor to the power-driven mechanism, also the transference of the skill of the real expert in management who trains and directs the persons who are permanently to manage. I believe this element can be better defined by stating that it is the conscious application of scientific methods to all phases of industry, or the conscious effort to build up a science of industrial management. The real science of management will apply research methods, not only to designing and testing but to all phases of industry.

DEXTER S. KIMBALL. Ever since the beginning of the present industrial era there has been a growing tendency to separate mental and manual processes and to again subdivide these by the application of the division of labor. The engineering and drafting department was the first direct result and is the best existing example of the separation of the mental from the manual. While the art of industrial management has lagged behind scientific design for natural reasons, its fundamentals are well known and basic data will no doubt soon be available so that we may expect to see it on a more scientific basis.

It is to be noted that the process of "functionalizing" any branch of industry involves no new principle. It is an extension of the general tendency to separate mental and manual processes and motion and time study are not new discoveries as the report clearly points out; but this should detract in no way from the credit due those who have so ably called our attention to the possibility of their more extended use. The ultimate extent to which these principles will be carried and the rate of progress that they will make will depend, however, not on their inherent value or effectiveness alone, but on the growth of public opinion that permits or demands them.

One phase of the discussion touched on in Pars. 62 and 63 deserves more than passing thought. Changed industrial conditions resulting from the separation of the worker from the ownership of his tools have introduced a difficult problem in the matter of the compensation of the employee. The efforts of such men as Halsey and Towne were the first steps toward new methods of rewarding labor. All so-called *systems* of management are based on the extension of the principles already mentioned with the addition of some special philosophy of management which invariably includes some variation of these methods of rewarding labor, mixed perhaps, with certain altruistic ideas on the relations between employer and employee and the general uplift of the workman. These altruistic ideas are fine and helpful, though not new, as they were introduced and used by Robert Owen more than a century ago.

Success in the use of these combined methods, whereby better wages and better conditions have accrued to small communities, has led some over-ardent advocates of these methods to the hasty conclusion that they really offered a solution of the industrial difficulties which press so heavily upon us. Statements similar to the following are often seen:

> The increase in wages which accompanies this type of management will largely eliminate the wage question as a source of dispute.

> The one cure, the only one for the condition which confronts us, is to increase the efficiency of the producer.

That is to say increased productive power *necessarily* means increased profits to the actual producer. But a diligent search through the literature of efficiency engineering will fail to disclose a single new regulative principle bearing on the equitable distribution of the fruits of industry either between the employer and employee, or between the industry as a whole and the ultimate consumer.

Stripped of all sentiment these new methods are exactly similar in operation to labor-saving machinery (Par. 37) and their initial and ultimate effects must be similar. They will enable those who first adopt them to obtain some commercial advantage and to pay better wages than their competitors for a time at least. They will also result, if universally adopted, in a considerable increase of productive power; but they in no way affect the fundamentally inherent advantage which must always accrue to those who control the tools of production. They can in no way affect the principle that knowledge of all kinds tends to become common property and for that reason no labor-saving device can forestall competition for any extended time. They can in no way affect the law of supply and demand; and even if all the manufacturers in the country were to adopt these methods at once we should continue to see in many places at the same time, storehouses filled with raw materials, idle factories equipped with the finest tools, and people walking the streets without food or clothes and yet willing to work. Labor-saving machinery opened the door to tremendous *possibilities* for humanity far greater in proportion than can ever be promised by labor-saving management; but it brought with it no self-regulating principle which insured equitable distribution of these advantages; and labor-saving management is at best a small extension of a great movement.

It is true that all classes of people have profited by the use of labor-saving machinery, the actual producer as much as any, and it also follows that in the long run we shall all profit to some extent by increased productive power. But the industrial problems with which we are now wrestling will all be with us till we have made some changes in the basic principles on which we now distribute the results of our labors.

True, all the new systems lay stress on the "square deal" and the coöperation of employer and employee, but these are old as mankind and have always been available as a basis of economic justice in common with all other welfare work. But these measures are optional with employer and employee and do not constitute basic principles. They are exceedingly useful and beneficial as they serve as a means of better understanding of the dual difficulty and as a basis of corrective legislation, which after all is a reflection of the sentiment of the community and grows with it. It is neither fair nor wise, however, to attribute powers and advantages to efficiency engineering which it clearly does not possess. I am not sure but what a small readjustment of some other of our economic problems would do as much for us as increased productive power. We need and need badly some *scientific distribution* and we shall be fortunate indeed if some of the reactive influences now at work on our social and industrial organization will offer some help in this direction before the strain becomes unbearable.

JOSEPH A. BURSLEY called attention to the fact that this was the first time the Society had devoted an entire session to the consideration of scientific management. He was particularly interested in the possibility of applying the principles of this subject to works of educational institutions, especially technical schools, and felt that there was a great field for applying this work in teaching in the engineering schools. The men in the shops connected with the universities, for instance, should be shown the best way of doing each particular piece of work, so that after they are graduated, they may transfer this knowledge to others.

This same scheme could be followed in the laboratories where various tests are made; and even in the class room in the solution of problems of various kinds there is always one way which is the best, requires the least time, and gives the smallest opportunity for mistake.

WILLIAM KENT. I hesitate to criticize so splendid a report, but I do object to the statement in Par. 37, "The expression 'labor-saving management' better conveys the meaning of the movement." Labor-saving management is but a fraction of the new movement. As I conceive it, the whole question is industrial management, and there are three kinds of industrial management, which someone has called, traditional or unsystematized, transitional or systematized, and scientific management. This third type is industrial management carried on in a scientific manner, and it refers not only to labor-saving management, but to saving of fuel, capital, machinery, wear and tear, lubricants, and everything that enters into the product. I think if a scientific expert were called in by the management of a factory and they should say, "We want your services to show us what we ought to do," he would have *carte blanche* to go into every department as well as the labor-saving department.

In regard to the statement that has been made to the effect that an engineer who dabbles in economics is going outside of his field, I wish to call his attention to the fact that the first paper, No. 207, written in 1886, was on the topic, "The Engineer as an Economist." The engineer was an economist in 1886 and long before that. Part of the education of the engineer, and no small part, is education in economics. The thoroughly educated engineer must be a political economist and when he dabbles in questions of economy, he is right in his own field and is not going outside of it at all.

H. H. VAUGHAN explained his objections to the majority report. He differed from the report because it definitely advocates certain things, such as the bonus system, the planning department, functional organization and time studies, as constituting the new way in which to run industrial establishments. No one could value Mr. Taylor's work more than he, but his methods had their limitations like most new discoveries. It is a mistake to think they will revolutionize everything and supersede all other systems.

One thing in the report was very interesting to him, the remarks of James Nasmyth, quoted in Par. 9, in which it is stated:

> The characteristic feature of our modern mechanical improvements is the introduction of self-acting tool machinery. What every mechanical workman has now to do, and what every boy can do, is not to work himself, but to superintend the beautiful labor of the machine. The whole class of workmen that depend exclusively on their skill is now done away with.

He thought that a good instance of how a man's ideas that a new discovery is going to take the place of everything that comes up is frequently limited by his subsequent experience. There are more skilled men in Nasmyth's shop today than there were at the time that Nasmyth wrote these comments.

In his minority report Mr. Vaughan used the phrase, "art of management." There is essentially an art in these things, and one cannot give the rules that make an art. There is more in the creating of a successful shop than the studying of a set of prescribed methods. There must be the peculiar intuitive judgment that comes from experience and from the contact with men.

He said further: "Transference of skill," referred to in the report, means in one place doing away with skill, in another the improvement of skill, and develops into the idea of telling the men how to do everything. It is commercially absurd to assume that we will reach the point where we instruct the men in everything. I believe in experts in the shop, but the experience of the men in the shop must be taken into account. Anybody who has started to build a machine or produce any other class of work with new and unskilled labor, has found to his cost the value of the skillfulness of their men as an asset.

The report advocated functionalizing. Instead, I believe in putting more responsibility upon the foreman, making him the head of the units. Functional management is very much like departmental management on a railroad, as opposed to divisional management. The most successful railroads are managed on the divisional system. We do not expect a divisional man to know everything, but we work through him with the staff department, and want him to be the boss of his unit as far as possible. In that way we certainly get results, quicker action in the case of emergency than where the departmental system is in use and where one must go through a lot of routine to get results. Suppose we have a rush order. One man is put in charge of the job, who follows it through department after department, to see that the work is properly done. We could not do that if each department had to be called upon through its head to coöperate to obtain the results. The best results in our shop have been obtained by putting the work up to the superintendent or foreman and leaving the matter in his hands.

With our piecework system the object is to advise the foreman of what is being done rather than of what has been done. We have obtained good results by putting on a man whose duty it is to advise the foreman from time to time as to what is being done so that he can take immediate action in case any men are failing to make the time expected, as governed by the records in the operation of the shop.

As to the question of fairness in dealing with labor and cutting prices, much of this is really due to the fact that the workmen of to-day will not stand cutting prices. A few years ago men were less independent, and many shops were operated satisfactorily on straight piecework and with cutting prices. There is no use in pretending to be altruistic in this matter. We have been forced to our present position by experience, and it is pleasant to know that we can truthfully say to ourselves that it does not pay to cut prices.

We have been building the same class of locomotives for five years under the ordinary piecework system, and by dealing with the men fairly and encouraging them and getting them interested, the hours have dropped from 100 per cent to 68 per cent.

We believe in the piecework system with a guaranteed day rate, and do not use the bonus system, although in my opinion it is better than piecework where the operations are comparatively simple and the conditions standardized. However, the system must appeal to the men, and if they do not understand it, the same degree of success will not be secured.

We are using time-study work to a large extent, and I think time studies are of great value in perfecting a shop. On the other hand we had a shop with a pay roll of $4000 a month get into bad conditions. We sent a couple of men there, with a few good demonstrators, picked it right up, and it began to turn out the output. That is better than if we had been depending on a long-drawn-out system; it is a question of personal influence and quick action. The influence exerted in that case will be felt for a long period to come.

As Mr. Gantt has stated, he introduced time studies in our shops, which we value highly. Our results in the time-study work have cost on the average $600 to $800 a month, since we started, and we are now saving $2000 a month on a pay roll of $35,000, contract work. There has been a satisfactory progression with time study, not a revolution; we would not be without it, but, on the whole, it has not been as important as the piecework system.

There is, moreover, certain work in which day work is preferable to piecework. We would not think of putting steam-shovel repairers on piecework. We would rather have them work day work. We must use day work in certain cases and we should then do all we can to help the men to get the results.

We believe that we should not have any more system in our work than we can get along with nicely. We would rather have too little system than too much in the operation of the shop. We think that the best results are secured not only by studying the conditions, but also by studying the men who are operating the shop.

THOMAS R. WOOLLEY considered that the benefits from scientific management had not been all that could be desired for the worker, the manufacturer or the consumer. The worker is dissatisfied because of the strain put upon him to increase his speed and the stop watch in particular causes dissatisfaction. If instead of taking the initiative away from the worker, the rule could be reversed and the initiative of the individual encouraged under the guidance of competent executives, the system would have permanent results.

While the manufacturer has been benefited in some cases, in other cases he has been driven into bankruptcy on account of the large overhead burden introduced to carry out effectively the system, particularly where the business fluctuates greatly from year to year and from season to season. Under such circumstances, it is questionable whether it pays to train workers only to let them go during a dull season or to carry them on the pay roll working inefficiently during that period.

Further, the public had not been benefited by the adoption of the system and the writer cited a case where a large order for steel was placed, after securing bids from different firms, one of which employed scientific management and whose bid was higher than those of its competitors.

Dealing with Mr. Taylor's example of training men to carry pig iron, he believed that a fraction of the money spent upon labor-saving machinery with an electro-magnet in connection with a crane would give better results at less expense.

In considering whether to install scientific management, a manager must determine whether there is enough of one class of work to make it pay him to train men; whether his plant runs continuously throughout the year; whether it will pay to add a corps of men to instruct his workmen; and whether he should consider that it would pay better instead to install the latest improved machinery for the particular class of work to be produced.

Mr. Taylor and his associates are to be commended for stimulating thought along the lines of eliminating movements, etc. Some of these principles can be applied in a plant but all can not be applied in all plants because of varying conditions.

H. K. HATHAWAY wrote that the essence of this report lay in the phrase (Par. 29), "The mental attitude that consciously applies the transference of skill to all the activities of industry," further qualified by the statement, "the novelty of the new management lies in this transference of skill from the management to the workman."

This viewpoint is so novel that one is led to question whether the older descriptions of the essence of scientific management may not have been wrong. The committee, however, are merely laying emphasis upon one of the elements which has heretofore been looked upon as rather of secondary importance.

Before skill can be transferred, the management must gather in and record the knowledge and skill which were formerly widely diffused in the possession of a great number of workmen, and much of which was an almost unconscious inheritance. Gathering in and systematizing this knowledge ready for use, constitutes the development of a science to replace the old rule-of-thumb knowledge: this is what has been called by other writers the first of the four principles of scientific management, and this point the committee recognize in Par. 47.

The writer's experience leads him to feel that the committee have not given sufficient prominence to the element of acquisition of skill or "the development of a science" as it has been termed. Such development goes farther than the acquisition of existing skill and results in additions thereto as well as improvement in methods and machinery, and the establishment and maintenance of standards.

It is impossible to transfer skill from the management to the workman without first choosing carefully the workman who is fit to do a particular kind of work, and then training him until he acquires skill: the second of the principles of scientific management. It is not only a transference of skill, but in one sense the creation of skill as well; perhaps a better expression would be the development of latent skill.

The third principle of scientific management has been called "bringing the science and the scientifically selected and trained workman together," which is merely another name for the committee's statement, "the mental attitude that consciously applies the transference of skill to all the activities of industry."

The fourth principle of scientific management has been defined as "an almost equal division of the work and responsibility between the management and the workmen. The management takes over all work for which they are better fitted than the workman, while in the past almost all of the work and the greater part of the responsibility were thrown upon the men." This principle also follows directly the moment the management accept as their duty the first, second and third principles of scientific management. The burden of developing a science where only rule-of-thumb knowledge existed in the past, and the burden of training, teaching and transferring skill from the management to each workman in the place, of necessity calls for an almost equal division of the work between the two sides. So that in the one definition of the new science, by the committee, are implied all of the four principles of scientific management.

It might be proper to point out, in order to avoid misunderstanding, that specialization of workmen on one comparatively simple operation is not necessarily in accord with the best and most economic practice in management. It is a serious mistake and a disadvantage to have operators "unskilled except in a single readily mastered operation" as in the instance cited in Par. 8 of the committee's report. The writer's experience has been that it is not only generally desirable, but in many cases necessary to economy in manufacture, that each operative become skilled in at least two and generally more of the operations making up a process of manufacture. This is an objection to over-specialization purely from the standpoint of production.

FRANK B. GILBRETH. The report is especially valuable for the reason that it emphasizes the fact, which has long been realized by those engaged in the work of installing scientific management, that transference of skill is one of the most important features.[7] They do not, however, make sufficiently plain that such skill and the experience which precedes it must be measured and recorded before it can be most efficiently transferred.

A better name for scientific management is "measured functional management." It is not sufficient to call it "labor-saving management" for it deals with more than labor and labor saving. It is a way for obtaining methods of least waste. It not only saves useless labor, but it improves labor conditions; improves quality of product; prolongs the period of the worker's productivity; conserves, teaches and transfers skill and experience. The committee have caused the Society and the world to recognize at last the importance of the feature of the transference of skill, but they apparently

[7] See *Primer of Scientific Management*, F. B. Gilbreth, p. 56; *Psychology of Management*, L. M. Gilbreth, chap. 8; *Motion Study*, F. B. Gilbreth, p. 36.

still lack appreciation of the even greater feature of the recording and transference of experience of Mr. Taylor's measured functional management and of micro-motion study. Mr. Taylor's system is best described in his writings entitled "A Piece-Rate System," "Shop Management," and "On the Art of Cutting Metals," published by the Society, and *Principles of Scientific Management,* published by Harper & Brothers.

As brought out in the report, the importance of transference of skill was realized many years ago. Studies in division of work and in elapsed time of doing work were made by Adam Smith, Charles Babbage, M. Coulomb and others, but accurate measurement and management became possible when Mr. Taylor devised his method of observing and recording elementary unit net times for performance with measured allowance for fatigue.

It is now possible to capture, record and transfer not only skill and experience of the best worker, but also the most desirable elements in the methods of all workers. To do this, scientific management carefully proceeds to isolate, analyze, measure, synthesize and standardize least wasteful elementary units of methods. This it does by motion study, time study and micro-motion study which are valuable aids to sort and retain all useful elements of best methods and to evolve from these a method worthy to be established as a standard and to be transferred and taught. Through this process is made possible the community conservation of measured details of experience which has revolutionized every industry that has availed itself of it.

Micro-motion study, presented for the first time at this meeting, is a new and accurate method of recording and transmitting skill. Based upon the principles of motion study and time study, it makes possible simultaneous measurement of both time and path of motions. It produces an entirely different result from any of the methods attempted by its predecessors, in that it shows a measured difference in the time of day on each and every cinematograph picture, even when the pictures are taken at a rate much faster than ever considered in work where positive films are printed and projected upon the screen.

The devices used in making micro-motion study are adaptable to the needs of the work. The kind of clock and camera used and the number of pictures taken per unit of time depend upon the nature of the work observed. For those interested primarily in the time study work of a machine shop, the clock that shows divisions of 1/200 of a minute is recommended; for ordinary problems of motion study, the clock showing divisions of 1/1000 of a minute is the best; and for those who desire to make the finest of motion and time studies for the purpose of obtaining ultimate methods of least waste, the clock showing divisions of $\frac{1}{1,000,000}$ of an hour or less is absolutely necessary. Such a clock is essential for discovering the method of least waste in cases such as handing instruments to a surgeon when operating. There is no case in the industries where the necessity for highest possible speed consistent with desired results is so great. For example, when operating for mastoiditis, it is necessary that the probe to lift the scalp be used within the shortest possible time after the skin has been cut, before the blood has had time to run down into the cut. Micro-motion study and stereocycle graphs are the only methods that will measure the times and paths of different motion methods for doing this portion of the operation. Micro-motion study has already determined that the combining of two or more instruments or tools for such cases and reversing the ends in the hand is much quicker than dropping one tool and grasping another.

Not only is it possible with micro-motion study to make more accurate measurements of shorter times than one could with any other method of motion or time study, it is also less expensive, even for ordinary work, than the older stop-watch method. Much of the work can be done by a less skillful man than the old time-study man; moreover, provision is made for stopping all photographic expense during any time the worker is resting, or doing work where no record except elapsed time is wanted.

Recent improvements in the method of taking pictures and of using half-width films, with nearly twice as many pictures to the foot and about one-third as many to the second as is used in motion pictures of the standard "movies," have still further reduced the cost of taking micro-motion studies.

Because of the flexibility of the micro-motion study apparatus the possibilities of its use are much extended. It is possible to take pictures as slowly as is desired, for such observations for example, as are required on time study of the machine's time, such as one picture per minute, while when it is desired to study the minutiae of motions the pictures can be recorded at any desired speed, even at the rate of 1,000,000 per hour, for short periods. Recording as it does rest periods as well as work periods, micro-motion study presents complete as well as accurate records of the skill displayed.

These records are not only indispensable to those who are to teach or transfer the skill or experience, and are in themselves useful as object lessons, but more important than all else they are the devices that measure and record the skill which is to be transferred. They are used by the man who makes standards to determine the most efficient method of doing work. By them he is able to "take any motion apart" and to think in elementary motions. Being provided not only with a record of the best method of the best man, but with records of the best methods of all most skilled workers, he can synthesize these into a standard method which will be better than any of the methods submitted, and is likely to be better than all combined.

To the worker this knowledge comes in various ways: He may be given photographic films depicting some method that he desires to acquire. These he can study at his leisure; making the demonstrator do the work as slowly as he pleases. The difficulty that most skilled workers find in making habitual motions slowly is a great hindrance to learning by observing them. The film records the swiftest motions, which can be taken apart and observed slowly. He may be given films on which are recorded methods of distant shops whose workers he would never otherwise observe. The worker may be taught not directly by the films, but by methods derived indirectly by them.

With records of skill that fulfil the three requirements of measurement, namely, (a) of proper units, (b) made by scientifically derived methods, (c) with devices that reduce expense, and with transference of skill that assures every worker an opportunity to acquire the best that has been thought and done in his line, scientific management can now look forward to fulfilling the ultimate demands, and justify itself from the economic viewpoint, and reduce the cost of the product to the consumer.

THE COMMITTEE. The large amount of discussion offered on the report on "The Present State of the Art of Industrial Management" shows the interest in this subject on the part of members of the Society. This, and the manner in which the report was received, are sources of gratification to the committee. Although a few points were singled out for objection, the report as a whole seems to have been approved. In fact, these objections as they appear in the printed discussion, in most cases can be directly offset by quotations from the same source.

The first objection is that the report gives "no more than a fragmentary idea of the conditions under which this art is carried on in the United States today," first paragraph of Mr. Going's discussion. Offsetting this, we quote from the first paragraph of Mr. Gantt's discussion, "The committee have caught fully the present spirit of the movement now in progress, and Pars. 45 to 58 of their report seem to me to be an excellent résumé of the subject." It was obviously improper for the committee to consider the details of the systems of the art of management as practiced, but it was essential to show the spirit of the movement and if possible the principles upon which it rests. This the report endeavored to do, and did do in the opinion of the member quoted above.

C. B. Thompson pointed out that there are several criticisms made by workmen against modern industrial management, and that labor unions are busily fighting its introduction. With further reference to these features is this sentence, "The report of such a committee as this should not have overlooked the opportunity to begin or extend the campaign of education in these particulars." And again, in regard to the dehumanizing effect on the workers of the methods of modern industrial management the same author says, "This committee must have had an opportunity to look into this side of the case; and it is to be regretted that they have not improved it more fully."

This author seems to have overlooked the necessity which compelled the committee to treat of their subject in a non-controversial manner. At the same time, the broad results from industrial management are clearly stated in Pars. 62 and 63. These seem sufficient to meet this criticism. In regard to the statement that the criticism of the dehumanizing effect should have been met, we need but quote from Mr. Coburn's discussion to show that the human side of the subject was found by one of the Society's members—"the committee have expressed in their report the human interest side of scientific or labor-saving management, which some of its critics say it lacks." Further, the entire discussion of H. L. Gantt develops the point that the workers are benefited by the best of modern management.

The term, transference of skill, is used frequently in the report and conveys one of the important ideas in the definition of the new element in the art of management. This term seems to have been misinterpreted, for near the end of C. B. Thompson's discussion we read, "In this report the committee emphasize the 'transference of skill' as the basic feature of the new labor-saving management. Unfortunately, however, it appears that this term is used with two meanings. Throughout most of the report it seems to mean the accumulation of skill by the planning department and its transference from this department by actual instruction to the workmen just as machinery is said to be the transference of skill, according to the report, from the designer and draftsmen to the machine. The idea intended to be conveyed is undoubtedly right, but the illustration chosen is unfortunate"; and in Mr. Vaughan's discussion, "the transference of skill referred to in the report means in one place, doing away with skill, in another the improvement of skill, and develops into the idea of telling men how to do everything."

The idea of the "transference of skill" is abstract, and these quotations indicate that their authors have failed to get the meaning of the term as used by the committee. "Transference of skill" is a process, and the expression might be expanded into "the process of transferring skill." It was the completion of this process that did away with hand looms and hand weaving in England. At the time of this completion, the skill in hand weaving was the personal possession of the last generation of hand weavers. Men of the succeeding generation did not acquire this skill for there was no economic advantage in so doing. Yet cloth was woven in greater quantities than before, leading at once to the question, where then was the skill? It is evident that the yarn was being manipulated by machines, thus, the former human skill was now in the metal fingers and arms and levers of the mechanism. But a new form of human skill was being developed as the process advanced; this is, the practical ability to tend the machine, keep it in order and producing to its maximum capacity.

The report pointed out that this process had advanced to a great length in the field of machine design, but had remained almost without application in the field of manufacturing. The best of modern industrial management applies this process to all of the activities of manufacturing, that is, a study is made of the steps of manufacturing in the same way that a study is made of the steps of designing. The results of handling and operation study are recorded for the instruction of the men engaged in manufacturing, in the same manner that the conclusions of the study of design are recorded on drawings as instructions for what is to be made. The parallel is exact.

It must be emphasized that this process applies to much more than the operation of machines, it applies to everything that is done in handling materials, machines, tools, and labor used in production. It is unnecessary to list these in detail, for everyone acquainted with manufacturing appreciates what is included. The training of the workmen is but one small, though important, part of the application of this process of transferring skill.

Regarding the discussion as a whole, there are two striking characteristics that attract and hold attention; the entire absence of exaggerated statement and the presence throughout of a humane spirit in keeping with the best trend of thought toward social justice. The first of these, the absence of exaggeration as to what industrial management has done or can do, was to be expected in any discussion before a body of engineers. The second shows clearly the development that has taken place within the last few years leading to a new appreciation of the needs and rights of employees.

But this commendable attitude of justice does not seem to have had its full influence on the relations existing between management experts. Among some of these, there is an unfortunate spirit of intolerance. This is in marked contrast to the spirit prevailing in all the great divisions of engineering. In these there is room for the cadet engineer as well as the recognized expert and for many others between these two extremes possessing varied degrees of knowledge and experience, as witness the membership of our own Society. The same is true in the field of industrial management. There is room and need for everyone who understands the principles upon which it rests and who will conscientiously and intelligently apply them.

This situation and these facts should lead to a tolerant attitude between all who are honestly trying to further the art of industrial management, and there should exist the same spirit of mutual helpfulness and encouragement which actuates those in other lines of engineering specialization. On the other hand, all who are trying to exploit the present interest in this important subject for mere personal advantage must be unsparingly condemned.

LEON P. ALFORD

*Ten Years' Progress in Management**

1913-1922

This Report stresses the thought that progress has largely to do with the human element—adding to the 1912 criteria the motive of service.

An interesting entry is the inclusion of a list of engineering schools which had begun including the new Science of Managing as part of their curricula.

* Alford, Leon P., "Ten Years' Progress in Management." Presented during Management Week, Oct. 16-21, 1922 and at the Annual Meeting, New York, December 4-7, 1922, of The American Society of Mechanical Engineers. No. 1876, *Transactions*, Vol. 44, 1922. Permission to excerpt by courtesy of the Society.

TEN YEARS' PROGRESS IN MANAGEMENT, 1913-1922

Leon P. Alford

TEN YEARS have passed since the Committee report on "The Present State of the Art of Industrial Management" was presented to The American Society of Mechanical Engineers. The request is now made for a review of the progress of management during the intervening decade. Unfortunately for the purpose of such a study, eight of these ten years were abnormal, many of the management changes and innovations introduced were of a temporary nature or were mere expedients, and it is difficult to separate them from other and more permanent developments.

2. The only satisfactory way to treat the review is to base it upon the report of 1912, which was well received and in large measure approved. This course has therefore been adopted.

3. At the outset we should recall and pay generous tribute to three of our late great leaders who aided in preparing that report and took part in its discussion: Frederick W. Taylor, the pioneer in management; Henry L. Gantt, who humanized the movement; James M. Dodge, the earnest, constructive supporter. During our ten-year period these men of vision and power completed their life work.

4. To obtain information on the worth-while changes which have taken place, letters were written to management and industrial engineers, to executives of plants in various lines of industry, and to educators familiar with industrial developments. Many interviews were held with men having industrial and managerial responsibilities. The response to these requests has been most generous. The author is deeply indebted for the information received and expresses his sincere gratitude to all who have given aid.

5. The report of 1912 declared the new element in management to be: "The mental attitude that consciously applies the transference of skill to all the activities of industry." It also quoted [1] and endorsed three regulative principles:

a. The systematic use of experience;
b. The economic control of effort; and
c. The promotion of personal effectiveness.

[1] *American Machinist*, vol. 36, p. 857, "The Principles of Management," by Church and Alford.

6. New interpretations and expanded meanings have been given to these principles, but they have in nowise been weakened or superseded. One correspondent writes: "Note, for example, the nearly universal acceptance of the principles. . . ."

7. In answer to the question, "What steps have been made in the progress of management since 1912?" a wide range of opinion was expressed as shown by the following sixteen quotations from correspondents' letters. The first gives a particularly well-balanced judgment of the situation.

It seems to me that management has very definitely progressed in the last ten years along certain main lines.

In the first place, good management is more insistent today on knowledge as a basis of judgment, rather than the old judgment based on personal observation. Management is more and more demanding costs, a knowledge of inventories, monthly profit and loss statements, statistics, and records of all kinds as pictures of events on which to base judgment.

In the second place, management is now undergoing a definite metamorphosis in the matter of industrial relations, and managers are waking up to the fact, as a practical element in their business, that they owe more to their employees than mere wages, and that whistle blow and hustle are not all there is to factory operation.

It is this belief and the spirit developing, rather than the volume of the action up to date, which is a matter of very definite progress in the past ten years of management.

8. Ten opinions, three to the effect that management has retrogressed or made little or limited progress, and seven stating the belief that progress has been made and mentioning certain details of improvement, are grouped to present a contrasting though in the main favorable picture.

Management (the directing group) has retrogressed in its acceptance of the principles of management, while labor has materially progressed toward a broader acceptance of these principles.

I believe that very little progress has been made in the adoption of scientific management principles in industries outside of metal working, with a few notable exceptions.

The main advance, and that lamentably slow, has been in putting into practice knowledge already available previous to 1912.

During the past ten years we have passed through the period of first glamour, then the reaction of a loss of confidence, and have finally evolved into the general recognition of the legitimate place of a new branch of engineering art and science—management engineering.

The important steps in progress in management during the past ten years have been from unintelligent rule-of-thumb management through scientific management to intelligent management. The latter has advanced steadily during the decade.

The greatest progressive step has been toward standardization of appliances and methods.

The most definite progress made during the past ten years is the universal acceptance of the merits of specialized production and standardization of design. These two steps have opened the way to a third simplification of method.

The reaction from destruction and waste incident to warfare and reconstruction has been toward the elimination of waste in industry as a management function. Waste in all forms has been more closely observed than hitherto, especially during the past two years. This effort to do away with waste has led to the fixing of budgets and the determination of cost standards.

Important steps in the progress of management since 1912 are:

a. Greater use of facts in the establishment of the standards by which business is conducted;

b. Broader recognition of the principle that industry exists for service to humanity;

c. Greater appreciation of the importance of regularization or control in the successful conduct of our industries;

d. Wider understanding of the economic value and importance of the management engineer in the operation of business.

There has been a great increase in the use of specifications not only to govern purchased materials but also to attain uniformity of process, quality and cost, and thus to insure reliability of product. Many plants now have well-equipped laboratories staffed by scientific men and some regularly employ consulting scientists. In the larger corporations research laboratories are not uncommon. Few of these departments are over ten years old and they evidence a rapidly growing appreciation of pure science as a tool of management.

The need of early and reliable figures as a mechanism of management has caused many companies to prepare monthly a complete statement of their business and earnings. A constantly increasing number of companies are publishing annually a detailed statement of their financial condition and many are publishing such statements quarterly. This voluntary publicity indicates a sincerity and frankness rare in management of an earlier decade.

9. The final quotations in regard to progress, five in number, discriminate between management form and substance. Progress is indicated in both of these aspects.

The biggest and most lasting accomplishment in the inculcation of management principles is that, like religious teaching whose significance has been forgotten during years of prosperity, they again, in the years of depression following the war, developed a new significance in the minds of the thoughtful. A principle is not established in the actual social inheritance of the race—as a step forward—until man has applied it to himself and seen whether its application makes him a better man in his social relations. So management principles are being used as yardsticks to measure individual industrial development. This means that these principles are becoming a subconscious part of the mental equipment of industry, and not only is this real progress, it is fundamental.

The development and use of the Gantt chart is the most important step of progress, because it calls attention to the movement of facts, to the necessity of basing decisions on facts rather than on opinions, and because it helps managers to foresee future happenings.

A second important step is the change in the method of installation from the old type which organized from the top down to the new type which builds from the bottom up.

A third important step is the development of the theory that the cost of an article includes only those expenses actually incurred in the production of the article, and that the expenses of maintaining one machine in idleness cannot be charged into the cost of the output of another machine. Along with this theory came the development of a method of arriving at costs of idleness and work.

Probably the greatest progress consists in a better understanding of the problems of management with a particular acceptance of the facts to which Taylor called attention, that management is an art which may be practiced advantageously through the application of certain principles and the scientific method. I do not think, as yet, that the great majority of men at the head of industries have anything like an adequate understanding of scientific management, nor that they are able to distinguish between form and substance in this respect. They have, however, apparently emerged from the attitude of opposition and mistrust of so-called scientific management, but are satisfied with a superficial application of the principles of management.

The important steps of progress made in management since 1912, I would say, are as follows. The order in which they are named is not significant:

a. A greater appreciation of the human factor in industry.
b. The growing recognition that employees should have a voice in the management as relating to those questions that directly affect them.
c. The recognition of the strategic position of shop foremen and the necessity of more carefully selecting and training them.
d. The increased recognition of the value of fundamental principles.
e. The recognition of, and in a large degree the adoption of, standard systems of cost accounting from the point of view of timeliness, as a barometer rather than history, as an instrument of production rather than a matter of finance.
f. A great development in mechanical equipment, combined with improved plant layout and building plants to fit manufacturing process.
g. A marked advance in sales policies.
h. A marked advance in substituting the trained, competent engineer for the old "cut-and-try" type of executive.

Using figures, which after all are most impressive, but basing those figures purely on my impressions, I would say that since 1912 industry has progressed in management by some 30 to 40 per cent in the appreciation of the fact that there is a management problem aside from the old concept, which was that the owner had simply to censor the things that happened within his jurisdiction. I should say that there had been a 20 to 25 per cent endeavor to install the mechanisms of management, considering in this figure the generally known stores systems, operation studies, wage-incentive plans, etc. In some cases, as for instance in stores control, the percentage might run a great deal higher, but I am refraining from increasing my estimate, for it is my belief that these mechanisms that we have installed are, for the most part, of a makeshift character, and that in industry as a whole and considering only the larger companies, I doubt if more than five or six per cent are possessed of mechanisms at all acceptable in the final scheme of what management should do and possess.

As to the real concept existing today of what management is, and what conditions must be considered, influenced and coördinated to bring about the situation which should exist, I doubt if more than one-fifth or one-fourth of one per cent of the companies in this country possess a knowledge or even appreciation of what is real management.

10. Combining and weighing these carefully prepared statements and adding to them certain well-recognized facts, there emerges a group of factors of varying importance which mark the progress of management during the past decade. These naturally arrange into three groups, of which the first concerns changes in mental attitude.

a. The ancient controversy as to whether management is a science or an art has subsided, with increased recognition of the scientific basis of management.

b. The attitude of opposition and mistrust toward management and the passionate antagonism to the installation of management methods have in general disappeared.

c. Among those responsible for the carrying on of industry there has grown an appreciation of the existence of problems of management. (The appointment of Herbert Hoover as Secretary of Commerce and General Dawes as Director of the Budget reflect an appreciation by the Government of the need for management in our national affairs.)

d. Acceptance of the principles of management has broadened among engineers, executives in industry, and educators.

11. The second group of factors of progress concerns the application of management methods.

e. The engineering or scientific method has extended in industrial cost accounting. Among the developments are uniform cost-accounting systems (64 manufacturers' associations which have adopted such systems), the theory and method of determining and applying standard costs, the methods of determining idleness losses, the forecasting of sales leading to long-term production schedules, and the budgeting of future expenditures.

f. Appreciation of the possibilities and advantages of standardization, simplification, and elimination of waste has spread rapidly during the past two years.

g. The demand for knowledge, facts, as a basis for judgment has grown insistent in all good management. This has led, among other developments, to a widespread use of specifications and graphics as a means of recording and communicating management knowledge. (The first modern book on graphics in the English language was published as recently as 1910. The Gantt-type control chart has been developed into its present form since 1917.)

h. Management methods have been applied or installed in practically every manufacturing industry, in distributing concerns and in institutions. (The report of 1912 listed 52 industries in which some form of management had been installed. A similar list prepared in 1922 would group all the branches of American industry.)

12. The third and final group of these factors concerns especially significant developments, which after being stated are subject to explanation and comment.

i. Management activities have broadened far beyond the installation of those mechanisms which are usually associated with the Taylor System, and which were emphasized in the report of 1912.

j. Some eight or ten of the leading American engineering schools have established courses in management since 1912.

k. Appreciation of the importance of the human factor in industry and attempts at its study from a fact basis have been the most striking management development.

l. Management engineers have declared that the service motive must prevail in industry and that all questions concerning human relationships must be considered in a spirit devoid of arbitrariness or autocratic feeling.

Management Mechanisms

13. To secure information as to the use of management mechanisms, the question was asked, "What (if any) mechanisms of management do you consider as generally accepted (a) in principle, (b) in practice?" From correspondents' replies the following twelve quotations have been selected.

I do not believe that any of the mechanisms of management are generally accepted in principle or in practice.

I know also that even where some of these things (mechanisms of management) have been established and we hear about them and might conclude that the firm using one or more of them is quite advanced, it often is not at all so. The feature described is only an unrelated "stunt," not supported by a complete coördinated system of administration and usually begins to go to pieces not long after it is installed.

There is at the present time a retrograde movement in regard to the building up of stores and making operation studies. However, as I see it, this is merely a temporary depression in the curve, and I believe that the general tendency of this curve is upward with a very slow ascending grade.

Incentive wage-payment plans have had a temporary setback due to labor conditions caused by the war and to the reluctance of managers in general to consider such plans in any other light but of profit to the company. I do not think that the main service which the incentive plan can give—namely, that of stabilizing relations between employers and employees—has been given sufficient attention by the management.

I believe that such mechanisms as balance of stores, routing, operation studies, incentive wage plans, personnel work, etc., are generally accepted in principle, but that efforts to install them frequently (perhaps most of the time) miscarry, and either accomplish little or no good. This is often due to a failure to see to it that details connected with the mechanisms are fully understood and looked after.

In a general way, the mechanisms of management are widely accepted now in principle and much less widely in practice.

Undoubtedly, good storekeeping is becoming very generally accepted. We know that unless we keep accurate records of the materials used we cannot get the most satisfactory results. I think storekeeping is accepted both in principle and practice as well as the intelligent study of operations.

I believe that balance of stores is accepted in principle and in practice, that is, insofar as a written record of quantities in stores is kept in the office rather than in a storesroom, and that a minimum or order point is predetermined and an order placed when it is reached. It is generally accepted in principle, though not in fact, that an incentive wage-payment plan is desirable and effective. It is accepted in principle that facts are shown on charts better than in tables of figures.

In principle, undoubtedly, all of the main mechanisms of management have been thoroughly established.

In a great measure all of the mechanisms of management as developed by Taylor and his immediate associates have been generally accepted in principle. But while they are being widely applied, my impression is that in the great majority of the cases the application is half-baked in character, and the results, while they may be satisfactory to the companies concerned, are far from being as satisfactory as they should be, either to the management or to the employees. My experience indicates that in most such cases an application such as Taylor would have approved will almost invariably result in increased production ranging from 30 to 100 per cent or more, depending on the nature of the business.

The following management mechanisms have been accepted in varying degrees:

Stores Control. In principle and practice very generally.

Operation Standardization. (a) In technical aspects, generally in principle, fairly so in practice. (b) In personal aspects, fairly accepted in principle, to a limited extent in practice. [By (a) I mean speeds, feeds, equipment, tools, etc.; by (b) motion and time studies of human elements.]

Wage-Payment Incentives. Generally in principle and in practice so far as direct labor is concerned. But little application has been made to indirect labor.

Cost Accounting. Generally accepted both in principle and practice.

Selection and Training of Employees. Fairly well accepted as to principle, but little in practice.

Purchasing Control. Generally as to both principle and practice.

Scheduling and Planning. Fairly well accepted in principle. Limited in practice in some industries, well established in others.

I find mechanisms being accepted one by one without a full realization of the part they are to play in the scheme as a whole. That is to say, I will find a company suddenly appreciative of the value of operation studies. It will thereupon proceed to organize to make operation studies, and for the time being in its new enthusiasm it pursues what threatens to become a hobby rather than a part of its business. This pursuit at times leads into the installation of other mechanisms. It begins to recognize, from the operation studies, that a balance of stores is essential, and that a wage incentive is desirable. I find, however, that this progress is accidental rather than planned.

Mechanisms of management such as are discussed in the 1912 Report are generally accepted in principle, but poorly carried out in practice in the majority of establishments. On the other hand, a few, representing the best organizations, have developed these things to a degree which serve as valuable guides.

Planning and control are used more and more extensively in plant operation. The tendency of the majority, however, is to try to gain the benefits of more intensive control through partial makeshifts which record past accomplishments instead of actually planning the work. The importance of control, in fact, in increasing production through elimination of idle time, men, and machinery, is not yet recognized except in a few markedly successful establishments. The developments along these lines are being undertaken frequently through inexperienced, low-grade men, who adopt mechanisms as such, instead of developing existing methods on fundamental principles.

Balance of stores is accepted almost universally in principle and widely used in practice. Accountants have been quick to recognize its advantages, and have made it an essential part of their accounting mechanism. On the other hand, two of the most vital features for assisting in the control of production, the column of "stores apportioned" and the entering of "minimum" quantities of each item permissible, are apt to be omitted.

The development of time study and job analysis, while widespread, has been unsatisfactory; piece rates are more and more universal, but their determination is still largely on a basis of past performance, aided by time studies which simply record these performances in more detail instead of analyzing the operations and determining the methods and units which will give most satisfactory results. There is still lack of appreciation of the fact that the chief aims of time study and job analysis must be:

a. To resolve the operations into such units that they can be recombined to provide for all variables;

b. To take advantage of this unit study to eliminate unnecessary operations, substitute improved methods, and remove defects in equipment and in control;

c. To enable the workman to earn more money, often with less effort; and,

d. To indicate means for improvement in quality and practicable methods for making the improved quality routine.

14. To these statements of the acceptance of management mechanisms it is possible to add a few quantitative facts. It will be recalled that the field reports of six industries, given in the Report of the Committee on the Elimination of Waste in Industry of the Federated American Engineering Societies, were based on an extensive questionnaire. The replies in four of these industries—metal trades, boot and shoe manufacturing, men's ready-to-wear clothing manufacturing, and printing—have been studied to show the use of mechanisms of management. The facts brought forth are presented in Tables 1 to 6, inclusive. Table 1 records the results for 16 metal-trades plants where the entire questionnaire was used; Table 2 is from 12 metal-trades plants where a condensed questionnaire was used; Table 3 is from 8 boot and shoe shops; Table 4 from 9 men's ready-to-wear-clothing shops; Table 5 from 6 printing estab-

lishments; Table 6 is a summary for the 51 plants studied. The questions from whose replies the facts were drawn are given in Appendix No. 1.

TABLE 1

Name of Industry: *Metal Trades.*   No. of Questionnaires: 16

Note: The wide diversity in kinds of work, varying from machine-shop to shipyard, must be borne in mind, also a wide variation in size of plants.

Mechanisms of Management	None	Inadequate	Good	Questionnaire Reference
1. Selection and Placement	0	6	10	K7
2. Incentive Wage Plan	2	6	8	K13
3. Planning Centralized	3	8	5	U4
(a) Routing, order of work	5	6	5	U4. 9
(b) Schedules, machine assignments	4	5	7	U5. 6. h
4. Time Study	6	2	8	U4. ef
5. Cost Control	4	3	9	U7
6. Idle-Time Analysis:				
(a) Men	13	0	3	U8
(b) Machines	9	1	6	U3
7. Purchase Control	3	4	9	U11
8. Balance of Stores	2	4	10	U11, 12

TABLE 2

Name of Industry: *Metal Trades.*   No. of Questionnaires: 12

Note: This is additional information from 12 plants assayed more briefly than the 16 of Table 1. A condensed questionnaire was used.

Mechanisms of Management	None	Inadequate	Good	Questionnaire Reference
1. Selection and Placement	0	4	8	No. 10
2. Incentive Wage Plan	1	3	8	No. 13
3. Planning Centralized	1	2	9	No. 19
(a) Routing, order of work	2	2	8	No. 19
(b) Schedules, machine assignments	1	3	8	No. 19
4. Time Study	2	1	9	No. 19
5. Cost Control	2	6	4	No. 18
6. Idle-Time Analysis:				No. 22
(a) Men	8	0	4	
(b) Machines	6	0	6	
7. Purchase Control [1]	1	1	10	No. 4
8. Balance of Stores	1	1	10	No. 4

[1] Purchase Control *as such* was not covered in the condensed questionnaire, but this estimate was based on the general stock and store systems; whether there were maxima and minima in stores, and a control of raw material all through.

TABLE 3

Name of Industry: *Boot and Shoe Mfg.*   No. of Questionnaires: 8

Mechanisms of Management	None	Inadequate	Good	Questionnaire Reference
1. Selection and Placement [1]	0	6	2	K7
2. Incentive Wage Plan [2]	0	0	8	K13
3. Planning Centralized	4	0	4	U4
(a) Routing, order of work	4	1	3	U4, g
(b) Schedules, machine assignments	3	3	2	U5, 6, h
4. Time Study	5	2	1	U4, 3, f
5. Cost Control	1	3	4	U7
6. Idle-Time Analysis:				
(a) Men	7	1	0	U8
(b) Machines	7	1	0	U3
7. Purchase Control	1	4	3	U11
8. Balance of Stores	1	1	6	U11, 12

[1] Not important, as skilled operatives are always available
[2] Union control very strong in this industry.

TABLE 4

Name of Industry: *Men's Ready-to-Wear Clothing Mfg.*   No. of Questionnaires: 9

Mechanisms of Management	None	Inadequate	Good	Questionnaire Reference
1. Selection and Placement [1]	0	4	5	K7
2. Incentive Wage Plan [2]	4	2	3	K13
3. Planning Centralized	4	2	3	U4
(a) Routing, order of work	4	2	3	U4, 9
(b) Schedules, machine assignments	3	2	4	U5, 6, h
4. Time Study	3	3	3	K13
5. Cost Control	2	5	2	U4, e, f
6. Idle-Time Analysis:				
(a) Men	6	3	0	U8
(b) Machines	8	1	0	U3
7. Purchase Control	3	1	5	U11
8. Balance of Stores	3	1	5	U11, 12

[1] Not important, as skilled operatives are always available.
[2] Union control very strong in this industry.

TABLE 5

Name of Industry: *Printing*.   No. of Questionnaires: 6

Mechanisms of Management	None	Inadequate	Good	Questionnaire Reference
1. Selection and Placement [1]	0	5	1	K7
2. Incentive Wage Plan [2]	1	1	4	K13
3. Planning Centralized	3	2	1	U4
(a) Routing, order of work	5	0	1	U4g
(b) Schedules, machine assignments	3	2	1	U5, 6, h
4. Time Study	5	0	1	U4, e, f
5. Cost Control	3	2	1	U7
6. Idle-Time Analysis:				
(a) Men	5	0	1	U8
(b) Machines	3	0	3	U3
7. Purchase Control	3	2	1	U11
8. Balance of Stores	4	1	1	U11, 12

[1] Not important, as skilled operatives are always available.
[2] Union control very strong in this industry.

TABLE 6   SUMMARY FOR 51 PLANTS IN 4 INDUSTRIES

Mechanisms of Management	Boot & Shoe, 8 plants			Men's R. M. Clothing, 9 plants			Printing, 6 plants			Metal Trades, 28 plants			Totals, 51 plants		
	None	Inadequate	Good	None	Inadequate	Good	None	Inadequate	Good	None	Inadequate	Good	None	Inadequate	Good
1. Selection and Placement	0	6	2	0	4	5	0	5	1	[1]0_0	6_4	10_8	0	25	26
2. Incentive Wage Plan	0	0	8	4	2	3	1	1	4	2_1	6_3	8_8	8	12	31
3. Planning Centralized	4	0	4	4	2	3	3	2	1	3_1	8_2	5_9	15	14	22
(a) Routing, order of work	4	1	3	4	2	3	5	0	1	5_2	6_2	5_8	20	11	20
(b) Scheduling, machine assignments	3	3	2	3	2	4	3	2	1	4_1	5_3	7_8	14	15	22
4. Time Study	5	2	1	3	3	3	5	0	1	6_2	2_1	8_9	21	8	22
5. Cost Control	1	3	4	2	5	2	3	2	1	4_2	3_6	9_4	12	19	20
6. Idle-Time Analysis:															
(a) Men	7	1	0	6	3	0	5	0	1	13_8	0_0	3_4	39	4	8
(b) Machines	7	1	0	8	1	0	3	0	3	9_6	1_0	6_6	33	3	15
7. Purchase Control	1	4	3	3	1	5	3	2	1	3_1	4_1	9_{10}	11	12	28
8. Balance of Stores	1	1	6	3	1	5	4	1	1	2_1	4_1	10_{10}	11	8	32

[1] The two figures shown separately in the metal-trades columns represent totals for the 16 plants (upper figure) covered by the regular questionnaire, and the 12 plants (lower figure) which filled out only a condensed questionnaire.

15. Turning to Table 6 and arranging the eight mechanisms in the order of the number of plants in which they are installed *in some form*, we have:

Selection and Placement
Incentive Wage Plan
Balance of Stores
Purchase Control
Cost Control
Planning (routing, scheduling)
Time Study
Idle-Time Analysis.

Rearranging in the order of the number of plants where the installation is *good*, we have:

Balance of Stores
Incentive Wage Plan
Purchase Control
Selection and Placement
Planning (routing, scheduling)
Time Study
Cost Control
Idle-Time Analysis.

16. The weight of opinion and fact brings the conclusion that certain mechanisms of management have made decided headway in acceptance both in principle and practice, and from an assay of four industries the importance of application yields two groups:

A.	B.
Balance of Stores	Cost Control
Incentive Wage Plan	Idle-Time Analysis
Purchase Control	Planning
Selection and Placement.	Time Study.

17. In the installation of such mechanisms a significant change is becoming evident. In the early days of management the mechanisms concerned the physical means of production. They were originated by the executives and were ordered into the shop.

18. At a later date, as emphasized in the report of 1912, the value of methods which concerned the worker was appreciated. Training was the first to have any widespread trial. But the attitude was still the developing or forcing of a mechanism from the top downward.

19. Within the decade under review, another attitude has been adopted in a few instances. It seeks to make the foremen and even the workers consciously parties to the development of the plans before they are put into effect. It endeavors to arouse

interest, to inspire to achievement, to release creative energy. Its effect is to install methods and mechanisms from the bottom upward with celerity and improvement in personnel relations.

Management Education of Engineering Grade

20. Where there was probably but a single college course in management in 1912, there are now eight, in these institutions:

> Columbia University
> Massachusetts Institute of Technology
> New York University
> Pennsylvania State College
> Purdue University
> University of Kansas
> University of Pittsburgh
> Yale University—Sheffield Scientific School

In addition to this form of instruction, management subjects have been introduced in mechanical-engineering courses. Examples are the pioneer work at Cornell University —Sibley College, and at the Worcester Polytechnic Institute.

21. The growing importance of this branch of engineering education is shown by the number of men enrolled. Appendix No. 4 gives the enrollment of all students in colleges of engineering in the United States for the school year 1921–22. The total is 53,414. The number in management courses is 1123, identified as

Administration Engineering	725
Industrial Engineering	389
Industrial Management	9
Total	1123

22. The 277 students in "Commercial Engineering" courses have not been included, although they undoubtedly receive some instruction in management subjects.

23. While these management courses in the beginning were based on mechanical engineering, their character seems to be changing, so that it can now be said that they are based on engineering broadly, with emphasis on fundamental subjects. There is a tendency to lessen or limit qualitative instruction in details of production. Without doubt, the character of the instruction is improving as teachers gain a wider and sounder experience in the application of management principles.

24. The significance of this new branch of engineering education is not its extent as measured in numbers of students, but in the fact that at least eight leading institutions have added it to their regular and older courses.

25. It is unfortunate that no common name has been adopted for these courses; at least four are in use.

The Human Factor in Industry

26. The report of 1912 presented the human factor in industry with particular emphasis on the responsibility of managers and executives to train their workers and the same thought was prominent in the discussion. According to the comment of the Committee in its closure, one of the striking characteristics which had already gripped attention was "the presence throughout the discussion of a humane spirit in keeping with the best trend of thought toward social justice," and "the development that has taken place within the last few years leading to a new appreciation of the needs and rights of employees."

27. Henry P. Kendall in his discussion of the report [2] outlined the operation of an employment department which he had initiated. The employment man interviewed applicants, selected workers by tests, placed them in positions for which they were fitted, required medical examinations, kept records of each employee, kept in touch with the foremen in regard to the deportment, skill and earning power of the employees, had charge of discipline and discharge, and gave advice, suggestions, and sympathy to the workers.

28. These disclosures in outline foreshadowed a great wave of industrial relations work which swept through American industry after the outbreak of war. The movement received its impetus from the demand for workers in a time of extreme shortage, and was influenced by emotionalism and social theory. With the return of a labor surplus in 1921 the unsound features have in the main disappeared, leaving but vestiges of the methods and devices which were initiated in such profusion.

29. The present situation as regards personnel work is appreciation that personnel problems exist, recognition that their solution is a responsibility of management, and a growing realization that job analysis, selection, placement, and training can be put on a scientific basis.

30. Associated in thought, though not necessarily a part of any employment or industrial relations plan, is the rise of works councils in American industry. Several hundred have been established during the past decade. In August, 1919, there were 225, in February, 1922, approximately, 725.[3] Their development has been in response to a desire on the part of the workers for a means of expressing their beliefs and wishes in regard to matters arising in employment, and on the part of the management for a means of communicating with their employees and gaining and holding their confidence and good will. The movement but emphasizes the fact that the development of the relationships of employer and employed is a responsibility of management.

The Service Motive

31. Management engineers as a group have declared that the service motive must prevail in industry, that everything planned and done must be directed to securing

---

[2] *Transactions*, American Society of Mechanical Engineers. Vol. 34, p. 1208.
[3] See Reports of the National Industrial Conference Board.

the worthy result of producing useful goods with a minimum expenditure of time, material, and human effort. One of the clearest statements was written by Henry L. Gantt a few weeks before his death: [4]

> We have proved in many places that the doctrine of service which has been preached in the churches as religion is not only good economics and eminently practical, but, because of the increased production of goods obtained by it, promises to lead us safely through the maze of confusion into which we seem to be headed, and to give us that industrial democracy which alone can afford a basis for industrial peace.

32. This disinterested purpose has been accepted as an ideal for the entire engineering profession, by becoming the challenging thought in the preamble to the constitution of the Federated American Engineering Societies.

33. To the factors dealing with the steps in the progress of management which have been discussed, should be added a consideration of the extension and growth of management societies which has taken place during the past ten years.

34. The earliest was the Society for the Promotion of Scientific Management, founded informally in 1910 and organized in 1912. In 1916 the name was changed to the Taylor Society, and in 1918 it was reorganized. See Appendix No. 2.

35. The first national organization to deal with personnel matters beginning with the training of workers was the National Association of Corporation Schools, founded in 1913. By 1917 its work had broadened to include all of the activities classified as human relations. In 1920 the name was changed to the National Association of Corporation Training. In May, 1922, it was merged into the National Personnel Association. See Appendices Nos. 3 and 7.

36. In May, 1917, in response to a war demand, The Society of Industrial Engineers was founded. In 1919, it was functionalized and has carried on the activities of a professional engineering society. See Appendix No. 4.

37. A second personnel society was organized during the war, May, 1918, under the name of the National Association of Employment Managers. On March 1, 1920, the name was changed to The Industrial Relations Association of America. May of that year registered the peak of the movement, the Chicago National Convention being attended by 5000 persons. The change in business conditions affected it adversely and in December, 1921, the Board of Directors voted to disband the organization. Early in 1922 it was merged into the National Personnel Association. See Appendices Nos. 5 and 7.

38. Although The American Society of Mechanical Engineers provided the forum for the presentation of the earliest papers on management, no part of that Society was particularly devoted to management matters until the formation of Professional Divisions in 1920. In July of that year, the Management Division was organized. It soon led all of the other Professional Divisions in membership and has held that position ever since. See Appendix No. 6.

[4] *Organizing for Work*, p. 104.

39. There are, therefore, four Societies concerned with management—three in its engineering or technical aspects, and one restricted to personnel matters. The combined membership, not discarding duplications known to exist, is 4041.

Management Division, A. S. M. E.	1,740
Society of Industrial Engineers	1,032
The Taylor Society	769
National Personnel Association [5]	500
Total	4,041

40. This membership is growing rapidly; more than one-half has been gained during the past two years, for that period spans the founding and growth of the Management Division of The American Society of Mechanical Engineers.

41. Within the last two years joint activities have been originated among these and other societies with the promise of benefits to all who are concerned with management. Included are: Development of a management terminology; development of a classification for management literature; standardization of management graphics; and development of methods for the measurement of management.

Management Results

42. The report of 1912 stated that the results of good management had been: "A reduced cost of product, greater promptness in delivery with the ability to set and meet dates of shipment; a greater output per worker per day with increased wages; and an improvement in the contentment of the workers." There was no evidence at that time that goods had been reduced in price to the consumer.

43. To a degree this evidence has now been supplied. There are examples where good management has held down prices during a period of inflation and reduced prices as soon as business conditions changed. These acts benefited the consumer. Therefore the management movement has earned its economic justification.

44. Management as developed through a generation of effort stands today as a great body of knowledge and practice to facilitate the operation of industry and the conduct of business. Through organization it determines policies, plans basically over long periods of time and fixes impersonal relationships; through preparation it plans in detail how, when, and by whom work is to be done; through direction it initiates and maintains the process of production and distribution.

45. Here, then, is a tremendous, hitherto unknown engineering tool. What is it for? The answer is a spur to every engineer and industrial executive.

46. *Industry and business* as developed in modern civilization must continue, else infinite misery will overtake the human race. Management is the agency by which community, state, and nation shall endure.

[5] The National Personnel Association also has 129 company members.

APPENDIX No. 1

Questions Concerning Management Mechanisms

48. The questions in the Waste in Industry questionnaire, whose answers supplied information to prepare Tables 1, 3, 4, and 5, dealing with the use of the mechanisms of management, are as follows:

K7 Are your workers selected carefully on basis of interviews, trade and other tests?

K13 How is wage remuneration, determined: union scale, competitive market, etc.; day work, piece work, or other form of incentive wage?

U4 Is your planning of work centralized or distributed among a number of shop executives and workers?

U9 Do you compare production performance with production standards, with reference to worker, job, department and equipment?

U5 Does your shop administrative mechanism enable you to anticipate idleness of machines and workers and provide against it?

U7 Have you a good current cost system tied in with the financial books?

U8 Do you compile a record of idle workers' time by amount, cost and causes?

U3 Do you compile a record of idle machine time by amount, cost and causes?

U11 To what extent is purchasing done to standard specifications, and does it clear through a purchasing agent?

U12 What control exists over receipt, issuance, and return of materials?

49. The questions in the condensed questionnaire whose answers supplied information to prepare Table 2, dealing with the use of the mechanisms of management, are as follows:

4 Storekeeping: (a) General methods? (b) How are stock records maintained up-to-date? (c) Where are storesrooms located with reference to producing departments? (d) How is material transported?

10 Employment Methods: (a) What examination or tests are used? (b) How are discharges or quits handled?

13 Wage Scale: (a) By classes of labor? Ratio of day workers to piece workers? Is any form of incentive system used?

18 Production and Cost Control: (a) Is there a budget by departments? (b) Are periodic comparisons made between output by departments or trades and labor costs? Is overhead standardized periodically, or is *all* overhead distributed monthly?

19 Planning Functions: (a) Is there a central planning department, or does each department do its own planning and follow-up of schedules? (b) How are schedules and standards set? (c) Are work tickets given out ahead of workers' needs?

22 Idleness: (a) Are records kept of idle machines and causes? Of idle men?

APPENDIX NO. 2

The Taylor Society

50. This brief statement of the founding and development of The Taylor Society (originally the Society to Promote the Science of Management) was prepared by Harlow S. Person, the Managing Director of the Society.

51. *The Background.* In 1886 Henry R. Towne presented the paper, "The Engineer as an Economist," before the A.S.M.E. Thereupon followed in that Society a series of papers relating to management, chiefly on wage systems, ending with Taylor's "A Piece-Rate System" in 1895. Then followed seven years of no papers on management before the A.S.M.E. In 1903 and 1904 several papers were presented, among them Taylor's "Shop Management." In 1906 Taylor's "On the Art of Cutting Metals" was presented before the A.S.M.E., followed by one paper on a phase of management in each of the years 1907, 1908, 1909, and 1910. In 1911 the A.S.M.E. had no paper on a management subject.

52. The group of young engineers associated with Mr. Taylor felt during this period that it required a struggle to get a paper on management before the A.S.M.E.; that each time a paper of significance was presented (Towne's in 1886, Taylor's in 1895 and 1903) consideration of the subject was stimulated, but the interest soon waned; that the dominant group in the Society did not believe management subjects should engage its attention and put obstacles in the way of such attention; that there was in the Society possibly hostility to the Taylor theories and methods and that they could not receive adequate consideration; and that in general the A.S.M.E. was not giving adequate attention to the subject of management as compared with the growing public interest.

53. On the following page is a tabulation of the number of items relating to management by years, and whether presented before the A.S.M.E. It has been prepared from *Scientific Management;* a list of references in the New York Public Library, compiled by Walter D. Brown, Technology Division, N. Y. Public Library, 1917.

54. This group therefore decided that to secure a discussion of management problems to an extent warranted by the importance of the subject and public interest in it, a forum other than the A.S.M.E. would have to be found.

55. *The Founding of the Society to Promote the Science of Management.* On November 11, 1910, a meeting was held at the Athletic Club, New York, to consider the matter. There were present Morris L. Cooke, Frank B. Gilbreth, Robert Kent, Conrad Lauer (representing Charles Day), and Wilfred Lewis. Mr. Gilbreth was the host.

56. It was decided to organize a society for the discussion and promotion of scientific management. A formal organization was not effected, but from then on James M. Dodge presided at meetings and Robert Kent acted as secretary-treasurer. For two years, with such informal organization, meetings were held approximately once each month, usually at Keen's Chop House, where management subjects of live interest

were discussed. The membership during this period increased to some twenty-five or thirty.

57. As a result of the increasing public interest resulting from the Eastern Rate Case Hearings (winter of 1911–1912), it was decided to make the organization more formal and to make more of the Society. Accordingly a meeting was held at the Hotel Astor, November 7, 1912, and a formal organization effected. The Society was named The Society to Promote the Science of Management. James M. Dodge was elected president and Robert Kent, secretary. Meetings were thereafter held less frequently (three times a year) but were more carefully planned. The place of meeting was usu-

	Year	Presented before A. S. M. E.	Not presented before A. S. M. E. Published in periodicals such as *Engineering Magazine* and others
Towne's "The Engineer as an Economist" ...	1886	2	0
	1889	1	0
	1891	1	0
	1893	1	0
Taylor's "A Piece-Rate System"	1895	1	1
	1896	0	1
	1897	0	4
	1898	0	2
	1899	0	10
	1900	0	12
	1901	0	24
	1902	0	17
Taylor's "Shop Management"	1903	5	20
Taylor's "On the Art of Cutting Metals"	1904	1	22
	1905	0	17
	1906	3	17
	1907	1	22
	1908	1	46
	1909	1	30
	1910	1	57
	1911	0	219
Committee Report, "The Present State of the Art of Industrial Management"	1912	1	165

ally New York, Philadelphia, or Boston. In 1913 H. S. Person was elected president, and succeeded himself annually until 1919. In December, 1914, was begun the publication of a small journal for members called *Bulletin of the Society to Promote the Science of Management.* By 1917, when the United States had entered the war, the membership had increased to about 110.

58. *During the War.* During the war the activities of the Society were in abeyance, the officers and over fifty per cent of the members of the Society having been absorbed into the war organization of the United States.

59. *Reorganization and Change of Name to Taylor Society.* Immediately after the Armistice in 1918, members of the Society in Washington and the vicinity held a meeting to consider the resumption of activities of the Society. It was felt that the Society should undertake more serious work, in view of the probable larger public service possible during reconstruction, and it was decided to establish a central office with a salaried executive. The name of the Society had been changed in 1916 to Taylor Society, in honor of Frederick W. Taylor, who had died in 1915; an office was established April 1, 1919, in the Engineering Societies Building, New York; H. S. Person was chosen the managing director, and John Otterson, Winchester Repeating Arms Co., was elected president. Mr. Otterson was succeeded by Henry S. Dennison, and Mr. Dennison by Richard A. Feiss, who is president at the time of this writing, August, 1922.

60. The objects of the Society as stated in the Constitution are, through research, discussion, publication and other appropriate means:

1. To secure an understanding and intelligent direction of the principles governing organized effort, for the accomplishment of industrial and other social purposes for the mutual benefit of

   a. The Community
   b. Labor
   c. The Manager
   d. The Employer

2. To secure the gradual elimination of unnecessary effort and of unduly burdensome toil in the accomplishment of the work of the world.

3. To promote the scientific study and teaching of the principles governing organized effort, and of the mechanisms of their adaption and application under varying and changing conditions.

4. To promote general recognition of the fact that the evaluation and application of these principles and mechanisms are the mutual concern of the community, labor, the manager and the employer.

5. To inspire in labor, manager, and employer a constant adherence to the highest ethical conception of their individual and collective social responsibility.

Appendix No. 3

The National Association of Corporation Training

61. The National Association of Corporation Schools was organized on January 24, 1913, to formulate a definite and constructive educational program for firms engaged in industry and commerce. Its officers and directors were drawn from repre-

sentative firms including: The New York Edison Company; Burroughs Adding Machine Company; General Electric Company; The Pennsylvania Railroad Company; The Curtis Publishing Company; Yale and Towne Manufacturing Company; Consolidated Gas Company of N. Y.; Dodge Manufacturing Company; National Cash Register Company; and the Westinghouse Electric and Manufacturing Company.

62. At the first meeting of the Executive Committee, an Educational Committee was appointed "to devise courses and recommend best how to teach: salesmanship, advertising, manufacturing, transportation, accounting, financing, purchasing, general office work, stenography, clerical work, filing, correspondence, physical efficiency, hygiene, sanitation, recreation, exercise and the elements of psychology. The general purpose was to assist firms having established educational work, or about to start such work. Through reports, members were informed as to what others were doing and what they might and should be doing.

63. For the first three years the emphasis of the work of the Association was directed toward preparing the new employee for his first working duties. In 1916 the scope was enlarged to develop employees old in point of service. By 1917 the work had broadened to include "all of the activities classified as human relations." This meant that the Association was definitely in the personnel field. In 1919 it was declared that the Association "has become a great clearing house for all authentic information on the subject of Employee Relations in Industry."

64. In 1920 it was believed that the Association faced a crisis brought on by the increased service being rendered and rising costs. A plan of reorganization was therefore developed providing for incorporation. The name of the organization was changed to The National Association of Corporation Training. The object was stated to be "the founding of an organization that shall contribute in every way possible to the mutual benefits of all concerned in industry and commercial enterprises; to develop the efficiency of the individual employee and to coördinate his best interests with those of employers; to develop the highest standards of efficiency in industrial operations; to have the courses in established educational institutions expanded to meet more fully the needs of industry and commerce; and to encourage all branches of literature, science and art, or any of them that pertain to industry and commerce." Three classes of members were provided for:

A—Commercial, industrial, transportational, financial, or governmental organizations

B—Any employee of a Class-A member

C—Individuals not eligible as a representative of a Class-A member, or as a Class-B member.

65. However, this reorganization did not modify appreciably the work of the Association, which continued until May 20, 1922, when the plan of merging with the Industrial Relations Association of America into the National Personnel Association was approved.

APPENDIX No. 4

The Society of Industrial Engineers

66. In May, 1917, the Western Efficiency Society held a national convention in Chicago on "The Importance of the Human Factor in Industry." On the day following the close of this convention, a group of engineers and executives met to discuss the human factor in preparedness and to consider the part which the expert could play in winning the war. At this meeting the Society of Industrial Engineers was organized. Before this meeting, the Council of National Defense had strongly urged the organization of such a national society and had indicated how such a body could assist the Government in the emergency of war. In June, 1917, the chairman of the Aircraft Board invited the directors of the Society to a conference in Washington. As a result the Society was called upon to gather through its members information on the personnel, financial and industrial resources of firms capable of building aircraft parts. Later work was done for the Ordnance Bureau of the Army. Until the Armistice, the activities of the Society were devoted to furthering the carrying on of the war. Two-thirds of the first board of directors filled positions in Government service; a majority of the members were engaged in organization and production work incident to the war.

67. During this period the activities of the Society were devoted to the first object for which it was founded:

> To furnish a vehicle for bringing together in closer relationship persons who are actively engaged in promoting efficiency in business and for making the training and ability of such persons available in the emergency arising out of the present war.

68. At the close of the war the second object became the guide for Society work:

> To furnish a medium for bringing out original contributions to the science of management;
> To provide an organization through which persons who are applying scientific methods to the solution of the problems of production and distribution may exchange views and coördinate their efforts;
> To coöperate with other societies;
> To codify and standardize professional principles and practice;
> To develop the professional standards of the industrial engineer;
> To promote efficient, energy-conserving management;
> To enhance the efficiency and prosperity of American industry.

69. In July, 1910, the board of directors put into effect a plan of functional organization which has continued in force. The membership (September, 1922) is 1032, divided into six classes: patron, professional industrial engineers; professional technical engineers and accountants; managing executives of commercial and industrial activities; educators in engineering economics, psychology and other lines associated with management; juniors and students.

APPENDIX No. 5

The Industrial Relations Association of America

70. This brief statement of the founding and career of the Industrial Relations Association of America (originally the National Association of Employment Managers) was prepared by Mark M. Jones, the first secretary and a director of the organization.

71. Sporadic attempts to organize the relationship between manager and men, rendered impersonal by the division of labor and the introduction of automatic machinery, can be traced as far back as the 80's. At first the development of this management function was slow. Somewhat later the number of specialists in the personnel field increased. It was not made up entirely of persons specializing in employment management. The growing importance of the whole problem of industrial relations had much to do with the formation of this Association and while the majority of the members were specialists in the personnel field, a large number were either in the general management field, or outside of industry but directly interested in industrial relations.

72. Between 1910 and 1917 other local organizations for the discussion of employment problems developed in New York, Philadelphia, Chicago, Pittsburgh, Cleveland, Newark, and Rochester.

73. The inter-city aspect and the beginning of the national movement dates back to 1914, when men responsible for hiring held a meeting in Minneapolis for the purpose of exchanging ideas. The success of this small meeting was such that it resulted in a second meeting in the same city in May, 1915, which was attended by persons from a much wider area.

74. In May, 1916, a general meeting was held in Boston, and in the same month of 1917 a conference at Philadelphia was attended by several hundred.

75. At this Philadelphia meeting it became apparent that some medium for coöperation, a clearing house for the experience of local groups, was needed, and a committee of ten was appointed to consider the advisability of forming a national association. The committee reported that it believed the time inopportune for such action but recommended that a national committee be created for the purpose of arranging an annual convention, as well as continuing the study of the desirability of a permanent national organization. Adoption of this recommendation resulted in the creation of the National Committee of Employment Managers' Associations.

76. A meeting was immediately planned for Cleveland, Ohio, to be held during the following year. The war situation, however, caused a change in plans. The National Committee arranged to hold the convention in Rochester, in May, 1918, in recognition of the pioneering work of Rochester University in graduating the first class of employment managers trained under a special course for the United States Government.

77. An attendance of over 800 men and women at the Rochester convention was

evidence of the need for a more formal national agency, and after considerable discussion it was voted to organize a national association. An organizing committee was elected for the purpose of so doing.

78. When the National Association got under way during the closing months of 1918, it was mainly an organization of organizations. Its control was in the hands of representatives of local associations, for while there were three other classes of members, the group members representing local employment managers' associations held the balance of power and determined the policies of the National Association of Employment Managers.

79. The task of the National Association when first organized was stated as follows:

(1) To arrange and manage an annual convention;
(2) Issue a bulletin;
(3) Promote the organization of local employment managers' associations;
(4) Assist local employment managers' associations then in existence;
(5) Operate a free employment service which would assist specialists in the personnel field to secure positions;
(6) Establish and maintain a central clearing house for employment information;
(7) Conduct such research work and surveys within the employment field as might be approved by the Board.

80. The first convention after the formation of the National Association of Employment Managers was held at Cleveland, Ohio, in May, 1919. An attendance of 2000 was an indication of the stimulus to the movement provided by the war.

81. As the result of a widespread demand arising out of the widening scope of the employment manager, with the result that his activities comprehended many more functions than could be described through use of the word "employment," the name of the National Association was changed on March 1, 1920, to The Industrial Relations Association of America. It was under this name that the first peak in the movement was reached. The annual meeting in Chicago, in May, 1920, attended by 5000, was one of the very great national conventions of that period.

82. Soon after the 1920 meeting the change in the business situation was reflected in the personnel field and a decline in interest and support set in. As personnel work had in many cases been the last addition to specialized management functions, there was a widespread belief that it would be the first to be discontinued. Experience has since indicated that such apprehension was not well founded. There were but few cases where that policy was applied in retrenching or where intemperate action destroyed a sound piece of work. Personnel work was decreased greatly, but not often to the same extent as other management functions. Wherever a severe reduction took place it came more as a result of individual work than an inherent weakness in the idea or plan.

83. In the first discussions of a national organization there was present a small

group which was anxious to decentralize the unit of association membership to the utmost by placing membership on an individual basis. The majority did not look with favor upon this departure, and the concentration of power and control in a group membership was the result. The experience of the organization ultimately established the fact that the group basis could not be entirely satisfactory. It did not provide the foundation for coöperation which was necessary if the Association were to make a real contribution to the progress of its members. It required many months, in fact, several years, for the advocates of individual membership to prove their case. However, at the 1921 convention of the Industrial Relations Association of America, held in New York City in November, a committee, widely representative of the whole country, presented a report which strongly advocated reorganization on an individual basis. The problems of the individual members of the National Board of Directors were so numerous, however, that they had little opportunity to apply themselves to the problems of the Association.

84. Finally, the Board of Directors recognized the need for a considerable alteration in the structure of the Association and decided that the way might be cleared for the most expeditious action if the Association were dissolved and an organization established along the lines suggested to the convention by the Reorganization Committee. The necessary steps to that end were taken and the Industrial Relations Association of America ceased functioning on December 31, 1921.

85. An organizing committee for the new association was then at work, and out of the whole situation a merger with the National Association of Corporation Training was arranged. This crystallized in the formation of the National Personnel Association in April, 1922.

APPENDIX No. 6

The Management Division of
The American Society of Mechanical Engineers

86. The Management Division of The American Society of Mechanical Engineers was organized in July, 1920. In the first annual report, the following definition of management was given:

> Management is the art and science of preparing, organizing and directing human effort applied to control the forces and to utilize the materials of nature for the benefit of man.

87. Interpreting the thought of that definition into a program, the same report stated the purpose of the Division:

> Inasmuch as the problems of management are of the utmost complexity and difficulty, the Management Division of The American Society of Mechanical Engineers, in seeking to render disinterested service, therefore declares its purpose to be the formulation and declaration of the fundamentals of management, both regu-

lative principles and accepted practice, and the dissemination of Management knowledge.

In working toward this object, the Management Division can thus not only be of service to the other Professional Divisions of the Society, to the individual members of the Society and to other societies of like aim, but also to all who are in responsible charge of human effort, and therefore, through them, can benefit society at large.

In carrying out such a broad purpose, the activities of the Management Division will vary with changing need, thus no comprehensive listing can be made to cover the present or the future. It is only possible to suggest a few already in project, namely:

The standardization of management terminology, units of measurement, the improvement and development of management education; the elimination of management wastes in industry; the elimination of unnecessary fatigue in industry and engineering; and lastly, management research.

88. Almost from the start, the membership of the Management Division has exceeded that of any other Professional Division. It now (September, 1922) numbers 1740.

Appendix No. 7

The National Personnel Association

89. The National Personnel Association was formed to take over the activities of the National Association of Corporation Training and the Industrial Relations Association of America. The possibility of such a union was discussed informally at a joint meeting of the Executives Club of New York and the New York Chapter of the National Association of Corporation Training, held on February 17, 1922. On the following day a letter of invitation was drafted and signed by 20 men who supported the suggestion of union, requesting attendance at a meeting to be held on March 9. On that day 34 persons were in attendance out of about 100 invited.

90. It was unanimously decided to form a national organization devoted to employment or personnel activities, provided the two existing organizations could be combined. A committee was appointed to consult with the officers of these two organizations and report a plan.

91. This committee reported on April 7, submitting a plan for the new Association and providing for an organizing committee to put it into effect. This committee was appointed and met on the same day. Anticipating this action, the officers of the I.R.R.A. had secured authorization to enter the merger. An expression of opinion from Class-A members of the N.A.C.T. was overwhelmingly in favor of the union.

92. On April 21 the articles of incorporation were completed and signed, putting the union into effect and bringing the National Personnel Association into existence. Its purpose is:

To advance the understanding of the principles, policies and methods of creating and maintaining satisfactory human relations within commerce and industry:

1. By assisting administrative executives, those engaged in personnel work and others who are interested in problems of personnel administration through providing opportunities for conferences, coöperative research, and exchange information among members.

2. By studying the problems of personnel administration, including employment, training, development, health, employee service and coöperation.

3. By assisting established educational and other institutions to interpret the personnel needs of commerce and industry by maintaining reciprocal relations with them.

93. Two kinds of members are provided for: individual and company. The membership is (September, 1922) 500 individuals and 120 companies.

DISCUSSION

FRED J. MILLER. Mr. Alford's admirable paper is, I think, very comprehensive, especially as a review of what may be called the tangible or measurable advances that have been made in the past ten years within the field to which the paper relates. I think, however, that the most important progress that has been made, mostly within the ten-year period, cannot be measured nor weighed, for it is manifested mainly in a changed attitude of mind.

At a time, about twelve years ago, when I, as factory manager, came into an intimate and responsible relation with the leading exponent of the art of Scientific Management then in active practice, and was in daily contact with his work, the dominant idea was that a new system of management was to be handed to the body of factory executives; they were expected to learn by rote to do each little part in working the system, and to ask few if any questions as to the whys or wherefores. This did not go very well, especially with our large group of department foremen who had been accustomed to be consulted, to have their opinions more or less deferred to, and to be left pretty much with a free hand in the management of their departments. Some of them resisted passively; others of them somewhat actively; scarcely any of them really liked it, especially at the beginning. Questions of discipline arose and a considerable proportion of previously satisfactory minor factory executives would have been dismissed if the advice of the industrial engineer had been followed. Eventually this led to an agreement that all matters of discipline and of bringing factory men into line were to be left to the regular factory executives. This worked much better, and the installation was completed with entirely satisfactory results. But it was not until we had entered the World War and the necessity arose for devising a method that would immediately, almost from the first day, without change of personnel, bring about an improvement in efficiency and promote smooth working of an organization already in being, that the difficulty was entirely overcome.

Just here, stimulated by patriotic motives, Mr. Gantt, assisted by his staff, did, in my opinion, his most important piece of work. He had the breadth of mind needed to perceive that he was confronted by a new set of conditions that, so to speak, compelled the enlistment and active participation of the foremen and others already familiar with the technique of the work they were engaged in. Many of the things formerly done by clerks were then done by the foremen or men working under their direction,—and much better done; but, better still, the foremen no longer felt that they were being shelved or sidetracked. On the contrary, they realized that their status was improved in many ways. Thus the war led to Mr. Gantt's conversion to our view, that foremen and others in the factory ought to be more actively engaged and their interest enlisted in the new methods of administration.

Mr. Gantt rose to the occasion magnificently. He entirely abandoned his earlier method of approach in installing his work, and found, what most intelligent shop men already knew, that factory men respond quite as readily and heartily to considerate and fair treatment as do other people.

I look upon the development of a method which is compatible with the facts cited above and in harmony with them, and which promotes coöperation instead of arousing opposition and antagonism, as being the most important advance of the past ten years and as being at least one superlatively important result of our participation in the war. This is so for the reason that aside from the fact that it is the decent, human thing to do, a method by which we attract and secure the hearty coöperation of those whose coöperation is vital to complete success is, obviously, scarcely less important than improved management methods themselves. In the earlier days especially, there was far too little of real management in the installation of management methods; and their adoption was—and for that matter, still is—much retarded by that fact.

H. S. Person. I think Mr. Alford showed a great deal of commendable bravery in tackling this particular subject. Ten or twelve years ago when the first report was made regarding progress in management, the problem was relatively simple, for the reason that there had been, during the preceding twenty years, marked advance in the development of management, and particularly marked advance in the statement of principles of management. Now, when one tackles the problem in 1922 of measuring the advance during ten years, over the achievements of 1912, one has a very much more difficult problem—in my judgment, almost an unsolvable problem; and, therefore, while I admire Mr. Alford's bravery in attacking this particular subject, I am not of the opinion that the achievement, in the very nature of the case, is comparable with that of ten years ago.

As I recall the printed paper, the first pages are devoted to proof on the basis of opinions. Now, I do not think much of proof on the basis of opinions. It is true that the report of ten years ago had a certain amount of proof on the basis of opinions, but it was a very much smaller proportion of the whole, so for a moment, I want to eliminate that.

Then, in the appendix and the latter part of this report is a very considerable amount of what I should call not exactly irrelevant matter, but matter which is over-stressed and does not seem particularly impressive as proof, in proportion to the amount of space devoted to it.

That leaves us what I may call the central part of the paper—the more substantial proof based upon certain data secured by the Committee on Elimination of Waste in Industry.

Now, with respect to that I have two particular observations to make: First, those data had been used once before by the Committee on Elimination of Waste in Industry to prove that industry is not so very efficient, from the point of view of management, and, of course, one has to be cautious in using it over again as a sort of proof that there has been very considerable advance in management. Nevertheless, in the second place, it does indicate an advance in management during the past ten years, but not in a positive, a precise and what I would call a measurable way.

We have, as evidence of advance in management, the existence of these various mechanisms which are tabulated in that part of Mr. Alford's report, but the mere existence of these mechanisms is not sufficient proof to me of a great increase in the art of management. It is simply proof that there has been some increase; for the excellence of management, in my judgment, is a result of these elements in combination, and when one counts them and tabulates them as isolated phenomena, one does not get that measure of proof which one would get by counting them and tabulating them in combination, because one plus another means a very much greater advance in management than two times either one alone.

In my judgment, a real measure would be an analysis of the existence of these mechanisms in combination, and that I conceive to be an almost impossible task at present.

I think, as Mr. Miller has said, that our greatest measure of advance in management is that more or less intangible, but very real, thing which we all feel in the industrial atmosphere—a new point of view, a new approach—and, in my judgment, that is the big thing; so that while I cannot say that this paper compares in significance to that of ten years ago, I think Mr. Alford is to be commended and congratulated for attacking the problem.

J. P. JORDAN. The question has been asked, "Why does the industrial or management engineer fail to have the standing of a mechanical, civil, electrical, mining, chemical or any other engineer of like class?" Is not this question pregnant with wide opportunity for much discussion? And can we not find in this paper by analysis a possible answer?

Par. 10d states "Acceptance of the principles of management has broadened among engineers, executives in industry and educators." May I ask what are these principles? Has any individual or any group of individuals fixed any such principles which have been generally accepted? and if so, who? Frankly I personally do not know of any such principles which can be accepted as such at one hundred per cent value, with the exception of two or three of very general import.

In Par. 15 we find in the arrangement of the eight "mechanisms" in the order of the number of plants where the installations were good, that cost control is seventh or next to the last. We then find in Par. 16 that cost control is again in the rear rank. This conclusion seems to me to be a most serious and damaging flaw in management progress, if it should be really true that such a condition exists generally in industry. Do we class general or financial accounting as a mechanism of management? Certainly not. Why, then, should we class cost control as a debatable mechanism rather than an absolutely indispensable organ of enlightened management?

Par. 19 states that an attitude seeking to make foremen and even workers conscious parties to the development of certain mechanisms has been noted, the effect of which is the installation of methods and mechanisms from the *bottom upward*. This is invariably so in plants where recognized and properly executed cost control is in effect; and it is not only a perfectly natural result, but probably it will be found that the upward demand for various so-called mechanisms occurs *only* in plants where cost control has clearly indicated the need for such mechanisms.

Under the general heading of "The Human Factor in Industry," Pars. 26 to 30 inclusive, I feel that Mr. Alford has restricted his consideration to but one phase of industry. The confining of thoughts respecting the human element to actual workers, to the exclusion of superintendents and foremen, seems to me to miss the biggest point of all. And this again leads us to cost control.

The first and greatest step is to humanize the foremen by giving them full and complete cost statements—something which exists in comparatively few companies today. And a continual neglect of this feature will rob industry of a most powerful and necessary means of progress. The lack of such backing for foremen has probably been a leading reason for the handling of workers on a bluffing basis, with no definite facts to work on or show. Without such facts efficient work was subjected to the same pressure as the inefficient work which was actually causing high costs. Therefore, those workers who were unfairly borne down upon, resented it; and we deliberately created the conditions of labor calling for the works councils and other movements mentioned under "The Human Factor in Industry."

It is to be regretted that "management" has not awakened to the realization of the necessity to "Know Thyself"; that the advisers of management have failed absolutely as a class to recognize cost control as *the control;* that all such things as time study, incentive wage plans, planning, idle time analysis and such are but means to the end of reducing costs; and that management is so blind to the creed that facts and facts only should guide their every action. Then—when facts are known, and known month in and month out, put into operation such necessary adjuncts of management as may be clearly indicated as necessary.

I want to express my regrets to the Management Division of The American Society of Mechanical Engineers, the Society of Industrial Engineers, the Taylor Society, and the National Personnel Association, that Mr. Alford did not include with you our little organization of about 3,000 members, called the National Association of Cost Accountants, of which I have the honor to be President, which is dealing with the problems of management along the lines as brought out in this discussion.

Perhaps we are wrong in our premise, but we believe in taking the position that the managements of industrial institutions are fully capable of fairly proper action, if they know, through accurate and usable costs where action is most needed. If figures show enormous costs in burdens for handling materials, management surely will cure it; if inventories are mounting on account of congestion in shop, management will surely take steps to use the standardized records and put in planning methods to reduce the congestion; and so on with all other mechanisms which may be indicated as necessary.

Management can progress only as it sees the light; and notwithstanding the apparent apathy of management, and perhaps also its professional advisers in the past, I feel that the future progress of management will come only through the guidance of cost control, accurately determined, properly presented, adequately interpreted and effectively used.

Dexter S. Kimball. My view of this matter is somewhat different from those presented by the preceding speakers, perhaps for the reason that I was long in close touch with industry and later have had a chance to stand at one side and see it pass by.

The great idea that sprung from the mind of Mr. Taylor has often reminded me a great deal of religious growths. Some great prophet gets an inspiration and teaches, through parables, what he essays to get before men's minds. Mr. Taylor's great paper, which is the fountain-head and will probably remain so, of this movement described a specific form or piece of mechanism of management. Many interpretations, however, have been put upon this paper, just as many and diverse interpretations have invariably been made of the work of all religious prophets. One man finds in one particular item the thing that he considers the vital truth, while another pins his faith for salvation on an entirely different passage of Scripture.

The question then as to whether we have or have not made progress cannot therefore be measured by the progress made in any one portion of the field, and I agree with Mr. Miller that it is very difficult to find criteria to tell us whether we have made any progress. This much is certain, however: the human race has never had before it for any length of time any great economic principle, and seriously considered and pondered over it, but that it has emerged with the truth. And out of the movement Mr. Taylor started there will surely emerge certain basic principles. Of course, some of the practices that Mr. Taylor advocated have already been discarded by forward-looking managers, but nevertheless as time goes on, it becomes increasingly clear that this classic document contains certain important truths, basic and fundamental, that are destined to influence industrial management for many years to come. Mr. Alford's paper, if I interpret it correctly, is an effort to bring out more clearly to our view the most important results that are emerging from this movement.

It is not difficult, I believe, to recognize the most important of these basic fundamentals as such, but it is not so easy always to see just how and where they should be applied. What is applicable to one shop is not applicable to another. The plan that may operate well with one set of men may not operate at all with a group having different personality. This is essentially true of cost keeping which is nothing more or less than one form of recorded experience so strongly urged by Mr. Taylor as a basic requirement for predicting results. Mr. Taylor did not invent cost-finding, however, though his work and writings no doubt gave an impetus to its development. As a matter of fact, cost-finding has been a matter of steady growth for many years. Not so long ago this science, like many others, was almost purely empirical in its character, and I have seen bids on great battleships worth at that time four million dollars prepared by a single individual with only such data as he himself had gathered during a busy life and contained mostly in personal note books and similar records. Today cost-finding forms a part of the education of most students of engineering.

This in general is true, also, of other economic industrial principles. Mr. Taylor himself disclaimed the invention of any new thing in management. In effect he said: Here are some things that are true: here is a combination of principles that will produce results, though no doubt there are other variations and combinations of these basic principles that will produce equally good results. I consider Mr. Alford's paper, therefore, a very important one since it presents a clear résumé of the progress made in interpreting and applying Mr. Taylor's gospel of management.

I agree fully with Mr. Person that it is difficult to mark progress. As time goes on the curve flattens out and it becomes increasingly difficult to see what principle should be applied next to keep the movement progressing. But I do believe that as time goes on the fundamentals that underlie successful management will be made clearer and clearer and that these laws will be as well known as those that underlie engineering or any other well-founded science. I have every confidence that the industrial engineer and the cost accountant will eventually come into his own. Not the least important index that this is true is found in the fact that every progressive educator believes that no man should leave college without some training in economics and in the fundamentals of industrial engineering and all good technical schools are now teaching these fundamentals as they conceive them to be at present.

DAVID B. RUSHMORE. In the number of points that are open for discussion on this paper I wish to add only one thought, and that is that in management there is need of a definition as to what management is. Broadly, I conceive it to be a function connected with industrial organization, but we need a definition as to what organization is. It is something made up, in part, of human beings, and we certainly need more or less, a definition in this work as to what a human being is, as to what he is composed of, as to the motives which actuate him, as the results of certain forces that play upon him.

If we do as Professor Kimball said—enunciate the fundamental underlying principles—we are doing the best we can in any line of work.

It has been my experience to see in a large number of organizations men attempting to function as executives without having devoted any thought of their own as to what an executive is. I am very sure that Mr. Alford and this committee will accomplish a great deal in bringing to the attention of the younger men who are going from the colleges into industry the suggestion that they acquire a clear appreciation of what an executive is before they undertake to function as executives.

Some of our young men, the moment they get a stenographer, become executives. We find a great many men in industry, large and small, who are not making the most of themselves, and many remain in the same positions much longer than they ought. In general we blame the man, but to some others it seems that where a man is not getting the best out of himself, the man to whom he reports—his executive—is, in part at least, responsible. One of the great needs of industry is a clear vision on the part of the younger men of the province of an executive, the functions of which are rapidly changing; as to what the possibilities are, what the responsibilities are, what the opportunities for accomplishment are, and what the line of future development should be, along the line of these fundamental principles for making the best executives. A large number of men who are trying to function in this way are, as I see it, many of them, doing it without any analysis, without any thought of their own, and doing it in about as many different ways and acting on about as many different principles as there are individuals; and this committee will indeed do a great work if it can inject into this situation a sense of the desirability of the development of executives along fundamental lines, which will be a real constructive work for industry.

FRANK B. GILBRETH AND LILLIAN M. GILBRETH.[6] Mr. Alford's plan of basing the progress report on the report of the Committee of 1912, of which he was a valued member, has both advantages and disadvantages. It furnishes a definite method of attack. On the other hand it restricts observation. New developments may be omitted; or, if observed and recorded, emphasis may be incorrectly distributed, thus both recording and weighing of data may be affected. It necessitates a thorough review of the 1912 Report, with its discussions and closure, before the new report can be adequately criticized.

The four points specially emphasized in the 1912 Report are:

1. The advance in unskilled work and the trades. (Par. 1) "The unquestionable proof of the advance that can be made in unskilled work . . . and in ancient trades. . . . These are the most striking phenomena of all."
2. The change in mental attitude toward the problems of production (Par. 22) which is called "the most important change and one that comprehends the others."
3. The transference of skill (Par. 41). "We have pointed out that the underlying principle, that is, cause in the widest sense, the application of which has built up modern industry, is the transference of skill."

[6] Very much abridged.

4. The making of utility the aim of laboratory methods (Par. 56). "The end and aim is utility."

This being the basis of the 1912 Report,—and a careful study will make this clear, we may expect to find these four points extensively discussed,—in fact made the basis of the 1922 Report.

What do we find when we turn to the 1922 Report? It starts with an account of the limitations of the report; states its methods; notes the loss of three great pioneers; and outlines the method of acquiring data. It then states as the chief subject the "new element," "the mental attitude that consciously applies the transference of skill to all the activities of industry." Then follow quotations from answers to the questionary as to progress since 1912, deductions from these plus "certain well-recognized facts," a review of progress in use of management mechanisms, a summary of management education, a statement of the results which affect the human element, of the acceptance of the "service motive," and of results that affect production and ultimately industry, business, community, state and nation.

The only strong emphasis noted is on consideration of the human factor. This is one of three factors introduced as concerning "especially significant developments, which after being stated are subject to explanation and comment"—and it is stated later that "appreciation of the importance of the human factor in industry and attempts at its study from a fact basis have been the most striking management development."

The questionary method is always open to objections—as those who have used the questionary, or are acquainted with its use in the field of education well know. It is difficult to select those to whom to send the questions; only a small per cent respond; and only a small per cent of responses are of value.

In examining the four factors of application of the 1922 Report (Par. 11), we note that they have to do largely with the keeping of records,—cost accounting, specifications, graphics; also with the extent to which management has been introduced. We find no list of measurement units, measurement methods or measurement devices introduced or developed. Yet we find stressed "the demand for knowledge, facts, as a basis for judgment."

Among the significant factors (Par. 12) it is well stated that management has expanded beyond the mechanism of the Taylor System. It might be appropriate also to list those mechanisms of the Taylor System which, while obviously antique, obsolete and superseded, are still in use—telling where, by whom, and especially why.[7]

In the review of the college courses, the nature of the work as it concerns technic might well be mentioned.

The study of the human factor "from a fact basis" has gone far beyond "attempts" (Par. 12k). Detailed discussion should be invited on this point.

In the discussion of management mechanisms that follows (Par. 13) the con-

[7] June 1921 Taylor Bulletin

sensus of opinion seems to be that these are generally accepted in principle, but not in practice. The final sentence of Par. 13 states admirably the reason why this is the case.

The tables discussed (Par. 14) are interesting, but the vital point is—*why* are the results as they appear to be? Why is Time Study, for example, sixth, seventh and eighth on the lists?

The 1912 Report stressed the human element. The 1922 Report states that the human factor is today the important element—yet the report places only five short paragraphs (Pars. 26-30) under this topic. This is not because Mr. Alford underrates the importance of the subject, but because he reflects the customary failure to realize that *training the worker is the real key to industrial relations.* The work of an employment department (Par. 27) and of "works council" (Par. 29) is not to be disparaged, but the *training of the worker,* instead of being dismissed in a few phrases in a paragraph or two, should cover that transference of skill which is stressed in the 1912 Report.

It is necessary to note most carefully the results of progress listed (Pars. 42-46). The only new result claimed since 1912 is the reduction of cost of the product to the consumer.

It is claimed that, through the work of "generations of effort" management now has "a great body of knowledge and practice," by which it directs both planning and performing.

But has skill been transferred during this period? If so, to what extent? If not transferred, has it been recorded? Are the data available to be formulated into transferable form for transference later? If not, why not? The report fails to say.

Real progress has been made. Skill can now be, and is being, recorded and is being transferred. The demands of those who wrote and discussed the 1912 paper have been met to an extent sufficient to prove the wisdom of that report.

The appendices are valuable as bringing much material into brief reviewable form.

A most unfortunate and serious error occurs in Appendix No. 2,[8] where an account is given of the founding of the Taylor Society (Pars. 52-57). As the writers of this discussion thought of and planned this first Society of Management, selected and invited those who were to attend a dinner which was the first meeting of any Management Society, and then and there disclosed and outlined the purpose of the gathering, we may therefore speak with authority.

We can state without question that the Taylor Society was not founded because of dissatisfaction with the attitude of The American Society of Mechanical Engineers toward management. The idea in mind in calling the group together to form the Society was to furnish an opportunity for men intensively interested in the principles and practice of Scientific Management and occupied in installing such management to discuss not only the theories and philosophy of management, but the technic. It

[8] Contributed by H. S. Person.

was to furnish opportunities for the exchange of experience and for best utilizing such time as Mr. Taylor had to give those interested in the new type of management. There was no feeling of criticism toward The American Society of Mechanical Engineers; no desire to withdraw from the Society, in any way or in any sense, and, so far as we know, all members of the original group were, always have been, and are at present enthusiastic and loyal members of The American Society of Mechanical Engineers.

We have noted that the keynote of the 1912 Report was the transference of skill. This idea was not new, as Mr. Alford himself acknowledges, but it was very well phrased, and its appreciation, and emphasis in the Report mark a milestone.

Too much emphasis can hardly be laid on the transference of skill, because the further developments during the last ten years have proved beyond doubt the importance of emphasizing everything that has to do with the most efficient transference of skill with the least loss in transmission. Naturally, to transfer skill it must first be recognized, recorded, and put in such form that other people than those who *have* the skill, or *notice* the skill, or have the ability, facilities and opportunity to record the skill can actually leisurely refer to, visualize, and evaluate the data that contain the skill.

This transference of skill does not mean the transference of skill of a laborer or mechanic only—it also means the skill of the manager, the executive, the artist and everyone from the super-expert, to the novice of all classes. There is skill in performing manual operations, and there is skill in performing managerial functions and operations, the laws of acquiring skill and automaticity in manual laborer's work and that of the mental laborer are identical, even though the results and their behavior are entirely different.

The transference of skill is a very great conception, as Mr. Alford realizes, and obviously, if we are to emphasize the transference of skill we must observe those who are the most skillful.

There must be great emphasis placed on the type of method which is used for recording, otherwise "transference of skill" becomes mere words, as it often has.

There will be no transference of skill until the method of work is recorded *in detail*. This is a fact not mentioned in the 1922 Report.

The recording of the method in measured errorless detail is the step precedent to any attempt at the transference of skill. Because of the lack of recording of the method in detail, Taylor was obliged to discard all of his time study data and the data of his associates when he started planning his book on time study which was finally written after his death by Dwight Merrick.

The state of the art in 1912 can be seen where it is advocated that the end and aim of management investigation be utility, and consideration of any other purpose than immediate utility is deprecated. There is no comment on this in the 1922 Report. The fear, in 1912, was that there would be too much time study and motion study. There was no recognition at the time that, inasmuch as all accurate motion study records not merely so-called elementary unit times, but actually the elements of the motions themselves, therefore all observations are absolutely transferable to other work immediately, besides being of the same value for all future work. This answers any possible criticism of the management investigator using his laboratory methods to discover facts apparently other than those for immediate use. All knowledge of any trades that has to do with elements of motions is *usable in all other trades,* for the reason that information regarding each of the sixteen subdivisions of a cycle of motions is usable in every kind of cycle of motions.

On every hand are found words emphasizing the training of the worker, but where and in how many instances are found those who train the workers, knowing in detail how the work should be done, and how they should be trained? There is but one thing that will hold the respect and the attention of the worker permanently, and that is training in the one best way to do work, based on measured facts together with original data that he can look over just as an engineer can look over the derivation and source of a formula given to him.

The respect of the worker will never be obtained when data are accumulated only on the fastest or most strenuous or most continuous worker, instead of the worker with the best method. No one thing has done so much to kill progress in scientific management among the workers as the misplaced emphasis on the time it takes to do work, instead of the one best way to do work. Usually the one best way to do work will produce the quickest time, but this is not necessarily so.

We desire to emphasize the fact not as yet generally recognized, that any information regarding methods where the motions are recorded in their most elementary details is usable for synthesis in making the one best way in any other kind of work, and also permits the prophecy of times, even when automaticity in the new synthesized method has not yet been acquired and is not yet in existence, and therefore cannot be actually demonstrated in practice. This is of vital importance, for time study must include the prophecy of the time it will take to do work after the worker has become highly skilled, not merely the time the work did take during the timing period.

It must never be forgotten that the quest for the one best way and the search for records of skill worthy to be transferred have the same object in view: The former simply adds the thought that the skill shall embody the best elements of method to be found, thus offering a method to be transferred that may excel any skilled method in actual existence. The one best way is not only an adequate answer to the demand of the 1912 paper for records of skill and their transference, it gives more than was there demanded.

We maintain that stop watch time study, although much better than nothing, will not give information on details of method. These can be obtained only through details of motions, which must, therefore, be completely separated from time study both in description and definition.

The realization that method, consequently detailed motions, must be considered, studied and recorded, placed new emphasis on the importance of considering super-standardized equipment and tools. An important new condition of the new type of management is the emphasis on furnishing the best tools procurable to the worker, instead of having the worker use such tools as he may desire, or he may provide for himself. This is important under all types of management, and is stressed under scientific management, but it is vital if the one best way is to be used and maintained, and the resulting skill to be utilized.

It may focalize attention upon distinct and definite advances since 1912 to list some which are the direct result of emphasis on the one best way to do work, as follows:

1. The recognition that management consists of definite fundamental units and that the greatest progress in management can come only by the selection of the right units to measure, the right methods for measuring these units, and devices that will make the cost of measuring the units accurate and cheap.

2. The recognition that the sixteen elements of a cycle of motions and not the motions are the true fundamental units for the one best way to do work.

3. Process charts and other devices that show the sequence and relation of operations of making, inspecting and moving, in a form that makes possible easy visualizing, as a whole and in detail, of the problems confronting the management in the plant, the office and the sales or any other department.

4. Instruction sheets for operations based on accurate knowledge of the one best way to do work.

5. Graphical control on the exception principle for executives, with provision for those executives to write and sign causes of deviation from class, task or program.

6. Standing orders for executives as well as others, with provision for notification, inspection and enforcement, together with the reason for the standing order, that all members of the organization may coöperate intelligently. This results in one best way maintenance.

7. Change orders with standard provisions for changes in the procedure and practice of management, together with the reasons for the change.

8. Suggestion systems and the proper accompanying mechanism for obtaining, absorbing and enforcing the benefits of the craft and managerial knowledge and skill of all of the individual members of the organization.

9. Superstandardization that will permit working in the one best way for the highest wages combined with the lowest costs.

10. Recognition that automaticity resulting from standardization is the greatest free asset of the worker.

11. Recognition of the mnemonic classification as a necessity for the filing of information regarding the one best way to do work.

12. Recognition that data on skill for current use only, is an unnecessary eco-

nomic waste, and that, for maintenance, records must be in such form that, once made, they are usable forever.

13. Recognition that for recording skill, it is an economic waste to observe any other than the best men obtainable.

14. The application of and conscious and intentional use of psychology to solve the problems of management.

15. Devices for obtaining, synthesizing and transferring the precious skill of super-experts.

16. Devices for an efficient learning process for all, including those who have neither the opportunities, technical knowledge or apparatus to record or to derive the one best way to do work.

17. Provision for each member of the organization to share in the management according to his ability.

18. The recognition that the percentage of labor turnover is a measure of the efficiency of the management.

19. The recognition of the economic value of the placing of all workers, including the handicapped worker, in the highest positions that they can fill.

20. Standard opportunities for fitting for promotion that maintain stability and at the same time recognize individual aptitudes.

21. The recognition that the waste from unnecessary fatigue is as definite and as real as the waste of tangible material. The organization of the Fatigue Committee of the Society of Industrial Engineers to attack the problem of the elimination of all forms and instances of unnecessary fatigue as an economic and social duty as well as a philanthropic act, and to disseminate the information that any fatigue elimination means more output or more comfort, or both, and that fatigue study is a first step in motion study.

22. The recognition of accident prevention and the safety first movement as a managerial duty.

23. The recognition of the value of professional management engineers as executives.

24. The recognition that all blank forms that have not been observed in accordance with the laws of motion study are entirely obsolete.

The above twenty-four advances in management have been either entirely omitted or merely hinted at in Mr. Alford's report. They are the memorable fundamentals on which management has progressed. They will be the fundamentals on which management will progress, because they are economically sound and conform to the laws of psychology, the greatest law of which is the Golden Rule.

MAX SKLOVSKY. It is well at the start to dispose of the skepticism that has existed on the subject of scientific management. As in the medical profession, there has developed what might be called quack engineering, and patent medicines have from time to time been prescribed by so-called engineers, one of them having as many as twelve patents which he has seen fit to classify under the dignified term of principles of efficiency. Mr. Alford very wisely ignores all of these and adheres strictly to the legitimate endeavor.

It is no reflection to recognize that many of the engineers that followed in the trail of such pioneers as Frederick Taylor and Henry Gantt have failed in the fulfillment of their claims. Their chief weakness lay in:

   a. Too great a generalization;
   b. A lack of appreciation of "inertia" in human enterprise;
   c. A lack of appreciation of the human element;
   d. Lack of understanding of executive viewpoint;
   e. Lack of knowledge of selling methods.

The result of the work of these men has been that many industries have started on a series of experiments in methods and management, resulting in a series of disappointments in many instances with disastrous results. These disappointments were the result of assuming the presentation of the engineer as a practical plan, and the failure to materialize had, therefore, cast a reflection upon so-called scientific management. In the long run, however, it may be said that these experiments have been a fore-runner of real progress that has since been and is further to be made, so that industry as a whole, has gained as a result of the efforts of these men notwithstanding the many blunders and disappointments resulting in many cases of a far-fetched and unwarranted claim. The engineering profession will, however, live down these mistakes and possibly some day hail as heroes and benefactors the men that we have in more recent years whole-heartedly discredited as false prophets. The chief error on the part of these engineers has been that they endeavored to reconstruct industry quickly by revolutionary methods in place of recognizing that the slower evolutionary method was the path by which the greatest progress would be made. This haste in the endeavor to establish new conditions has resulted in the use of undigested and unreliable data with the result in damage as followed. It is no surprise, therefore, to note in Mr. Alford's paper under Item 8 that opinions on progress in management vary widely and also that in cases reaction had set in. This, however, is a temporary attitude which will correct itself by time. There is a healthy index in the endeavor on the part of engineers through special study courses to attain a better understanding of business enterprise. The engineer has been usually weak in this direction. His business equipment had been very close to the vanishing point and as a consequence he has ignored the selling side, the financial side, and the human side of business enterprise. This attitude on the part of the engineer is shown to be itself weakest in dealing with intangibles, particularly with the human factor. It is no secret that on the whole, men without formal training have succeeded better in dealing with men than the engineer, but the engineer is waking up.

The data given by Mr. Alford in the tables indicate conclusively that *control* of industry has made substantial progress in dealing with the physical side of the business, but comparatively little progress has been made in dealing with the intangible or human side. Just what progress may be made in the future in that direction is difficult to predict. In fact it appears that it may be wisest for the engineer to leave that field entirely alone and apply himself to the development of the physical in industry, holding at all times in mind, however, that the human element is a factor that should always be taken into account and that to a large degree it is an uncontrollable item.

THE AUTHOR. Ten years ago, when Mr. Dodge gave the closure for the Committee, which reported on the status of management, he said substantially this: It was unnecessary for the Committee to make any closure, because the points of objection which had been raised, on the one hand, by certain speakers, had been adequately answered, on the other hand, by other speakers. I feel like taking the same position.

However, I should like to correct Dr. Person on at least one point: He referred to the tabular matter dealing with the mechanisms of management, saying it was material that had been used in the Waste Report, and, therefore, lacked value in being represented. As matter of fact, that matter does not appear in the Waste Report, and was not in the possession of the committee that wrote that report. To secure these data, it was necessary to go back to the original questionnaires, about 125 in number, and make a careful study of all of them to secure the information presented in those six tables. It is new information and never has been presented before.

Dr. Person objected to the presence of quoted matter—opinions—but mentioned that the same method was used by the Committee in 1912. The methods used in developing these two reports are identical. The matter presented as quotations, grouped under a number of headings, gives background for the actual experience of men who are engaged in industry, as to the progress which has been made. From those, and other fact material, a number of conclusions have been drawn.

Dr. Person objects further to the failure to present the matter in combination, referring particularly to that absence in the matter of mechanisms. It appears, however, that the matter presented is in combination, for there are twelve items of progress grouped under three heads. Or from another point of view, there are twelve items in combination, although only four are explained in detail.

Mr. Jordan brought out the lack of agreement or acceptance of principle. Par. 5 states three so-called regulative principles of management, which were a part of the Report of 1912, and seem to have stood the test of ten years' study and discussion. He also criticized the position of cost accounting, saying it does not deserve to be considered as one of the mechanisms of management. That may be true, but there is a difference between presenting that which you discover, and that which you would like to discover. The position which cost accounting occupies in the six tables is by the results of the 125 questionnaires.

He also regretted that the National Association of Cost Accountants was not included in the list of management societies. I concur with him in that regret, merely saying, however, that that organization has lived largely within itself, is not well known at the present time in the management field, and that this report was written before the Society honored itself by electing Mr. Jordan as its president. I am sure that any consideration of management organizations from this time on must include the National Association of Cost Accountants.

Dean Kimball presented the detached point of view which any report of this kind must seek to take.

Dean Sackett emphasized the educational advance, which unquestionably is one of the most significant and most striking developments of the last ten years. Today some eight or ten of our great national engineering educational institutions have highly organized courses in management, in connection with mechanical, civil, and electrical engineering.

Mr. Rushmore very properly emphasized the need of definitions—of a language of management which we will all understand and use in the same way. A report,[9] one of the first of a series which will attempt to define management terminology and give the common language or grammar which we need, has been presented to the Society.

Mr. Wallace emphasized the points brought out in Pars. 17, 18, and 19—the necessity of working from the bottom up—and laid particular stress upon economic knowledge. Without doubt, if a study of this kind be made ten years hence, the development in economic knowledge will be found to have been one of the great steps taken in the development of management in industry.

[9] Progress Report of Committee on Standardization of Terminology.

LEON P. ALFORD

Ten Years' Progress in Management, 1923-1932*

1933

This Report appeared at the end of a decade in which more widespread progress was made in the field of Managerial Work than had occurred in all the preceding years, since Taylor had first conceived his scientific approach to this field of human effort.

Progress included more effective technical procedure, and better human relations as well as wider public service—especially national planning.

* Alford, Leon P., "Ten Years' Progress in Management, 1923–1932," American Society of Mechanical Engineers, *Transactions*, Vol. 55, 1933. Permission to excerpt by courtesy of the Society.

TEN YEARS' PROGRESS IN MANAGEMENT, 1923–1932[1]

Leon P. Alford

INDUSTRIAL MANAGEMENT has undergone a severe test in the decade 1923–1932 due to violent fluctuations in industrial activity and sharp contrasts in the results of operating performance. Despite these changes it has made steady progress. It has been extended to all human activities where work is done. It has contributed to the accelerated rate of industrial development of the first six years, and its principles and practices have withstood the decisive trial of the deep depression of the last three. As an outcome of its application, well-managed concerns have passed through this period of business recession better than all others; as a result of its progress, management is now firmly established as a function in industrial operation. An examination of the changes in trends of some 25 industrial-management developments supports this major finding.

This paper is the fourth of its kind to treat of the progress of industrial management for the attention of the members of The American Society of Mechanical Engineers. The first was a committee report of 1912 under the title, "The Present State of the Art of Industrial Management." The second, a paper of 1919, was on "The Status of Industrial Relations." The third, a paper of 1922, a review of ten years' progress, was founded on the report of 1912 and was titled "Ten Years' Progress in Management." This paper seeks to review the changes and progress of another period of ten years, the decade just closing. For its foundation it reaches back to the three preceding summaries.

On the whole the ten-year period, 1923–1932, has been marked in the United States by sharp contrasts in results of industrial operation. The mid-point recorded the greatest peak of peacetime activity that industry has ever experienced. As this paper is being written operation is estimated to be only a little more than 50 per cent of normal. There have been three movements of the business cycle in this decade. These are dated as expansion to May, 1923, contraction to July, 1924, expansion to October, 1926, contraction to December, 1927, expansion to September, 1929, contraction to

[1] Contributed by the Management Division and presented at the Annual Meeting, New York, N. Y., December 5 to 9, 1932, of The American Society of Mechanical Engineers.
NOTE: Statements and opinions advanced in papers are to be understood as individual expressions of their authors, and not those of the Society.

date. Physical volume of industrial production surged up to its highest point in 1929 and then dropped sharply. Commodity prices and manufacturing costs have likewise receded. Statistics of production of the Federal Reserve Board are:

Year	Industrial Production Combined Index, Unadjusted
1923	101
1924	95
1925	104
1926	108
1927	106
1928	111
1929	119
1930	96
1931	81
1932 (January through June)	65.6

A comparison of the relation of profits to capital investment for 432 manufacturing concerns gives averages for 1920–1921 and 1929–1931. The figures for the latter period show the decline in profits during the present business recession.

Year	Percentage of Profits to Capital Investment
1920	9.89
1921	1.17
1929	12.82
1930	6.55
1931	2.47

A remarkable increase is shown in the productivity of American industrial wage earners. The percentage rise for all industry from 1899–1919 was 4.7 per cent; that is, productivity had changed but little during the first 20 years of the twentieth century. The change from 1919–1927 is a 53.5 per cent increase. For many industries this change became manifest in the year 1921, thus placing most of the advance in the decade under consideration.

Upon the surge of prosperity that these increases indicate was founded the belief that economic poverty in the United States was almost banished. Some of the more optimistic prophesied that by 1931 or 1932 everyone would have an abundance of the necessities of life. In gloomy contrast with this prophecy is the hundreds of millions of dollars already paid out for relief during the past two years and the organization of national relief agencies on a scale never before attempted to mitigate the human misery impending during the winter of 1932–1933.

Unemployment in the United States has fluctuated widely during the past ten years. The estimated minimum number of unemployed among non-agricultural wage and salary earners was at its lowest point in 1923, with an average of 1,532,000. The corresponding estimate as this paper is being written is 11,000,000, with well-founded fears that this number will be increased by 1933. During the first seven years of this decade, employment for industrial executives was quite stable. Shifts in business connection were comparatively few. Beginning with 1930 this situation changed, and the turnover of management personnel has since been rapid.

These circumstances have brought a reversal of belief in regard to American industrial achievement. At about the mid-point of the decade statements like the following were commonly made concerning us: America has made an "immense advance" industrially, "America has experienced a period of unusual industrial prosperity. Millions of people have found their earnings increasing at a more rapid rate than their standard of living." America has become "the first power in the world." As the decade closes this quite different matured judgment of the situation has been publicly declared by engineers:

> The problem of the relation of consumption, production, and distribution is one of supreme importance. More and more it will command the attention and devotion of the most intelligent, unselfish, and far-seeing men and women of the body politic. There is no human problem which compares with it in difficulty, in magnitude, in hopefulness. . . . what is being contemplated is nothing less than a purposeful changing of the course of history.

In spite of these violent fluctuations, management has made steady progress during the decade ending in 1932. It has extended to all human activities where work is done. It has contributed to the accelerated rate of industrial development of the first six years, and its principles and practice have withstood the crucial test of the deep depression of the last three. Increasing recognition is being given to the fact that well-managed concerns have come through the period of business recession better than all others. As a function of industrial operation the art of management is now firmly established because of the general acceptance of its fundamentals. The promise of the future is to lead on to a higher professional standing through the development of intellectual, societal, and moral attitudes and values. Should a report like this one be written at the end of the next decade, much of its narration may well be a stirring epic of human achievement.

The nature and extent of the change make the task of reviewing the decadal progress of management difficult. But this difficulty is somewhat relieved by the availability of certain management literature, no prototype of which existed in 1912 nor in 1922. The items which have been most helpful in the study are: *Bibliography of Management Literature,* published by The American Society of Mechanical Engineers first in 1927, and revised in 1931; *Progress Reports of the Management Division of The American Society of Mechanical Engineers* from 1925 to date; and parts of the *Report on Recent Economic Changes.*

In these contributions two trends in management are definitely pointed out—the one toward increased specialization, the other "more management per man." The Bibliography lists in round numbers 800 references (827 by count) covering the 35 years prior to 1923. The comparable figure for 1923–1932 is 5000 items (3915 by count for eight years, 1923–1930). This record indicates an amazing expansion in the volume of management literature. Its character has also changed. Quoting from the foreword of the 1931 edition:

> . . . the trend of the development of management [is] indicated by its literature during this period. No longer are there many works dealing with the broad subjects of shop management and scientific management, but rather do they treat of specific phases or branches of management, such as economics, material handling, research, and safety. This, of course, is a logical result of the widespread tendency toward specialization.

Henry S. Dennison, in the chapter on "Management" in *Recent Economic Changes*, commenting on the increasing release and utilization of creative and managerial abilities, has this to say: "There is today not only more production per man, more wages per man, and more horsepower per man, but more management per man as well." [2] The reference date is 1928, the mid-point of the decade under consideration.

The approach to this review, as already indicated, is through the emphasized points in the three preceding studies of like nature. From this background the exploration has been broadened to include the activities and developments of management which were found worthy of comments in the annual progress reports. An advantageous difference in treatment between this paper and its predecessor lies in the rather generous introduction of quantitative evaluations. Facts and data of this kind were unavailable in the preceding report years.

Important Findings in Report of 1912

1. Advance in doing work. "The unquestionable proof of the advance that can be made in unskilled work . . . and in ancient trades . . . . These are the most striking phenomena of all." (Par. 1.)
2. Change in mental attitude. The shift in viewpoint toward production was declared to be "the most important change and one that comprehends the others . . . seeking for exact knowledge and then shaping action on discovered facts." (Par. 22.)
3. Transfer of skill. The application of this principle was emphasized as "the prominent element in present-day industrial management." (Par. 29.) And "we have pointed out that the underlying principle, that is, cause in the widest sense, the application of which has built up modern industry is the transference of skill." (Par. 41.)

Important Findings in Paper of 1919

The major lines of development in the effort to work out better industrial relations were indicated as:

(a) Profit-sharing plans;

(b) Methods of wage payment;

[2] *Recent Economic Changes.*

(c) Methods and laws to reduce the hazards in industry and mitigate the effects of injurious and occupational diseases;

(d) Employment management;

(e) Systems of mutual or joint control by employers and employees (Par. 18.).

Important Findings in Paper of 1922

1. Management principles. "Acceptance of the principles of management has broadened among engineers, executives in industry, and educators." (Par. 10.)

2. Management methods. ". . . demand for . . . facts as a basis of judgment has grown insistent in all good management. Appreciation of the possibilities and advantages of standardization, simplification, and elimination of waste has spread rapidly during the past two years. . . . The engineering or scientific method has extended in industrial cost accounting." (Par. 11.)

3. Significant developments. Especially significant developments include broadening the applications of management far beyond original Taylor mechanisms, establishment of management courses in colleges, "appreciation of the importance of the human factor in industry," and declaration that the "service motive must prevail in industry." (Par. 12.)

4. Economics of industry. "Without doubt if a study of this kind be made ten years hence, the developments in economic knowledge will be found to have been one of the great steps taken in the development of management in industry." (Author's closure).

No similar group of significant developments and trends is offered from the annual progress reports, for the reason that they deal principally with current evaluations rather than trends, but numerous quotations are included to show points of view and steps of progress.

It is unlikely that any two investigators would pick identical items to present as significant in a decade of progress, nor give, even approximately, the same emphasis to each one, nor the same interpretation to the surrounding facts. In this paper the first situation is made partially impersonal by the choice of the items. Of the twenty-five that are discussed separately, only one, "National Planning," lacks a reference in the preceding reports of The American Society of Mechanical Engineers. As to the second situation, a free use of quotations and citations tends to broaden the area of opinion and to impersonalize the comments.

From this place on, this paper gives a series of summary word pictures of the circumstances of change and progress of the selected developments of management in action. Each is considered separately, although none is independent. "The art of management today [1928] is in large part the progressive adjustment and integration of conflicting needs, conflicting influences, and conflicting purposes."

National Planning

Management is faced with the greatest challenge of its career in the need and demand for national planning and world planning. This summons to still greater achievement comes from the profound influence of the depression that broke like a storm in 1929. More questioning and searching has ensued, directed at the organization and operation of industry, than at any other similar national institution. H. S. Person[3] presents the issue, clearly outlined like the ascending steps of a vast pyramid:

> Stabilization of material factors is not sufficient; human relations must be stabilized. Stabilization of production is not sufficient; merchandising must be stabilized. Stabilization of production and merchandising is not sufficient; general administration must be stabilized. Stabilization of an individual enterprise is not sufficient; all enterprises in the industry must be stabilized. Stabilization of one industry is not sufficient; all industries of a nation must be stabilized. . . . stabilization of national industry alone is not sufficient; international economics must be stabilized. Achievement of any of these ends is a step toward a more balanced and harmonious industrial and social world life; each end is but a means to another and greater end.

International planning as a matter of fact must be dismissed at this moment as a stimulating speculation. National planning for the United States is in quite another situation. The idea has grown directly from the experiences with shop planning and the application of Taylor's theories.

The objective of national planning in its economic aspect is to attain and maintain "in the United States a standard of living that is high, broadly distributed, and free from severe fluctuations;"[4] in its industrial aspect it is to stabilize the operating performance of industrial enterprises; in its national aspect it is to minimize the fluctuations of business and avert disaster.

The principles to apply are the enduring fundamentals of management. Methods and technique must be evolved to satisfy insistent needs. Their prototypes are here in the mechanisms and procedures now applied successfully in hundreds of individual plants and in many coördinated industries.

Numerous plans have already been proposed. In general they vary between these extremes:

1. Those that seek to make industrial and business planning a function of the National Government. A governmental bureau, for example, would tell manufacturers what to make, how much to produce, and at what price to sell;
2. Those that seek for voluntary regulation of the operation of industry by industry itself, under some governmental supervision to safeguard the rights and interests of the public.

We may confidently look forward to attempts at national planning during the coming decade. Management will give a good account of itself in this new test.

[3] "Principles and Practice of Scientific Management," World Social Economic Congress, 1931.
[4] Progress Report [1932] of Committee on the Relation of Consumption, Production, and Distribution of the American Engineering Council.

Service Motive in Industry

Scrutiny of the literature and programs of conventions dealing with management reveals that "profit management" has been a favorite topic of discussion. Industrial executives have, in the main, felt and expressed their responsibility toward their own organizations and their investors, and to a lesser degree toward their customers. Toward their employees there has been little evidence of a sense of managerial accountability. This situation might seem to indicate that the fine idealism of Taylor and Gantt had been lost in the general emphasis on profit making. Taylor had the welfare of his fellow man at heart, and spent much of his life's energy in trying to establish mutually satisfactory relations between employees and employers. Gantt challenged industrial leaders with the statement that the life of the community depends upon the service it gets, and that the community needs service first, regardless of who gets the profits.

The statements of two industrial leaders that now follow show that the motive of service is still recognized, although applications may seem to be few.

Gerard Swope (1925): [5]

> The reason for the existence of industrial organizations is not first and primarily for profit, but to furnish the community with something the community desires to have. If an organization furnishes something that the community wants, of good quality and at a fair price, it will always be rewarded for that service by an adequate profit.

Benjamin A. Franklin (1926): [6]

> Every industrial executive and every owner in an industrial enterprise, whether in whole or in part, strives for and desires a profit. This is the essential reason for ownership. But ownership is no longer, if it ever was, a warrant for profit, for profit must come from the public and from nowhere else. The public is only willing to pay a profit for service, and, with the wider spread of industry, for the best service; therefore, essentially and fundamentally, industry is a service.

No facts can be presented to show how far the ideal of essential service is shaping industrial policy. But the feeling of responsibility toward employees is manifesting itself in operating procedures. The unemployment payment plan of the General Electric Company (1930) and the Unemployment Allowance Act of the State of Wisconsin (1932) recognize such responsibility. Numerous bills to set up unemployment insurance may be expected to be introduced at the 1933 sessions of state legislatures. It will be surprising if some do not become law. The sense of responsibility of industrial executives toward their workers seems to be increasing.

Change in Mental Attitude: Adoption of Scientific Method

The change in mental attitude which was noted 20 years ago is still going on. It is a shift to the scientific method. The adopted viewpoint is one that seeks for exact

[5] From an address before the Illinois Manufacturers' Association, December 9, 1925.
[6] *The Industrial Executive*, p. 100.

knowledge, and shapes action upon discovered facts. As a doctrine of management it has had great prominence during the past decade. But no one has presented it more forcefully than Gantt: "We have no right morally to decide as a matter of opinion that which can be determined as a matter of fact." [7]

This doctrine has had an influence in developing management procedures. Examples are forecasting, budget planning, and standard cost systems. Management reports, the result of studies and investigations, have been numerously produced, both by organizations and individuals. A few indicate their nature. A complete list of such studies is beyond the scope of this paper.

American Engineering Council:
> *Safety and Production* (1927)
> Industrial Sections of *Recent Economic Changes* (1928)

Management Division, American Society of Mechanical Engineers:
> *Economic Life of Equipment* (1931)
> *Measurement of Management* (in process)

National Association of Cost Accountants:
> *Cost Reports for Executives* (1928)
> *How to Set Standards* (1931)

National Industrial Conference Board:
> *Supplemental Bonuses* (1927)
> *Industrial Standardization* (1929)
> *Budgetary Control in Manufacturing Industry* (1931)

Industrial Relations Counselors, Inc.:
> *Vacations for Industrial Workers* (1927)
> *Pensions for Industrial Workers* (1928–1929)
> *Unemployment Benefits in the United States* (1930)

A. G. Anderson:
> *Industrial Fatigue* (1931)

Charles W. Lytle:
> *Collegiate Courses for Management* (1932)

Economics in Industry

Studies of economic problems in industry with the purpose of resolving into mathematical formulas relations formerly expressed qualitatively in words have made substantial progress. The efforts have been directed principally toward the establishment of rates and optimum levels. The mathematical expressions derived are simple in themselves, but because of the large number of variables involved, and unstandardized economic and accounting practices, which provide many of the numerical quantities, the symbolization adopted has been complex. Simpler expressions must follow before general application of these economic formulas will be possible in industrial practice. Generous appreciation is due to those who have pioneered in this field, and

---

[7] *Industrial Leadership*, pp. 88–89.

who are thereby assisting in laying the foundation for a new economics. In this group those listed here deserve mention, most of them members of this Society.

INVESTIGATORS	ECONOMIC PROBLEMS STUDIED
Kimball	Minimum cost point
Davis, Lehoczky, Pennington, Raymond	Economic manufacturing lot sizes
Coes, Hagemann, Kurtz, Norton, Raymond, Shepard, Vorlander	Economic life of equipment
Roe	Economics of small tools
Davis	Economic purchase quantities
Shewhart	Economic control of quality of manufactured product
Knoeppel, Rautenstrauch	Break-even point

Management Principles

Continuing attention has been given to the fundamentals of management. Two codifications of principles and laws have appeared during the past decade. These contributions have important differences when compared with their predecessors. They recognize a comparatively large body of fundamentals rather than a few; they have been stated to connect cause and effect. Three principles have had their first formulation during this period: the Law of Simulation, by Blanchard; the Law of Motion-Time, by Segur; the Law of Operating Rates, by Alford and Hannum. None of these principles as now formulated nor the codes into which they have been combined can be considered as final. Statements of fundamentals need to be brought under review and revision at recurring intervals to keep them abreast of the advances in theory and practice.

Advance in Doing Work: Transfer of Skill

The most striking single industrial advancement in this decade is the increase in the productivity of the individual industrial worker. From 1919 to 1927 this increase, as represented in the physical volume of product, was about 50 per cent. The corresponding increase in utilization of primary horsepower per worker was some 30 per cent. A recent study made by Hannum and the author indicates that in well-managed concerns the increase in the productivity of the worker is continuous, is not affected by business depressions, and is of the order of 4 per cent *per annum*. These increases are evidence of the expanding mechanization of industry, the widening use of machines and tools, and the extension of the application of the principle of transfer of skill.

The number of references in the *Bibliography to Production and Production Control* is 16 times more for the decade 1923–1932 than for the 35 years preceding

1923. The comparative figures are 52 to 875; in the latter figure the totals for 1931 and 1932 are extrapolated. This bursting increase in the literature on how to do work suggests the advancement in productivity—namely, the further application of science to the work of manufacturing. Wesley C. Mitchell[8] in answering the question, "What is the prime factor in prosperity?" says: "Since 1921 Americans have applied intelligence to the day's work more effectively than ever before. . . . The old process of putting science into industry has been followed more intensively than before; . . . ."

The Human Factor in Industry: Employment Management

Taking the recurrence of the items in the Bibliography as an indication of interest and importance, labor and personnel matters, the human factor in industry, rank with production and production control. The number of items for the decade 1923–1932 is 871. No one has more succinctly presented the development of man management in industry than Henry S. Dennison.[9] At first

> . . . men were called to personnel management who were new to the problem . . . Their experience was academic but their outlook was fresh, their sympathies and earnestness were high, many of them had keen and well-trained minds, and they knew enough to begin at once to learn from each other by pooling their experiences. They overcentralized and overelaborated the job, as is always likely at the installation of a new functional department; and in this case all the more so because of the intense pressures.
>
> With the business stagnation and glutted labor market of 1921, they were virtually swept away, but they left behind them new practices, and old ones modified, psychological and trade tests, job analyses and classifications, rating scales, systematic training, and shop committees. What is of more importance is that they left a habit in the business mind of considering personnel management as a difficult, distinct, and major function of business management. Previously such little selection, training, health and safety work, insurance and social contacts, and joint relationships as had been attempted, had often been administered with no coördination . . . seldom as serious projects of human engineering.

The process of sweeping away personnel activities, which was so widespread during the depression of 1920–1921, has recurred during the present business recession but in a mitigated form. The situation indicated by the Progress Report of 1931 has not materially changed down to the present time.

> Modern labor management as a whole has by no means been abandoned. Most companies have maintained their industrial-relations programs, and some have even extended and liberalized their labor policies. Unemployment of personnel directors and their associates has probably not been greater than that of other supervisory and staff employees.
>
> This situation, which is strikingly different from that which characterized the depression of 1921, is to be accounted for largely by the growing usefulness of modern labor management, and by the increased recognition of its usefulness by the leaders of industrial enterprises.

[8] *Recent Economic Changes,* vol. 2, p. 862.
[9] *Ibid.,* p. 518.

This gain in usefulness has been due in part to the gradual acceptance of the theory that personnel management is properly a staff or advisory function in the industrial organization, and in part to the rising professional status of industrial-relations directors.

Management Methods: Organization

Three developments in organization have commanded the attention of industrial executives and management engineers: the operating structure itself, the functionalization of duties and specialization of the personnel, the measurement of operating performance.

The depression of 1921 with its disturbance of business relationships gave a new importance to the internal structure of industry and business. Examinations of the principles of organization and the mechanisms whereby they are made effective and are coördinated have been made afresh. One result is the placing of more reliance upon the personnel of an organization, and less upon the static design of that organization as indicated by the regulation organization chart.

Functionalization of types of activity has spread and with it the specialization of individuals. Managers have recognized that to take full advantage of the national aptitudes and exceptional abilities of executives, problems and duties must be narrowed in scope and submitted to special consideration and action. Apart from the Taylor installations, the most significant applications of functionalization have been made during the decade just ending.

Once the structure of an organization has been perfected there arises the need for measuring its operating performance. Numerous studies, but little real progress, have been made in this field. An extensive, though uncoördinated, group of ratios, turn-overs, rates, efficiencies, engineering and experiential factors has grown up, the work of many investigators. It is reasonable to expect that a satisfactory mechanism of measurement must be a part of a system of control.

Shewhart,[10] in establishing a mathematical basis for quality control by random sampling, has shown the application of scientific theories to the solution of every-day management problems. But he has done more. He implies that for every function of management, standards of performance can be established in accordance with the normal distribution of each characteristic of the function when influenced solely by a constant system of chance causes.

Three widely used mechanisms of control employ standards as an integral element in their procedure. The Gantt chart plots requirement against actual performance for the same interval of time, a day, week, or month; budgets estimate expenditures for a year, for example, and divide the amounts into weekly or monthly subdivisions; standard costs compare the actual costs with a predetermined standard. In each of these mechanisms means are provided to set a standard performance, to compare the actual performance against it at specified intervals, and to analyze the causes of failures and variations.

[10] "Economic Control of Quality of Manufactured Product."

The most recently devised mechanism of this nature is based on a somewhat different theory. It is the system of kmh-rates of Hannum and the author, and is based on the principle of operating rates which is stated as: Operating performance is controlled most directly through control of the rates of expenditure of labor, materials, and expense.

In the comparison and harmonizing of actual performance with present standards, or in the control of the rates of input of production factors in industrial operation, may lie a means for the direct measurement of management.

Management Methods: Cost Accounting

The most significant development in management procedure that has taken place during the past decade is in cost accounting. The major credit for this progress is due the National Association of Cost Accountants and that organization's able leaders. This Society was founded at the end of 1919, thus the major part of its work is included in the decade under review. Three of its contributions are particularly noteworthy:

1. Raising the status of cost accounting;
2. Promoting the use of budgets and developing budgetary procedure;
3. Extending the use of standard costs.

Budgets made extraordinary progress following the publication in 1922 of "Budgetary Control" by J. O. McKinsey. No other mechanism of management of similar scope and complexity has ever been introduced so rapidly. A 1931 publication of the National Industrial Conference Board analyzes 162 budget systems. It is estimated that 80 per cent of the budgets installed in industry have been put in since 1922. The depression years 1930–1932 have created situations which have made budgeting difficult in many instances, and have shown the necessity of introducing adjustable means to make the estimates correspond with the possibilities of changing conditions. It is likely that the budget as a master plan will emerge from these troubled years a more useful and effective management mechanism.

Standard cost procedure is second only to budgeting in its growth in cost-accounting practice. Although the first presentation of its methods by G. Charter Harrison was made in 1918, the literature of the art and extension of the methods have come principally since 1922. Standard costs have now been applied in nearly every kind of industry, both intermittent and continuous. The concept behind the development is scientific, the prediction in advance of what the cost of product is to be.

Management Methods: Waste Elimination

Three developments in the economy of industrial operation which have had a rise to a position of prime importance since 1923 are: the elimination of waste in industry, simplification of manufactured products, and engineering standardization. The "Waste in Industry" report of the American Engineering Council was issued in 1921. From the impetus given by its presentation and recommendations have come the movements for waste elimination and simplification. In engineering-society circles no other management topic has received more attention, been the subject of more meetings, and the object of more special effort than that of waste elimination. The concept of preventing or avoiding wastage, a distinct contribution to national economy, has been accepted far beyond engineering and management circles, and has become a part of the directive thinking of many non-technical individuals and groups. President Hoover, when Secretary of Commerce, said of the Waste in Industry report, that if the American Engineering Council produced only one such engineering economic document in fifty years, the existence of the organization would be justified.

Simplified-practice recommendations have eliminated unnecessary variety in sizes, dimensions, models, and types of over 130 commodities. About 20 new projects are constantly before the Bureau of Simplified Practice, which is the coördinating agency for the developments and promulgation of the recommendations.

Some elimination-of-waste surveys in manufacturing plants have indicated a possible saving of $50 per employee *per annum*.[11] ". . . the savings of American manufacturers from simplified practice and the application of the recommendations of the report on Waste in Industry [is estimated] as upward of $600,000,000 annually." On the basis of this estimate the total saving for the decade 1923–1932 is of the order of five billion dollars.

Standardization, while well established before 1923, has made substantial progress since that date. The work has been participated in by individual plants, trade associations, technical societies, and governmental agencies. The movement to create "American Standards" was initiated by a group of technical societies which founded the American Engineering Standards Committee. In 1928 this committee was reorganized to include a broader industrial scope, and the name changed to the American Standards Association. It is now a federation of some 40 national technical societies, trade associations, and Federal Government departments, with numerous affiliations abroad. Up to January 1, 1931, it had approved 181 American Standards, of which only 10 antedate 1923. The economic advantage of standardization cannot be evaluated. The automobile industry claims a saving of $750,000,000 per year. A survey made in 1926 showed that 91 trade associations and technical societies were expending $2,600,000 annually on standardization activities. At the same time the yearly expenditure of the Federal Government was $4,250,500.

Management Methods: Wage-Payment and Profit-Sharing Plans

Financial-incentive wage-payment plans have made steady progress in the extent of application. C. W. Lytle gives a comparison of the distribution of such incentives and day work for industrial workers:

[11] *Recent Economic Changes*, Vol. 1, p. 119.

A rough idea of progress can be gained by comparing data from the Gemmill [12] survey of 1922 with those from the Jucius [13] survey of 1932. The former was from representative plants in and east of Chicago, while the latter was from representative plants in Chicago. Both surveys include all sizes of plants and all types of product. Despite differences in scale and location, the figures are probably representative of the progress in the better-managed plants during the last decade.

The comparisons are:

	Number of Employees		Per Cent of Whole	
	1922	1932	1922	1932
On time wages	15,630	44,674	53.5	29.4
On financial incentives	13,600	107,489	46.5	70.6

The invention of wage-payment plans has continued. A listing of 1924 recorded 17; a similar compilation of 1932 showed 32. It is becoming more generally recognized that many of these are but variations of more basic plans that are well known.

Five of the annual Progress Reports of the Management Division comment on incentives. From them excerpts have been selected to show progressive changes.

1926: There has been a revival of interest in this subject. . . . Group bonus has become common, especially in the automobile industry. . . . The prejudice which formerly existed against piece work has lessened as such rates have become guaranteed and employees are learning that piece rate gives them *all* of the wages saved from decreased time.

1927: Interest in incentives seems to be gaining. . . . The cutting of piece rates or commission rates has become uncommon, and the response to such incentives is therefore more wholehearted than ever before.

1929: For some time a tendency has been developing to make more and more group applications of incentive plans. This is a natural accompaniment of mass production in that more and more work is interdependent. As in all new things, there is, however, a danger of this change swinging too far. Since task standards need only be set for the whole assembly and the subordinate parts merely balanced, it is an easy way to avoid some of the preliminary job standardization and much of the paper work of operating. If equal results were possible, there could be no objection, but it is well established that group effort is neither that of the least efficient nor that of the most efficient, but a mean between.

1930: There has been a revival of interest in financial incentives. This is undoubtedly due to the fact that the high-wage principle has come to the front, and also somewhat to the mature stage which job standardization has now attained.

1931: Incentives have continued to spread into lines of work formerly considered too difficult of job standardization.

Incentives for executives, fostered by prosperity, were freely introduced up to 1929, and as freely dropped after the beginning of business depression. The Progress Report of 1929 makes this comment:

[12] P. F. Gemmill, "A Survey of Wage Systems," Industrial Management, October, 1922.

[13] M. J. Jucius, "The Use of Wage Incentives," Journal of Business, University of Chicago, January, 1932.

Here the incentive is coming from two directions; first, from profits in the form of a fund and distributed according to the estimated contribution of each executive; second, from measurable achievements such as departmental standards of quantity, quality, delivery, and the all-inclusive costs. . . . the type of incentive based on measured results is infinitely superior for all minor executives, and usually so up to the general manager.

Profit-sharing plans have had a negligible record during the decade under review. There is no reference to them either in the *Report on Recent Economic Changes* or in the annual Progress Reports.

Management Methods: Job Standardization

The high wages that prevailed during the first seven years of the decade just closing stimulated the study of operations and jobs with the purpose of reducing labor costs. Much consulting work has been done in this field. The controversy over the relative merits and possibilities of time study and motion study, which was alive in 1923, has subsided. The harmonizing of these methods of job standardization by Roe and Lytle in *Management's Handbook* has been an important influence in bringing about the change of attitude. In addition to the extension of the utilization of time and motion study, important developments are improvements in the technique and devices for time and motion study, and in motion-time analysis. Segur has based the technique of the latter on the principle of motion time.

Three of the annual Progress Reports contain these comments:

1928: There has been a pronounced tendency toward a better understanding of time study.

1930: The application of time and motion study is now spreading in the textile industry, especially in the South. . . . Some of the most progressive labor organizations have begun to insist upon the establishment of standards in their operations.

1931: There is definitely a revival of interest in the micromotion method of job standardization. This has arisen from the General Electric Company's practice of using the full micromotion method to train its analysts, and of allowing the work of the analysts to be done without the full use of the method. . . . when analysts are trained by the full micromotion method they are so familiar with the principles of correct motions that they are able to make drastic improvements without taking elaborate measurements of existing work methods.

The Society of Industrial Engineers has completed a survey of time-study devices and methods, but the report has not been published.

Management Methods: Inventory Control

Inventory control has been refined and made more effective during the decade of this paper. Concentration upon methods for its accomplishment was stimulated by the shortage of materials during the World War and the excess of stocks during the depression of 1921. Control is sought to hold quantities within prescribed limits, to reduce the risks of damage and obsolescence, and to save the wastes of handling.

> One of the dramatic developments . . . is to be found in some automobile plants, where the average inventory has actually decreased from several months' to a three or four days' supply. . . . materials . . . are planned to be taken directly from the freight cars and placed in the manufacturing departments where they are to be used, thus eliminating handling and the expense of stores control.[14]

Management Methods: Materials Handling

An indication of the creative energy directed toward better handling of materials is given by the number of references in the Bibliography before and after 1923. The record is: before, 8; after (1923–1932 adjusted) 251. Improvement has been in the economics and control of handling, in the equipment available, and in organization of material-handling departments. Economies in many instances have been substantial. Thirty-seven installations reported in 1928 had aggregate annual savings of over $850,000. Under this general head is the extension of assembly equipment to allow "straight line" production. Numerous installations in many different kinds of industry show the wide possibilities of applying this principle.

Management Methods: Accident Prevention

The seriousness of the industrial-accident problem began to be appreciated in the United States some 12 years prior to 1923. Workmen's compensation laws were passed, the safety movement initiated, and thousands of persons began to give their attention to ways and means to reduce accidents. The effect of this work was significant. The prevailing number of accidents was cut in half, or to a third, in many industrial establishments. But following the revival of business in 1923 an alarming situation became evident, brought about by the increasing frequency and severity of compensatable accidents and mounting accident costs. The real situation was at first masked by the great increases in production and productivity. While there had been an increase in the hazard of industry per man-hour, production had increased so much more that the hazard in terms of production had decreased.

Following 1923, therefore, the accident problem became this: Can accidents be controlled under modern industrial conditions of high productivity? The National Bureau of Casualty and Surety Underwriters asked the American Engineering Council to investigate this matter. The report of 1928 on Safety and Production presented the results of the study. In brief the findings are:

1. Industrial accidents can be controlled under modern conditions of highly efficient production;
2. Safety and production are shown to have a coefficient of correlation of 0.835; "a 'safe' factory is eleven times more likely to be 'productive' than an 'unsafe' factory";
3. Major industrial executives have as much responsibility to initiate accident prevention as to initiate improvement in productivity.

[14] *Recent Economic Changes*, Vol. 2, p. 509.

The situation has changed but little since the issuance of this report. The industrial-accident problem is still of major importance. But the attitude toward the question has improved, and the means for its progressive solution are more clearly defined.

Management Methods: Works Councils

Employee-representation plans, or works councils, spread rapidly after the recovery of business following 1922. By 1923 some 700,000 workers were included in these plans. By 1928 this number had doubled. In the management survey of 1928 for the *Report on Recent Economic Changes*, 20 per cent of the plants studied had active, formal employee-representation plans, 10 per cent dealt occasionally with especially elected employee committees, and 6 per cent were working under union agreements. One of the consequences of the rise of these plans has been the retarding of the growth of organized labor. What the effect of the present depression will be ultimately on works councils cannot be foreseen. It may not be so far reaching as that experienced in 1921–1922.

> The year 1921 saw the discontinuance of many arrangements for joint relations, both union agreements and independent employee-representation plans. The serious unemployment at that time and the weakened position of the unions resulted in the abrogation of many arrangements made during the war and boom years. Many plants closed, and when they reopened the employee committees which had previously existed were not revived.[15]

Wage Levels

No other theory of management has ever had such a meteoric rise of acceptance and seemingly an equally meteoric drop in favor as the doctrine of high wages. The theory that high wages accompany high production was practically unknown in 1921, although it had been suggested by a few management engineers. In that year "more than 300 articles appeared telling of methods used in cutting wages and speculating on how far they would fall. By 1922 articles of this sort had disappeared and those about wage incentives had taken their place."[16] By 1926 the doctrine was well established and had been accepted by many able business executives and trade-union leaders. The high wages of these years down to 1930 were an impelling force in the management progress that this paper records. As the depression of 1929 began to be felt, the high-wage doctrine was invoked to maintain wage rates, with considerable success through 1930. The Progress Report of that year states:

> The principle of high wages is standing the test of the depression better than many expected. . . . Relatively few of the leading large companies have cut wages per piece or per hour. . . . The very fact that so many leaders are deliberately trying not to cut wages is enough to vindicate the statement that the high-wage theory has come to stay in this country.

However, during 1931 and 1932 wage cuts became common.

[15] *Recent Economic Changes*, Vol. 2, p. 529.
[16] *Ibid.*, p. 529.

A study made by the National Industrial Conference Board of the record of 1718 industrial concerns employing 3,358,666 workers in 1929, and 2,391,009 in 1932, yielded these facts:

Nature of Reductions	Per Cent of Companies
Executive salaries	80.5
Other salaries	81.0
Wage rates	75.4

Extent of Reductions	Average Reduction in Per Cent
Executive salaries	20.3
Other salaries	15.9
Wage rates	13.9

In general, salary reductions have preceded wage-rate reductions. In 1930, 212 of the companies reporting reduced salaries; 148 reduced wage rates; about 12 per cent of the reported reductions in salaries and 11 per cent of the reported reductions in wage rates were made during this year. More reductions occurred in 1931. The peak seems to have been reached early in 1932.

The ultimate fate of this doctrine cannot be predicted. It has not been abandoned. It may return to general favor and acceptance with the modified meaning that high wages can be paid only for high productivity. The Progress Report of 1931 gives an excellent summary of opposed points of view:

A veritable storm has raged between the orthodox economists, including many of our bankers, and the progressive manufacturers, including most of the engineers. The former group believes that the sooner wage rates are reduced to the same extent that commodity prices have been reduced, the sooner will be the recovery of industry. The latter group, while conceding that a proportionate reduction in money wages need not affect adversely the economic status of the worker, maintains that the real strength of American business lies not in the maintenance of an even balance between wages and cost of living, a continuing equilibrium from year to year, but in a steady advance toward the higher standards.

Working Hours

In 1926 the Ford Motor Company startled industrial executives by announcing the adoption of a five-day week. The move was a natural result of the higher productivity per machine and per man-hour which had been attained. A report of the National Conference Board published in 1931 showed that 270 establishments employing in the aggregate 216,921 wage earners were operating on a year-round five-day-week schedule at the close of 1928. The annual Progress Report of 1930 carries this item:

While a few companies have lengthened the working day in order to pay the same daily wage, in general hours have been shortened and the five-day week has been given greater trial than ever before. In 48 national and international unions there are 532,894 employees on this basis.

347

Continued agitation for shorter working hours and a flexible working week is active, and the practices have many advocates.

> Shorter normal working hours would constitute a permanent spread of unemployment. . . . For instance, it is reasonable to believe that if in an industry normally operating 50 hours per week, the working hours were shortened to 40, with 50 per cent overtime pay up to 45 hours, and 100 per cent overtime pay beyond that, the influence of the change would be in the direction of maintaining good business. . . .[17]

The trend toward shorter working hours is one of the most pronounced in industrial management today.

Working Conditions

Increasing attention has been given to working surroundings and conditions during the past decade. Evidence of this fact is offered by the following tabulation of items in the Bibliography:

Item	References before 1923	References 1923–1930
Air conditioning	0	60
Artificial lighting	2	80
Fatigue	7	30
Fire prevention	0	26
Noise elimination	0	6

Ventilation and air conditioning have been utilized to remove dust and fumes and to control temperature and humidity that working spaces may be more comfortable and better adapted to manufacturing processes. Artificial lighting has tended to use brighter and higher unit intensities and is credited with substantial increases in productivity. The situation in regard to the elimination of fatigue was characterized in the Progress Report of 1926 in these words:

> This matter has had more propaganda than research. . . . there has been practically no advance in our knowledge of the nature of fatigue and the part it plays in efficient production.

Since that statement was written, fatigue has had intensive study with a reversal, or substantial modification, of former common beliefs. Anderson's investigation (1930–1931) was under actual working surroundings and conditions. He shows that with good management fatigue is not a major consideration:

> Progressive, modern manufacturing methods and management are rapidly eliminating real fatigue from industry. At the present time satisfactory outputs at low cost may be had without unduly timing workers, and in industrial work can be, and probably will be, of little importance.

Fire prevention and protection in industrial plants has kept pace with the improve-

[17] Progress Report of Committee on the Relation of Consumption, Production, and Distribution of the American Engineering Council.

ment in maintenance. Noise elimination is just beginning to receive attention, with as yet no tangible results to record.

Industrial Plants

Two possible tendencies in the locating and planning of industrial plants are worthy of attention, although neither is strongly evident at this time. The first is toward the locating of industries in small centers; the second is toward selecting the small unit as most economical in operating performance. In regard to the one, the American Engineering Council says:[18]

> The decentralization of manufacture which is engaging the attention of industrial leaders offers a useful method of striking a balance between agriculture and manufacturing. While a few industries, like the manufacture of steel, must be organized on a scale so large as to surround themselves inevitably with urban conditions, this is not true of the greater number. They can properly be divided into smaller units. The present tendency is to locate units in smaller communities in closer contact with rural conditions.

In regard to the other, recent studies strongly indicate that the optimum size of plant for effective operating performance is much smaller than is commonly believed. On the operating side, plant maintenance has assumed new importance because of its influence to increase production when bad-order machines are avoided and its effect in arresting depreciation.

Obsolescence of Equipment

Management has begun to deal with the obsolescence of equipment from two points of view. The one is that far too much machinery and other physical property is in use, or held for use, which actually is obsolete and should be disposed of. The other is that, due to the depression, actual values of previously acquired plants are lowered and assets should be written down accordingly. Two comments appear in the annual Progress Reports:

1928: The replacement of obsolete equipment is considered to be one of the principal factors in good management.

1929: Probably the most important questions that confront the manufacturer today are the relation between the condition of equipment and profits and the replacement of machinery which in point of service may have many years of usefulness but which is incapable of satisfying the latest fancies of the consumer market or competing with more recent and improved machinery. . . . Experience is showing in these competitive days the mathematical relation between obsolete machinery and profits is an inverse ratio. . . . The important phases of the industrial-equipment studies are: (1) to bring out facts showing the relation of equipment obsolescence to production costs, and (2) to discover, if possible, a means for correctly evaluating and providing for obsolescence in cost accounting.

[18] Progress Report of Committee on the Relation of Consumption, Production, and Distribution.

349

Industrial Research

Industrial research has as fully demonstrated its value during the months of business depression as any other management function. In spite of bad conditions, expenditures for research in well-managed plants increased in 1931 over 1929, laboratory efficiency has improved, and research has aided in these definite ways: by reducing costs, improving products, developing new products, increasing customers' goodwill, and in some instances is credited largely with the earning of profits.

The demands of the war gave a great impetus to research through the physical sciences. A report of the National Research Council of 1920 lists 300 organizations for research. Included are company, joint, consulting, commercial, trade association, and university laboratories. A further report in 1927 lists 999. Rough estimates of expenditures for basic production research as of 1928 ranged upward to $200,000,000 annually. Since 1921 business procedures and economic forces have been added to chemical and physical research. Numerous references in this paper are evidence of the work already done in these newer fields. Methods for statistical research and market analysis are examples. An assay made by the National Research Council in 1928 gave the major emphasis on items of industrial-research programs in this order of frequency:

1. Improved product or service;
2. Reduction of production costs;
3. Development of new fields of application;
4. By-products and new materials;
5. New products.

A similar, though less extensive, assay in 1932 gives indication of the effect of the depression.

Expenditures for research in percentage of establishments, comparing 1931 with 1929:

Increased 75
No change 15
Decreased 10

Laboratory efficiency, comparing 1931 with 1929, expressed in percentage:

Increased 87
No change 10
Decreased 3

Emphasis in research programs in 1931 expressed as percentage of frequency of appearance:

New products 38
Improved quality 37
Reduction in production costs 19
Development of new fields of application 5
By-products 1

Industrial-Engineering Courses

The major change in industrial-engineering courses of engineering grade has been the increase in number and in enrollments. The number of institutions giving this work has increased from 10 in 1922 to 35 in 1932. The number of graduates in 1922 was 311, and the number of graduates in 1931 from 30 institutions was 596.

In 1923 the Society for the Promotion of Engineering Education undertook a comprehensive study directed to the improvement of engineering education. The investigation was completed in 1929. In the fact-finding stage of this study engineering-college graduates were asked what subjects they regretted missing in college. Seven of these and the number of men mentioning them follow:

Business administration	456
Economics	226
Accounting	179
Psychology	122
Salesmanship and advertising	118
Industrial management	104
Production and production methods	33

This record is an indication that graduate engineers feel the need of courses such as are included in industrial-engineering curricula. An indication that engineering educators are alive to the situation is found in the fact that industrial-management subjects occupied a prominent place on the program of the summer schools for engineering professors, held under the auspices of the Society for the Promotion of Engineering Education at Purdue University in 1930 and at Stevens Institute of Technology in 1932.

Lytle [19] has summed up the major purposes of industrial-engineering courses as:

1. To formulate the principles of an emerging profession;
2. To prepare more adequately many men who are to enter this profession.

The situation seems favorable for major advances in the teaching of industrial engineering in the years immediately to come.

Marketing

Among the new problems that assumed importance during the decade 1923–1932, none has led on to more discussion than management of marketing. One-fourth of the section on management in the *Report on Recent Economic Changes* is devoted to this topic. In the Bibliography there are seven items on sales management up to 1923. From 1923 through 1930 the total is 181. Marketing is commented on in each of the annual Progress Reports beginning with 1926. The Taylor Society has been the leader in developing the science of marketing and in applying scientific management principles to selling. The American Management Association has a division devoted to

[19] "Collegiate Courses for Management," International Management Congress, Amsterdam, 1932, and Engineering Education, (S.P.E.E.), Vol. 39.

distribution problems and has made marketing practice a major topic in its programs. However, the progress made must be judged as slight. Marketing technique is crude both in its planning and execution. A few tendencies have asserted themselves: functionalization of selling activities similar to that which has taken place in manufacturing; adoption of the sales budget; accounting for sales expenditure; scientific pricing of product; analysis of markets; setting sales quotas.

The year-to-year comments in the Progress Reports show something of the develments of the attack on the problems involved:

1926: . . . these principles [of management] are extending beyond the old engineering type of industries and are becoming popular in industries less accustomed to engineering methods. Offices and retail stores are resorting to them. . . .

1927: The trend is toward intensive rather than extensive marketing. . . . Part of the advertising budget is being taken for research to ascertain what the consumer really wants.

1928: There is a growing interest in the cost of marketing, and more specifically in the cost of marketing activities.

1929: Relatively little progress has yet been made in analyzing distribution costs from the standpoint of the cost of handling individual items or performing individual services. . . . Investigations in wholesale and retail distribution for several lines of trade, with particular reference to the small as well as the larger producer and also to the several methods of distribution, show the possibilities for reducing costs through more uniform methods.

1930: Experiments in distribution have continued and some progress has perhaps been made, but it has not been sufficient to allow much specific discussion. . . . There has been increased appreciation of the fact that as a rule it is necessary to market those commodities which the consumer wants or can readily be brought to want . . . industry is coming to realize that its raw materials are the needs and wants of persons.

1931: The field of marketing is now in the greatest need of sound common sense and engineering skill. . . . The demand for useful products cannot be forced into being. . . . It has been recently recognized, both in private investigations and by governmental analysis, that it is very nearly universal in industry today to find that approximately 80 per cent of the volume of production exists on approximately 20 per cent of the number of products in the line. . . .

Association and Society Activities

The open-minded interchange of trade and technical information has been a factor of importance in the progress of the immediate past, and promises to occupy an even more important position in the business practice of the future.

What is raising the whole standard of management in the United States is the habit among employers of discussing their problems openly among themselves, of comparing the methods of one industry with those of another, and of founding associations for research and conference. . . . They are not afraid to teach each other, nor too proud to learn from each other.[20]

[20] "American Industry and Its Significance," *Round Table* (London), 1926, Vol. 17, p. 264.

In 1926 the Department of Commerce listed nearly 9000 business associations; in 1928 the number was 13,000; by 1930 there were 19,000. Some are local in scope, others state-wide or interstate, still others national or international. Their activities range

> over almost the whole field of management, including especially statistical service, cost accounting, industrial and commercial research, simplification, standardization, credit information, traffic and transportation studies, and trade ethics. It is significant that several hundred business executives are members of some national association of the social sciences.[21]

The membership in management societies has likewise increased during the past decade, the influence of the organizations has widened and strengthened, and the reports and papers sponsored by them have greatly enriched management literature. Among themselves the societies have entered into close cooperation and have participated in numerous joint activities. Management Week meetings in the United States and Management Congresses abroad are examples. Management Week was instituted in 1922 to promote interest in the function of management and to further disseminate information on its principles and practice. During the week designated in 1926 meetings were held in over 200 cities. From that high point interest waned until the plan for a week of organized activities was abandoned in 1929. Five International Management Congresses held in Europe have been participated in through the American committee representing jointly The American Society of Mechanical Engineers, the Society of Industrial Engineers, the American Management Association, the Taylor Society, and the National Association of Cost Accountants. The meetings were held in Prague (1924), Brussels, Rome, Paris, and Amsterdam (1932). Fourteen papers were contributed to the Amsterdam meeting. In addition there were several American papers presented at the Management Session of the World Engineering Congress held in Tokyo in 1930. Still further, American support has been active in the establishment and maintenance of the International Management Institute, with headquarters in Geneva. These contacts in foreign countries have served to show, with new emphasis, that management is universal.

DISCUSSION

WALLACE CLARK. The Alford progress reports are of great value, not only as authoritative records of the history and practice of management, but as a source of inspiration to engineers and all others working in that field. The writer is impressed by the breadth of this report and by the certainty it gives that the influence of management on human life is greater than ever before and more widely understood.

It is good to hear that the service idea in industry has survived the grave difficulties of the last few years. All honor should be given to those companies that have made efforts to keep their workers and to spread their work. The most encouraging statement is that some real progress is being made toward national planning, for this

---

[21] *Recent Economic Changes,* Vol. 2, p. 497.

seems to be the best protection against the recurrence of another serious depression. Even then, our national planning must be coordinated with that of other countries or it cannot be wholly effective.

DEXTER S. KIMBALL. Mr. Alford again has presented in concise and clear form the progress of industrial management, and this paper is a most welcome addition to those that he has already written marking the progress of industry. The paper is well documented, indicating that as usual what has been written bears the marks of scholarly research and is not merely a passing opinion. Several of his findings are of more than usual interest.

First, he calls attention to the changed viewpoint of all manner of people at the close of this decade as concerns the ultimate good of the vast industrial machine we engineers have built up. Dismay and doubt have succeeded admiration and applause. The problem of distribution has transcended that of production, and as the author points out, this in itself challenges the engineer and the industrialist to so direct management that it will "lead on to a higher professional standing through the development of intellectual, social, and moral attitudes and values." The point is well taken and should command the attention of every engineer and industrial leader.

The next important impression gained from the paper is his findings to the effect that in spite of this industrial debacle the principles and practices of scientific management, so called, appear to be firmly established and have apparently suffered no loss of prestige. He notes rather that progress along these lines has been constant even during the last few years, and he concludes that "the change in mental attitude which was noted 20 years ago is still going on. It is a shift to the scientific method."

This is highly important when one considers the new ideas of industrial planning which he discusses and which have appeared for the first time in our literature during the past year. Mr. Alford notes quite correctly that industrial planning in an effort to make production and distribution balance is a natural outgrowth of Taylor's ideas of shop planning which are now so familiar to all industrialists. He quite properly dismisses international stabilization through planning as out of the question at present, but the writer agrees with him that we shall, in the next decade, hear much about industrial balance or stabilization through national or private planning or both. This is perhaps the greatest and the most difficult problem that confronts us.

Mr. Alford also brings to attention as a problem of management the theories of wages which are now so much discussed. Here we touch upon difficult economic theory which we as engineers are not as yet in a position to debate with much success. Yet this and the correlated question of the length of the working day are matters with which the engineer in general and the industrial engineer in particular must concern themselves, for no doubt they are intimately connected with industrial recovery and stabilization.

ROBERT T. KENT. The author has undertaken a task of no mean order when he attempts to evaluate the progress of management during a period that presents such contrasts in management problems as does the decade under review. That he has been able to trace real progress, notwithstanding the chaotic conditions that have tried the souls of management during the past three years, is a tribute not only to the author's power of analysis, but also to the soundness of the basic principles of management itself. The method that the author has adopted is unique. Nevertheless, it is probably sound, for the literature of a great movement undeniably reflects the thoughts of those who are participating in that movement. The facts and data are exhibited in the paper. The interpretation of these facts and the conclusions drawn therefrom are the author's own. It is with these interpretations and conclusions that others may disagree.

The writer does not wish to take the position of disagreeing. On the contrary, he agrees with most of the statements made by the author. He believes, however, that more stress could well have been laid upon certain points, and it is these points that the writer desires to discuss.

Under the head, "Advance in Doing Work, Transfer of Skill," the author refers to the increase in productivity of the individual industrial worker, and states that the increases in productivity are evidences of the expanding mechanization of industry, the widening use of machines and tools, etc. It would seem that an opportunity has been missed here to point out the necessity of the education of the people, as a whole, in the fundamental principles of political economy. The author has not only laid open himself, but the entire engineering profession, to the charge that he is giving evidence in support of the economic fallacy of technological unemployment. Every engineer who has studied industry, its history and its future, knows that the mechanization of industry does not permanently decrease employment, but in the long run increases it. At this point, where the author shows that the productivity of the individual worker has been increased by mechanization of industry, he also should show how this mechanization of industry has created more employment for more people in the long run, and that therefore the mechanization of industry still further is a desirable thing. This is true, notwithstanding the outcries of those who oppose the machine age, sometimes from political motives and at other times from pure ignorance.

In his section on "Machine Methods and Organization," the author speaks of the measure of operating performance. A careful reading of this section indicates that he refers more to the measurement of the operating performance of the personnel in the organization than to measurement of the performance of the management as a whole. The writer believes that the late and the present unpleasantness through which we are now passing has revealed as nothing else could do the woeful need that we have for some standard of measuring the effectiveness of management itself. This has been pointed out several times, but apparently no systematic study of this subject has ever been made. Several years ago J. W. Roe presented a paper before this Society outlining a tentative method for the measurement of management. It was offered as a starting point from which we could begin the development of a system or method or plan for the real measurement of management itself. So far as the writer has been able to discover, and he has made many earnest efforts so to do, no one has ever even attempted to apply the principles enunciated by Professor Roe, and one of the most valuable papers ever presented before this Society is an unused tool of exceptional value in a crisis such as we are now experiencing. The most important thing before management today is to learn how to evaluate itself and its own effectiveness.

Budget control is the subject of a single paragraph in the section on "Management Methods, Cost Accounting." Here again the experience through which we are passing has demonstrated that budgets are far from being the instruments of perfection that they were considered to be during the golden years that ended with 1929. This is not said in derogation of budget control. On the contrary, if it had not been for budget control, our experiences during the last three years would have seemed mild compared to what they would have been had not budget control been as well established as it was. The point is that budgeting has failed us only in the respect that we have not yet learned how to accumulate data which will enable us to make better forecasts—in other words, to make more accurate predictions of income. In a period of falling commodity prices, falling volumes of business, and all the other concomitants of a first-class business depression, those who have been in the management end of industry have seen the most carefully made budgets become worthless within a month of their completion, simply because of inability to forecast the income figures correctly.

Budgeting will not become an exact science until we have learned how to accumulate data and to interpret these data in such a manner as will enable us to forecast income as accurately as we can now forecast expense. The problem is thus simply stated. The solution of it is one of the major jobs ahead of the engineering and management professions.

Wages will always be a subject of controversy. Whether to keep wages high and maintain individual purchasing power or to cut wages and keep more people at work will always afford a theme for discussion between two different schools of economics. The author states that during 1931 and 1932 wage cuts became common. These wage cuts were made in most cases only in desperation, as the last thing that many manufacturers could do to save themselves from bankruptcy. More and more have manufacturers and leaders of industry come to the conclusion that the way to prosperity is to build up the purchasing power of the great body of industrial workers. Hundreds of manufacturers in the past three years have gone deeply into their surplus, and in some cases have wiped out their surplus, before wage cuts were put into effect. The table of percentages of reductions in wages and salaries given by the author is significant in that executive salaries were cut more deeply and in more cases than wages. This table shows very clearly that the executives in charge of industry realized not only their duty to their country, but to their employees as well, and that when punishment was necessary, they took their own punishment first.

Under the head of "Working Hours," the author calls attention to the decrease in the length of the work week or work day. While this has nothing to do with the paper except as a comment upon the last sentence—"that the trend toward shorter working hours is one of the most pronounced in industrial management today"—the writer believes that it is significant that every improvement in mechanization and in management has tended toward the shorter working day and the shorter week. It will be recollected that when the factory system first started, the 14-hour work day was common in England. The writer remembers, as a boy, of hearing of certain places where they still worked 12 hours a day, and in the 1890's the working week throughout industry was 60 hours. Inasmuch as consuming power can grow but slowly while productive power can be increased rapidly, it is only logical to assume that the remedy for our so-called over-production is to produce less; that is, we should follow the trend that has continued since the beginning of the factory system and use the greater productivity to give us more leisure in which to enjoy the increased earnings that better machines and better management will give us. The writer believes that the five-day week is inevitable within the next few years. It would not surprise him to see the four-and-one-half- or even four-day week become universal within the next quarter century.

The author gives considerable attention to the improvement in working conditions. Working conditions have a direct relation to costs. Improved working conditions have not been brought about particularly by any altruistic spirit on the part of management, but by the realization that with better working conditions, increased production and consequently lower costs are possible. In this same section is mentioned the reversal of ideas concerning fatigue. Arguments pro and con in regard to fatigue are rather academic. Fatigue automatically is eliminated by better working conditions and by good management methods. The fundamentals of good management, as stated by Taylor, in which he demonstrated that fatigue is an important element in the determination of the daily task, still hold good. The fact that fatigue does not seem to play so important a part today is simply due to the fact that machines, work places, working conditions, etc., are so arranged that fatigue is not engendered in the way that it was when Taylor wrote his classic.

In discussing the location of industrial plants the author quoted from the American Engineering Council, which says that the decentralization of manufacture is engaging the attention of industrial leaders. One of the things that management will come to in the near future is extensive decentralization of industry. From his experience in plants located in large cities, and also in the largest city in the country, and in plants located in the smaller cities, the writer will unqualifiedly put himself on record that the plant in the small community is far and away better located than the one in the larger community. Not only are there better opportunities for good management, but the workers are more contented and have more of an interest in their employers' business, have more leisure in which to enjoy themselves, and therefore approach their work in a better frame of mind.

Under this same subject, the author discusses the maximum size of the plant. The writer believes that in future the trend will be toward the smaller plant, and more plants in the larger companies. During the war, the writer was closely associated with the management of a plant where were employed 4500 to 5000 men and women in

357

diverse occupations, under a single directing head, the general manager. While this man was one of the ablest of managers, the multifarious duties involved in the management of such a large number of employees was beyond the capacity of any one individual. The writer then formed the theory that in every industry there was a definite upper limit to the size of plant that could be efficiently managed under a single head, and that when a company grew to a size larger than this, the proper procedure would be to subdivide it into two or more plants, each of which would be smaller than the economical management limit of size.

The author outlines in considerable detail the progress that has been made in industrial research. Extended comment on this is unnecessary, except to state that it might have been well to emphasize that research is the foundation stone of industry and that there cannot be too much of it.

The author gives some consideration to the subject of industrial engineering education. At the risk of being branded a heretic, the writer will put himself on record that, in his opinion, industrial engineering education is, *per se*, highly overrated. It is a mistake to train young men specifically in this branch of engineering. Engineering students should be grounded thoroughly in the fundamentals of science, in sociology, English, and good common sense. If they have this foundation, they will quickly absorb the principles of industrial engineering as soon as they get out into the world. The engineering educational schools seem to stress too much the mechanisms of management to make good industrial leaders.

The writer finds himself in complete agreement with the author's statements concerning marketing. We have much to learn on the application of the principles of management to marketing. While the fundamental principles of management are applicable to marketing and distribution, just as much as they are applicable to production, the application must be along different lines than those used in the shop. The standards must be different, and the technique must be built up. Nevertheless, if the principles of management as applied to marketing were as thoroughly understood as they are when applied to production, it is probable that much of the distress of the past three years would have been avoided.

In his treatment of association and society activities, the author does not make clear whether or not he includes in this category the trade associations. While some of these are mere price-fixing agencies, others, and the writer believes the majority, are powerful forces for the advancement and stabilization of management. The writer has had experience in several trade associations, and it is his observation that they are the one big factor that will tend to stabilize industry, prevent cut-throat price competition, lead to cooperation in the stabilization of markets, and that they will be the promoters of extensive industrial research that cannot be undertaken by individual companies. The trade association may well become to an industry what the planning or production-control department is to the factory.

CARL L. BAUSCH. Another item should be included as a part of the ten years' progress report and as an essential for recovery. This is unemployment insurance. In

February, 1931, the Rochester Chamber of Commerce reported that fourteen companies had adopted the unemployment benefit plan. The plan is as follows:

All employees receiving less than $50 a week are included. The benefit will be 60 per cent of the weekly earnings, with a maximum of $22.50 a week, payable after two weeks of unemployment. The benefit will be paid only to employees laid off on account of slack work.

The fund will be accumulated by the concerns laying aside up to 2 per cent of their pay-rolls for the year 1931 to 1932. No contributions will be made by employees during normal times. If after the plan is started and it seems to the management that the fund is inadequate, an emergency may be declared and a 1 per cent assessment made on salaries of those getting over $50 a week. In such cases the company will contribute an additional equal amount.

All plans looking toward business recovery must include means to bring about a feeling of confidence in the minds of labor as well as of capital.

WALTER N. POLAKOV. There is no reference in the report to the influence of power production in the changing aims and methods of factory management. In the machine age and prior to the appearance of machines, the object of management was to make the worker personally more efficient. Training of workmen in the habits of industry, time and motion studies, premium systems, and task work with bonus were designed to that end. With the advent of the power age, machines became emancipated from the shackles of belts and gears. Driven by individual electric motors, machines are now easily relocated to suit the sequence of operations, thus upsetting all traditions concerning material handling, partly finished stores, shop dispatching, etc. Electrified machines are now frequently automatically loaded, adjusted, driven, controlled as to dimensions, unloaded, and output recorded, wholly automatically. There is a definite trend toward the "automatic factory" where no human hand touches the product throughout the operations. There are numerous skelp mills, rolling mills, aluminum plants, paper and pulp mills, cigarette factories, etc., where the transfer of skill and transfer of power from worker to machine are so complete that the functions of workers are chiefly supervisory in their nature.

This changes the labor specifications from demanding trade skill and physical force to new requirements of a psychological nature: (1) sustained attention, (2) correct perception, (3) prompt reaction. These qualifications are becoming essential labor characteristics, since observations of instrument indications in continuous processes demand sustained attention to all such factors as pressure, temperature, humidity, concentration, speed, etc. Then, these instrument indications must be correctly perceived and interpreted, so that prompt action may be taken before any damage is done by the changing conditions. This new role which labor is now increasingly called to play eradicates the old distinction between manual and mental labor, fusing them as the machine itself is fused with a motor and electrical controlling devices. Consequently, the main function of management is the securing of an uninterrupted flow of production. This function is becoming the more important as the first cost of the automatic equipment, and hence the fixed portion of capital charges, is getting not only far greater than it was before, but it generally exceeds many times the pay-roll.

This definite aim of securing an uninterrupted flow of production largely depends upon the managerial function of planning. Within the last decade this problem of planning of production, originally evolved out of the principles laid out by Taylor and perfected by Gantt, is spreading beyond the walls of a shop or a plant and has become a grave problem of planning within an industry, within a nation, and even among the nations. Hence we observe the movement to modify the anti-trust law, to plan and control the production of oil and cotton and other commodities, to plan import-export trade and readjust the tariffs, and even to plan concerning international war debts. The management engineer who a few decades ago was confused with an "efficiency expert" is looked upon today as one peculiarly fitted by his experience in planning to give advice on major economic problems.

L. W. WALLACE. The paper has omitted any reference to the conference of the leading industrial and commercial men of the nation held in Washington in December, 1929; that in this conference they committed themselves not to reduce wages if it could possibly be avoided; that this action signified that the fundamental principles of good management have become embedded in the minds of our leaders; and that they recognized the importance of maintaining good personnel relations. As a result of this commitment and the sincerity with which it was followed, American labor realized that management was doing everything it could to safeguard its interests during this depression.

As a result of this, during these strenuous times there have been less labor disturbances than in normal years. This fact is a great credit to both labor and management, and will become historical. It is one of the most significant events in the realm of management during the last ten years.

In a broad sense and over a long period of years, there is no such thing as technological unemployment. Due to technological advance there has been a shift in occupations, all tending to elevate the position of industrial workers. More skill, intelligence, and judgment are required to construct and operate modern equipment than under old methods; hence industrial workers have been greatly relieved of drudgery and are receiving higher compensation.

LILLIAN M. GILBRETH. In his 1912 report on the progress of management, the author referred to the transference of skill as of great importance, and his writings ever since have shown that he continues to feel this. It is not easy to define skill. The best that we have been able to do is to define it as "knowledge, plus dexterity, plus adaptability." Psychologists and engineers would seem to agree that knowledge and dexterity are necessary for skill; there is as yet little realization of the great importance of adaptability. Yet this is fundamental, for intensive studies of skill show that the man who possesses it can adapt to changing situations, and it is this adaptability that distinguishes the skilled man from any machine that may be invented to take over the work that he does.

If adaptability is accepted as part of the definition of skill, then skill can never be transferred from a man to a machine, though it can be transferred from a man to a man. And we need have no fear that machines will ever make skill unnecessary. Machines may embody knowledge and furnish repetitive dexterity, but cannot adapt themselves to a changing situation, as can a man.

The implications of this are many. Materials, if they are to facilitate machine operation, must be carefully standardized. If they are to conserve and develop skill, it is thinkable that not such close inspection is indicated. Machines should take over drudgery and such repetitive work as requires no adaptability. Men should be assigned to work that will require as high a degree of adaptability as they can supply, if their skill is to be conserved and developed.

In motion study, we are careful always to keep the consideration of maintaining, developing, and using skill a part of the program. The chief emphasis is on developing men, rather than on making things or inventing machines.

As a Society, we have made great progress by adding economics to the subjects discussed at meetings. We could make similar if not greater progress by adding psychology. A study of our programs during the last 20 years shows that we are including the human element more and more in our discussions of management.

But as yet we do not include the principles and practices of psychology, which concerns itself with the developing science of human behavior.

Our great need today is to realize that we can develop the human element along with our machines and our materials. This can be most appropriately done by discussing skill, its definition, its transfer, and its development, and it is to be hoped that every program of the Management Division will contain a place for such discussion.

G. M. EATON. The writer challenges Mr. Wallace's statement that there is really no such thing as technological unemployment. As a statement of long-time average considerations, the writer agrees with Mr. Wallace on the job-creating achievements of technological advance. But we are evading the issue when we deny the more or less transient unemployment attendant on every broad technical advance.

To give one specific illustration, the interests with which the writer is connected laid off nearly 300 skilled men when, along with the rest of the steel industry, they replaced hand labor with machines for the removal of surface defects from steel blooms. Do you think you could convince those 300 men that technological unemployment is imaginary? As they tightened their belts, they would resent defining their hunger period as transient.

We have been told that the engineer must get off from the beaten trail in his economic thought and be guilty of appearing radical. Very well, let us be radical for a moment. We have been told of organized effort to train men of skill, men of knowledge, dexterity, and adaptability, so that they can apply their skill to carving a living in a new way. The writer wishes that it had been brought out that too much of this effort is now necessarily exerted after the emergency demanding the change has arisen.

There was time enough in the interval between the sure knowledge that hand chipping of blooms was a dying art and the commercial availability of the machines to plan the transfer of the men whose art was evaporating. But it was nobody's business to do this, and the job was left to the slow process of evolution.

Our attention has been focused on the uselessness of a budget where only the expenditure side has been forecast with accuracy and little is known about income. When we budget employment in terms of man power and know little about the coming demand for men, our budget falls into the same category. Unemployment can be foreseen in just about the degree that we organize for this advance knowledge.

When the Pennsylvania Railroad foresaw the end of wooden cars, it transferred the skill resident in the workers from wood to steel, and did this ahead of the emergency, so that no men were laid off.

We dare to disclose our epoch-making ideas to the Patent Office for our own gain. Will we ever dare to disclose them in some similar manner to a planning agency for the welfare of others? This is radical; but it is worthy of hard-headed thought.

ERIK OBERG. The paper presents not only a most comprehensive summary of what has taken place in the last ten years in management engineering, but a prophecy of the future as well. The parts relating to industry planning and the service motive in industry are especially important, dealing as they do with the broader aspects of management. We engineers have been so busy delving into the physical laws of engineering that we have almost forgotten the purpose of it all. We have begun to look on the means as an end, and the result has been all too obvious during the past three years.

Management has to do with the running of industry efficiently. Industry is not running efficiently when a large part of its machinery stands idle and millions of workers are idle also. To that extent, management has failed, because it has not been built upon a broad enough basis. It has not had an adequate conception of fundamental economic laws. To acquire such a conception, however, is the business of management.

Most of the investigations into our economic difficulties, it seems, have not been undertaken with the courage that the engineer displays in attacking engineering problems. In engineering, we are not tied to tradition; but when we deal with business or economics, we are too partial to the methods and practices of the past. We fear to examine too critically into established commercial and economic principles. We dare not question old institutions lest we be labeled too radical; and so, in our fear of mere words, we fail to see clearly that which is obvious.

Now management must learn to see a few of these obvious things, if we are to build a rational industrial system for the future. Suppose that for the moment we forget completely the intricacies of our traditional economic methods and examine a few of the obvious facts in the world about us, just as an engineer would examine a mechanical problem. Let us try to formulate a few economic axioms—facts on which management would build, if there were no past practices to be taken into account. It seems to me that a few of these axioms are as follows:

1. We are physically able to produce more food, more clothing, and more housing—that is, more necessities—than the nation is able to consume. In addition, we are able to produce an abundance of comforts and luxuries. Yet, millions who are able and willing to give their full share of useful labor to society suffer for lack of these very necessities, let alone the luxuries.

2. When labor applied to nature produces abundantly of wheat, cotton, or other products, we ought to be prosperous. These bounteous gifts of nature ought to be welcome. Yet, our economic practices are such that ample crops are a menace. Unemployment, hardship, and depressions follow the presence of abundance in the things we all need for health, comfort, and well-being.

3. When men work efficiently, their reward ought to be security and comfort. As it is, efficiency apparently causes overproduction, and to both the engineer and the manual worker, it appears that the more efficiently he works the more insecure is his job.

4. Mechanical means for production that save toil and labor should be a blessing to mankind; they should create more leisure, greater comforts, and greater security. Instead, they appear to create insecurity, unemployment, and suffering.

5. Money is not a commodity like wheat, cotton, or iron ore; it is a means of exchange. Pieces of paper or pieces of metal used as money do not, by themselves, satisfy our needs or add to our comforts. But our economic practices seem to have made of money something more than a means of exchange— something that by its mere "scarcity" or "abundance" may create abnormal and undesirable conditions, irrespective of the scarcity or abundance of the actual commodities that we want and that we make use of.

6. The object of engineering is to obtain the greatest amount of product with the least amount of work; the object of trade is to obtain the greatest amount of goods for the least amount of work given in exchange. Hence it should be advantageous for a nation, as well as for an individual, to obtain an abundance of goods from abroad, in exchange for the minimum amount of labor on its own part. Yet, our economic practices make it undesirable for a nation to obtain goods cheaply—that is, with the expenditure of a small amount of labor—if these goods come from abroad. Under our economic methods, nations believe that they promote their prosperity and well-being by working harder in order to produce greater quantities of goods to send out of the country (exports) than they are to receive in return (imports). Briefly, in international trade, by getting as little as possible in return for our own products, we are supposed to grow prosperous.

7. Property is clearly of two kinds: Property that has been created by the exer-

tion of man, and property that has been created by nature without human effort. Our economic practices deal with these two kinds of property largely as if there were no distinction between them. There is also a form of value generally termed "the unearned increment" that is not created by individual effort, but by the cooperation of society as a whole. This we label "private property," just the same as the products of man's individual exertion. Many of our economic ills may be due to this confusion of ideas in regard to property.

8. Waste of human labor, due to unemployment, is the most costly waste of our industrial system. If calculated in dollars and cents, during years such as 1931 and 1932, it mounts into figures greater than any other waste for which management is responsible.

It seems to me that management must face these economic facts squarely. Any discussion of the cure for our economic ills that avoids facing these facts courageously, particularly the first and last—the fact that we are physically able to produce in superabundance and that the waste due to unemployment is the greatest of all industrial waste—cannot lead to a rational solution. We must be as courageous in our economic thought as we are in our engineering research; otherwise, we can expect nothing but continued confusion of thought.

Because we see the problem clearly, we need not assume that the sudden abandonment of all past economic traditions would be advisable. That would probably make the cure worse than the disease. But an engineer owes it to his profession to recognize fundamental facts. What action he takes after having ascertained the facts is a matter for sound balanced judgment.

Author's Closure

The discussion of this report on a decade of progress in management takes up two aspects: (1) interpretation and emphasis on certain items differing from that of the author, and (2) indication of a few developments mention of which was omitted in the report. These will be rediscussed in the order in which they appear in the preceding discussion.

Clark, Kimball, and Polakov stress the importance and enlarge upon the difficulty of national planning. Kimball emphasizes the change in the nature of the major problem confronting management engineers from that of production to that of distribution, saying that the new need "challenges the engineer and the industrialist." With all this the author is in complete sympathy.

Kimball and Kent comment upon the controversial topic of wages. The report does little more than present the aspects of the changing situation in the consideration of industrial wages and state the nature of the problems involved. No one can differ with the point of view that the entire matter is complex, difficult of solution, and of the utmost economic importance.

Kent, Wallace, and Eaton discuss technological unemployment. The divergences in their viewpoints indicate anew the need of a thoroughgoing study of this matter and of the related development and application of productive machinery. No greater contribution to our knowledge of economic processes could be made at this time than the findings of such an investigation. The temporary hardship suffered by individuals who lose their places in industry due to technical and managerial progress is a matter of common, continuing observation. The long-time readjustment whereby the same individuals find a new place in industry needs to be evaluated, before we can judge the probable extent of unemployment in any future situation. Kent calls the author to account for not showing that "mechanization of industry has created more employment for more people in the long run." While the author believes that is a true statement of what occurs, satisfying, quantitative evidence of the process is not available.

Kent comments upon the measurement of operating performance, saying, "The most important thing before management today is to learn how to evaluate itself and its own effectiveness." The author substantially agrees with this statement. If too little emphasis was placed upon this topic in the report, the lack is perhaps adequately made up in the paper which he presented jointly with J. E. Hannum on "Applications of the Kmh Method of Analyzing Manufacturing Operations" at the session of The American Society of Mechanical Engineers which received the Progress Report.

The author finds no reason to differ with Kent over his comments on budgeting and on shorter working hours. The trend toward the latter is unmistakable. Kent questions whether trade associations are intended to be included in the treatment of association and society activities. They are comprehended in the classification "business associations," and, as Kent remarks, they "may well become to an industry what the planning or production-control department is to the factory."

Polakov comments on the absence of reference in the report "to the influence of power production in the changing aims and methods of factory management." This development is not disregarded, for under the heading "Advance in Doing Work: Transfer of Skill," in treating of the increases in the physical volume of product is this statement: "The corresponding increase in utilization of primary horsepower per worker was some 30 per cent." Further, the question is quite properly raised whether the increase in primary power is not secondary to the development of productive machinery. As a reply to this query the author agrees with the point of view expressed in the following quotation from the Second Progress Report of the Committee on the Relation of Consumption, Production, and Distribution of the American Engineering Council: "The substitution of mechanisms, the transfer of human skill to machinery and tools, rather than the increased amount of power applied, is the essential change."

Bausch suggests: "Another item should be included as a part of the ten years' progress report and as an essential for recovery. This is unemployment insurance." Strong forces are gathering behind the proposals for unemployment insurance in some form. Under the heading, "Service Motive in Industry," reference is made in

365

the report to this matter, and the enactment of laws to this end is foreshadowed: "Numerous bills to set up unemployment insurance may be expected to be introduced at the 1933 sessions of state legislatures. It will be surprising if some do not become law."

Mrs. Gilbreth in her comments takes up this matter of transfer of skill and gives an interpretation of the process in line with the most progressive modern thought. This topic deserves intense study that we may understand accurately what does occur both to man and machine when the process of transference takes place. This question groups properly under the broad heading of psychology which Mrs. Gilbreth urges for addition to the subjects in the range of interest of management engineers. The author strongly supports her suggestion.

Oberg challenges management engineers to face "economic facts squarely" and to be as "courageous in our economic thought as we are in our engineering research." He also gives eight "economic axioms" which formulate facts upon which management must build. The author accepts these axioms, as a presentation of the major features in our economic situation, and endorses the plea for courage in our economic thought.

Ten Years' Progress in Management, 1933-1942*

1943

With the death of Leon P. Alford, a committee from the Management Division of the American Society of Mechanical Engineers was appointed to complete his work on the 1942 Report.

After the most severe depression ever experienced and which had not yet ended when the most destructive and widespread war in all history engulfed the world, the preparation of a progress report on Management was a major problem.

Articles by various authorities in the field were combined into a Report that reflects the thinking of the decades. Some of these articles have been chosen for inclusion in this section.

* "Ten Years' Progress in Management," contributed by the Management Division and presented at the Annual Meeting, New York, N. Y., November 30–December 4, 1942, American Society of Mechanical Engineers, *Transactions*, Vol. 65, 1943. Permission to excerpt by courtesy of the Society.

TEN YEARS' PROGRESS IN MANAGEMENT, 1933–1942

Foreword

FOLLOWING A TIME-HONORED CUSTOM, and in commemoration of the one to whose foresight and leadership in the field of management this custom owes its origin—Leon Pratt Alford, able engineer, dean of management editors and historians, developer of men—this "Ten Years' Progress in Management" Report is presented by the Management Division, of which Dr. Alford was one of the founders. It is the fourth presentation of its kind, the three previous Reports having been written by Dr. Alford and delivered by him to The American Society of Mechanical Engineers at Annual Meetings, respectively, ten, twenty, and thirty years ago.

Frederick Winslow Taylor, Father of Scientific Management, and a Past-President and Honorary Member of the Society, began his pioneering achievements in 1881, and in 1895, 1903, 1906, and 1911 presented the results of certain of his important discoveries and developments at its meetings. The Society was thus the first organized association to recognize the vital significance of this new field of industrial and economic endeavor. The 1911 paper, "Principles of Scientific Management," caused considerable discussion within the Society, so much so that a Subcommittee on Administration was appointed to make a thorough investigation of Scientific Management, presumably to justify it, or recommend its rejection, as a part of the Society's activities.

The 1912 Report on Industrial Management

At the Annual Meeting in 1912, just thirty years ago, this Subcommittee presented its report on "The Present State of the Art of Industrial Management." [1] The chairman of the Committee was James Mapes Dodge; the secretary—who developed the report—was Leon Pratt Alford, then editor of The American Machinist; and other members were D. M. Bates, H. A. Evans, Wilfred Lewis, W. L. Lyall, W. B. Tardy, and Henry R. Towne. This report was a "Majority Report," a "Minority Report" also being submitted by those who disagreed with some of the majority findings.

NOTE: Statements and opinions advanced in papers are to be understood as individual expressions of their authors and not those of the Society.

[1] Previous Reports appear in the Transactions of The American Society of Mechanical Engineers for the respective years.

A reading of this first Report reveals, to those familiar in subsequent years with Dr. Alford's progressiveness in engineering and editorial endeavors, his clear conception and prophetic foresight, at this early date, of the vast opportunities ahead in applying scientific-management principles intelligently to bring about engineering, industrial, economic, and social progress.

Ten Years' Progress Report of 1922

In 1922, after the first World War and the subsequent 1920–1921 depression, Dr. Alford, whose career meanwhile had been marked by engineering and editorial leadership in the field of management, conceived the idea of preparing for the Annual Meeting of the Society a "Ten Years' Progress in Management" Report to summarize the widespread developments made since the first Report was presented. He was particularly interested in doing so because, in 1920, the Management Division had been formed, with his active participation, and he had been its first chairman.

The 1932 Report on Ten Years' Progress in Management

After the publication of the 1922 Report there followed a period during which more widespread progress was made in the field of management than had occurred in all of the years before, since Taylor had first conceived his scientific approach to this branch of human endeavor. National progress and prosperity continued until after 1929, when the long depression of the 1930's suddenly broke. In 1932, Dr. Alford, continuing his custom of reviewing the course of events in management, presented at the Society's Annual Meeting the second of his "Ten Years' Progress in Management" Reports, again summarizing, with his keen discernment, the high spots of advancement, assaying their value, and indicating their portent and potency for further industrial and economic progress.

The Ten Years' Progress Report of 1942

To those associated with Dr. Alford it was known that he contemplated a continuation of his custom by offering a third "Ten Years' Progress in Management" Report at the 1942 Annual Meeting. Unfortunately, his untimely passing from the scene of his labors, on January 2, 1942, while actively engaged in many Society undertakings, and in educational work as Head of the Department of Administrative Engineering in the College of Engineering, New York University, prevented the carrying out of his desire in person. At least four others prominent in the management field and in the Society also passed away during the last ten years: C. B. Auel, Robert I. Rees, W. L. Conrad, and Harold B. Bergen.

With his customary careful preplanning and his invariable foresight in discerning the outstanding developments, Dr. Alford had already begun to collect pamphlets, papers, articles, and data on subjects which he considered significant indicators of management progress. Close friends of Dr. Alford in the Management Division committees felt that no more important step could be taken, and nothing more pleasing to Dr. Alford could be done than to continue the practice of presenting a "Ten Years' Progress in Management" Report, at the 1942 Annual Meeting, along the sound lines for which he had already set an outstanding precedent. The plan, in fact, became the guiding consideration in selecting topics and speakers for all of the Management sessions at the Annual Meeting, thus unifying the program around the most significant management thinking of the day. Obviously, after the most severe depression ever experienced, which had not ended when the most destructive and widespread war in all history engulfed practically the entire globe, the preparation of a progress report on management became a problem of major difficulty.

Deep Debt Owed to Contributors

A committee appointed for the purpose began in January. While all members of the Management Division Executive Committee, and of its General Management Committee, were affiliated with the work, special acknowledgment is due those who untiringly selected authors for the various sections of the extensive Report planned, and then as untiringly co-operated in securing the delivery of manuscripts from men who unselfishly added to their pressing burdens that of writing parts of the Report. These committee members are: Prof. John R. Bangs, James M. Talbot, Gideon M. Varga, Joseph M. Juran, Lawrence A. Appley, Andrew I. Peterson, Dr. E. H. Hempel, Professor Carlos deZafra, and John A. Willard. To the contributors, whose names and professional connections appear at the head of the respective sections of this Report which they wrote, we are forever grateful. To the Report Committee Chairman, Dr. Lillian M. Gilbreth, is due full credit for envisioning the possibilities of the Report, directing the work of planning the sections and the selection of authors, arranging the method of presentation and steering the activity through its many vicissitudes during a time when demands upon managers and engineers heavily loaded them with unprecedented difficulties.

Through presentation of the Report by Prof. John R. Bangs, chairman of the Management Division, to Harold V. Coes, incoming President of The American Society of Mechanical Engineers, and by him to James W. Parker, President of the Society during the year 1942, as part of the Society's archives, we trust that the custom set by Dr. Alford may now become a precedent for future Management Division Committees to follow. Several of the sections were lengthy papers which had to be condensed for presentation in the Report, because of limited space. The originals are available, however, and may be read in full by anyone applying to the Editorial Department of the Society, where they will be on file.

The Management Division and its Committee preparing this Report submit it in commemoration of Dr. Alford's unflagging interest in Management, his outstanding contributions to the fund of management information, his active support in many new developments in advance of their general acceptance, his unswerving loyalty to the engineering profession and to The American Society of Mechanical Engineers through which he found a ready outlet for his varied creative energies, his devotion to his friends and associates in whose progress he many times exerted a helping hand, and his sincere interest in engineering education where his leadership and inspiration were constructive influences in shaping for many students broader and more useful careers. He has taken his place among the leaders who have placed the Society in a position of leadership in the Management field.

GEORGE E. HAGEMANN
Vice-Chairman, Ten Years' Progress in Management
Committee, and Editor of Report

Management Division

Executive Committee—1942

John R. Bangs, Chairman
James M. Talbot, Vice-Chairman
Gideon M. Varga, Secretary
Joseph M. Juran

L. A. Appley
Andrew I. Peterson
E. H. Hempel, Research Secretary
Frederick M. Gilbreth, Junior Adviser

General Management Committee

R. M. Barnes, William Loren Batt, C. W. Beese, F. B. Bell, H. B. Bergen (deceased), Wallace Clark, Harold V. Coes, K. H. Condit, Howard Coonley, Carlos deZafra, Norman E. Elsas, S. P. Fisher, Walter D. Fuller, William H. Gesell, Lillian M. Gilbreth, R. E. Gillmor, G. E. Hagemann, Charles H. Hatch, E. H. Hempel, Paul E. Holden, William F. Hosford, D. S. Kimball, William H. Kushnick, T. S. McEwan, L. C. Morrow, David B. Porter, Fairfield E. Raymond, Joseph W. Roe, Erwin H. Schell, Elliott D. Smith, A. R. Stevenson, Jr., L. W. Wallace, John A. Willard, A. Williams, John Younger.

ADMINISTRATIVE ORGANIZATION

By Lounsbury S. Fish [2]

Perhaps the most significant trend in the field of administrative organization during recent years has been an increasing recognition of the need and importance of a well-designed plan of organization in facilitating and expediting the direction, co-ordination, and control of an enterprise. Organization is the chassis upon which management is mounted—if adequately designed, the management job is made easier and more effective; if poorly designed, management is difficult and results often unsatisfactory.

Organization Often the Result of Mere Evolution

Most large organizations have just "evolved"—have "grown up like Topsy." Additions and changes have been made to meet specific problems on a basis of ex-

[2] On loan from Standard Oil Company of California as Director of Organizational Planning for War Production Board.

pediency with little consideration for over-all design or rationality. The difficulties of management under these conditions may be likened to those which would be involved in living in a house built one room at a time over the years by different tenants without benefit of architecture.

In some cases the rationalization of organization plan has been prompted by enlightened recognition of the advantages to be gained in increased management effectiveness; in others it has been forced by the problems of size, unwieldiness, lack of flexibility, and overburdening of top executives. Regardless of cause, however, an appreciable number of major concerns have overhauled and clarified their general organization plans within the last ten years, to their great subsequent advantage. Others recognize the need but are reluctant to move because of the complexity of the problem, lack of specialized assistance in this field, or hesitancy about changing the assignments of key personnel.

Trends During the Past Ten Years

In general, the trend and emphasis in organizational planning during recent years have been along the following lines:

1. *Freeing top executives of administrative detail to concentrate on policy determination, long-range planning, and over-all control.* In the case of large enterprises, this result is often accomplished by relieving a number of well-qualified top executives of operating and administrative responsibility to assist the president in the general management and direction of the business as a whole, defining over-all policies and objectives, deciding matters of major concern, co-ordinating the various aspects of the business into a successful whole, and appraising over-all progress and results. This arrangement proceeds from the recognition that in any very large concern it is virtually impossible for any one man, such as the president, to do full justice to the top executive job single-handed. While in a smaller business the operating executives are normally in a position to render such assistance to the chief executive, in very large organizations the operating heads are almost invariably so heavily burdened with day-to-day administrative problems that they seldom have the time and objectivity to assume a major role in the general or over-all management of the enterprise, and it is necessary to set up a separate group of carefully chosen men for this special purpose. These men function virtually as "assistant presidents."

2. *Decentralization of the burden of management by dividing and subdividing the enterprise into its logical, separable components, each of which can be held fully responsible and accountable on a proprietary basis.* Due to increasing size and the growing complexities of management there has been a distinct trend toward the subdivision of large enterprises into smaller components which are reasonably complete entities in themselves and which, therefore, afford the basis for effective decentralization. Examples of this type are the many companies which in recent years have subdivided on the basis of product divisions or regional divisions, each having, as a rule, its own product engineering, manufacturing, and marketing organization,

and thus constituting, in effect, a separate enterprise which can be held accountable on a profit and loss basis. This type of organization requires special provision for co-ordination of basic functions (product engineering, manufacturing, marketing, etc.) between divisions, usually through the medium of functional vice-presidents who serve in a staff capacity.

3. *Delegation or placement of the power of decision at the lowest practicable organization level, resulting in the elimination of unnecessary layers and levels of management, multiple handling, and red tape.* The importance of this fundamental concept in simplifying organization structure and relationships is just beginning to be recognized. When supervisors in immediate charge of operations are well selected and trained, given a maximum degree of responsibility and authority for making their own decisions within general policy and budgetary limitations, and finally held accountable for results, it is remarkable how well they usually perform, relieving their superiors of unnecessary burden and often eliminating the need for intermediate "layers" of management.

4. *Better co-ordination and integration of staff functions.* Another promising trend is the clarification and standardization of staff relationships. For many years organization of the comptroller's functions has served as a model of staff effectiveness in many concerns. The general plan has been for the comptroller to place a "sub-comptroller" trained in the over-all company system, in each department or subsidiary, with the acquiescence of the local manager. The subcomptroller is directly responsible to his manager for supplying necessary information and service in support of operations; at the same time, he is functionally responsible to the comptroller for compliance with the general company system and methods within his field. In recent years this well-proved plan has been increasingly used as a model for the organization of other staff functions which find application throughout the enterprise, such as personnel relations, engineering, purchasing, etc.

5. *Clear-cut definition and understanding of the basic functions, objectives, relationships, and extent of authority for each principal position or agency.* A well-designed organization structure or chart goes only part way in defining a sound organization plan. It must be supplemented by a thorough understanding on the part of each responsible executive as to just what is expected of him and his organization in relation to the rest of the enterprise. As a basis for such understanding there is an increasing tendency in well-run enterprises clearly to define the primary purposes, functions, relationships, and limits of authority of each principal position or agency within the organization—the board of directors, the president, vice-presidents, managers, committees, etc. These written statements can best be developed by staff representatives thoroughly familiar with the existing and projected plans for the organization as a whole, in collaboration with the executives concerned, thus assuring full understanding of the proper relationship of each part with respect to the whole.

In view of the increasing complexities of management and the difficult problems and adjustments which lie ahead, it seems probable that the next decade will witness further major progress toward rationalizing and clarifying industrial organization plans in order that management may be free to concentrate major attention upon broad needs and objectives and have effective means of their fulfillment.

DEFUNCTIONALIZATION OF INDUSTRY

By Henry H. Farquhar[3]

Summary

In the 1920's there was a trend toward "functionalization." Thus, in addition to the usual major departments (of production, of selling, of finance), various companies went much further in separating out certain over-all functions or activities common to each of these major operating departments—functions such as personnel work, public relations, cost and accounting methods, the setting of work standards, and so on—and giving a man in charge of each of these authority either within one of these departments or over all departments according to his location in the organization. But such a high degree of subdivision of labor and the setting up of these "functional" officials cross-cut and interfered with "line" operations of producing and selling, and the past decade has witnessed a decided straight-lining of industry back to one-man control at any one point in the organization.

Perhaps the most notable trend in organization during the past decade has been the widespread setting up of "staff" assistants to various officials, to advise and instruct operating men in handling these problems of personnel, public relations, finance, and the rest, but without authority to issue orders to operating men. In clear-cut organizations it is made plain to everyone that such staff men have no authority (except as may be specifically and publicly delegated on special occasions). A sharp distinction has been made between "line," "staff," and "service" or housekeeping functions. The natural tendency for staff men gradually to assume line authority has been reduced through definition of the staff's place in the organization, as well as through increasingly sympathetic understanding and use of the staff by line executives.

The other notable organization trends during the past decade connected with the movement away from undue functionalization, are the development of more adequate control over total operations; the integration of research and production through definite organization machinery; and the raising to the top levels and the building up of high-grade men and methods for collective bargaining and other personnel matters.

Organization

The outstanding over-all development during the 1930's is the great progress our leading corporations have made in revamping organization structure to meet the imperative demands of the times.

[3] Organization and Management Counsel.

Anyone who has not followed closely the recent trends in decentralization, and in the simplification of lines of authority supplemented by technical staff and service assistance at various points, will be impressed with the modifications which many companies have made. There is still, to be sure, considerable variation in the degree of formality of organization and control. In general, as might be expected, the close corporations usually have an informal setup, whereas those with wide stock ownership tend to develop a more formal structure and to minimize the danger of repercussions and drastic changes upon the withdrawal of any one individual.

Practices Among Progressive Companies

A few major points of emphasis, indicative of modern practices and trends among the more prominent and progressive business and industrial firms, are these:

1. In the larger companies, it is now customary to have one official, usually the chairman of the board, who devotes his undisturbed time to major matters of policy, contact, public relations, and long-time plans and programs, free from the many demands of the day-to-day running of the business. The actual operating is left to a chief executive—the president or an executive vice-president—the chairman concerning himself with current administration only in very exceptional cases. In some companies the chairman has no direct authority over operations.

2. Particularly noteworthy is the extent to which the staff has grown in prevalence and importance during the past few years. (By "staff" in this discussion is meant a group of specialists composing a part of an executive's own office, but outside of the line of authority, with no administrative or routine duties, whose principal job is to enable the executive more fully to exercise co-ordinating and other functions pertaining to his own office, and who also carry on broad constructive work, keep in touch, advise, inspect, and supervise with respect to their particular specialties, and act as delegated from time to time by their executives in definite fields, functions or projects.) These staff officers have charge of no departments, have no regularly recurrent or other duties except as delegated by the president or by the subordinate official to whom they are advisers. In some cases such staff officials are found at headquarters only; in other cases corresponding staff men are found at divisional or regional headquarters, and also at each individual subsidiary within each region. In some cases these distant staff men report directly to the corresponding headquarters staff men; in other cases, they are under the jurisdiction of the local manager. In either case, however, it is the practice for staff men wherever located to correspond and deal direct with each other in the discussion of programs, plans, and technical matters.

Among the firms which have taken the lead in modern organization, it is the universal practice that staff men have no regular authority except by virtue of their knowledge and position. When their recommendations are to be translated into action, they must persuade the line official concerned that such action is desirable, and all orders putting such action into effect are transmitted by and through line officials.

This keeps the lines of authority and responsibility clear, and enables the chief executive to hold one man responsible for results along specific lines.

An individual normally assigned to line work may be and often is transferred for a period to a staff position, the staff man meanwhile being assigned perhaps to the line. There is ordinarily much interchangeability between line and staff personnel. But the positions remain distinct; during the time the line or the service man is occupying a staff position, he is an advisory assistant to his executive and no longer exercises authority. He is not expected adequately to carry on both line or service and technical staff duties simultaneously, or switch indiscriminately from one to the other.

The staff thus neither exercises authority over the line nor performs line work for an operating official. [A staff assistant for personnel management, for example, does not do personnel work for the line, nor lessen any line official's responsibility for maintaining good industrial relations. This staff assistant helps his executive to see that all line and all service officials conduct personnel work in their own units in accordance with announced policy and procedure.]

In some notable cases this general staff principle embodies a definite group of advisers to the chief executive, each of whom is assigned as adviser also to one or more specific departments. It is the duty of such advisers to relieve the chief executive of many details in running the business, to keep informed of what is going on in the division to which he is assigned, to keep the chief executive informed regarding such activities, and to serve as a correlating and reference agency to which the particular department head is morally obligated to refer. In such cases many more officials report direct to the chief executive than has heretofore been considered practicable—it leaves the avenues of approach open, but removes from the chief executive innumerable conferences on minor matters. In fact the "span of control" has been immensely extended through such means as these.

A most important element in the full use of the staff, is the judicious use of advisory group discussions at various levels. Groups are becoming indispensable in big concerns for purposes of co-ordination, for developing high morale, for training younger executives, and for the simultaneous bringing out of all points of view. For these purposes advisory boards in a few cases extend throughout the personnel. They should not be confined to the top levels, although unfortunately this is where too many of them are found today. Their use has been materially increased during the last ten years; they are today of major service in helping determine company policy as a whole.

It is significant that such use of the staff, supplemented by advisers and advisory boards, has come about on a large scale almost entirely since the depression, and in the face of the necessity of economizing in every practicable way.

3. In large corporations with many subsidiary plants it is of course customary to have in the headquarter's office a vice-president of production, of sales, of engineering, and so on. It is the general practice, however, to allow utmost freedom of action to

the president or local manager of each subsidiary and, in effect, these vice-presidents in the headquarter's office are advisory rather than line officials.

4. All necessary authority for the accomplishment of specific work is delegated to one individual as directly and with as few limitations as possible; such authority being delegated in turn by the particular individual to his subordinates with a view of transmitting it as close to the point of action as possible. Certain exceptions and reservations, of course, are made in various cases, either in written form or in well-understood procedures evolved over long periods of time and controlled by headquarters in various ways as will be discussed under the next topic.

Control

As has been indicated, it is becoming increasingly the practice to delegate authority with as few limitations, overlappings, or indefinite areas as possible, coupled with the development of various means by which the exercise of such authority may be checked. Among the outstanding measures by which central control with decentralized operation is secured are the following:

1. The use of advisers as just explained. With an understanding on the part of each line official that he is not only to keep his adviser informed but also to secure his concurrence where possible in contemplated action, the chief executive has provided a series of spokesmen for himself in transmitting his desires downward, and a spokesman for each operating official whereby the latter's activities and wishes are transmitted upward. There is an understanding by line officials that such advisers have freedom to look into any activity at any time. There is thus provided a means by which the executive can secure sifted summaries of what is going on below, with the safeguard that lower officials can come direct to him or he to them; he thereby has multiple sources of information regarding each activity.

2. The creation of staff specialists at various levels throughout the organization with much the same effect as in the case of the advisers previously described. Such staff specialists have the additional function of specializing on current research or other problems referred by operating officials—problems which would otherwise occupy the time and attention of such officials and their subordinates at the expense of getting the work done. It might seem that such control through the advisers and the staff would result in a slowness of action, but as a matter of fact it has the opposite effect in that each line official is given full and unmixed authority under close inspection and advisory guidance, with the opportunity to reach his adviser or a staff man much more readily than he can reach the chief executive.

3. The increasing use of carefully prepared operating plans and budgets, whereby individual responsibility for expenditures and results is secured, with monthly or other short-term comparisons and measurements. Matters of budgetary control and of adjustments of funds are in but few cases entrusted to anyone other than the chief executive, or to his immediate personal or staff assistant delegated by him to make adjustments in all possible cases without reference to him.

4. The much more extensive use of advisory committees in the past few years. These committees consist of both permanent and special groups, selected with the definite purpose not only of getting a breadth of viewpoint, but also of serving as correlating agencies. In a few cases they are used definitely for the purpose of taking details of administration off the chief executive's shoulders by his delegating to the committee authority to take action where general agreement can be arrived at. Reports of the meetings of such groups, and reports covering subsequent action, are submitted to the chief executive.

5. In various companies the careful detailed definition of duties and authority of each individual; in most cases, however, such written instructions are couched in broad general terms only, and in some cases the attempt to draw detailed specific lines is not favored. The latter is more often true, however, with old established organizations than where recent changes in functions and relationships have been made.

6. The interchange of headquarters and outlying personnel insofar as practicable, and the detail of outlying personnel to the headquarter's office.

7. Inspection by specialized officials from headquarters, and particularly by staff men; in some cases through the medium of traveling inspectors who do nothing else; and in all cases by occasional field trips of top officials.

8. Encouragement of all important officials to go to the top for advice and guidance if they feel so impelled, without necessarily clearing through their immediate superior, and encouragement of the practice of the chief executive's calling directly on anyone down the line for information and advice. In such cases, the chief executive is careful to confine his contact to information and advice, and not give even *implied* instructions to any subordinate except through that subordinate's superior officer.

Research

Research plays and will play a vital part in the leadership, and in fact in the very existence of practically every large company today. It is particularly important to observe how operating officials and activities, and research officials and activities, are correlated and made of maximum benefit to one another and to the company as a whole. The following has become pretty much standard practice during the recent past:

1. With the exception of projects which might be termed "pure" research looking to long-term product or process developments which may or may not have an eventual commercial value, it is almost universally customary that all research projects are passed on either by the president, by the executive committee, or by a special committee-delegated authority for this purpose. In all of these cases each proposed project is "shot at" from all major angles—sales, production, finance, engineering. In some cases formal recommendations from each one of these officials are turned in to the central approving agency, in other

cases the president or agency calls in such affected officials as seems necessary for proper consideration of the special case.

2. Actual conduct of research projects is turned over by the central approving agency either to the operating or to the research end of the business, each of which thereafter has exclusive jurisdiction over the project under the established procedure that the other is to assist if necessary in an advisory capacity. In some cases technical men are borrowed from operating departments for temporary work under research, and *vice versa.*

3. It is quite generally customary for operating officials to conduct specified minor research projects through utilizing their own technical personnel, but with prior approval of the chief executive or of an appropriate official or group reporting to him. Such limitations, furthermore, are usually expressed in terms of maximum estimated cost, or left to the operating official to be carried on within his budget, or to be referred to the research division at his option.

4. It is customary that progress reports be required at short intervals covering each continuing or new project assigned. The progress reports go to the central approving agency, and to other interested or affected personnel. In various cases the extent to which research is to be prosecuted is defined in advance—for instance, in pharmaceutical manufacture, research is in one company limited to determining the medical practicability of the project, after which the president determines commercial practicability through conferences with various officials.

5. When a project is completed to a defined point the results go back to the approving agency, which through additional conferences determines the department (research, production, or sales) which is to have future responsibility for putting results of research into practice.

6. Some interesting variations of paragraph 5 above is where specific departments, removed from the jurisdiction of either research or operating, have the responsibility of converting the results of research into factory or other operating standards and instructions. Such departments have no authority to put standards and instructions into effect, these being finally approved by and executed through the line official affected.

7. In many cases much of the work of research dealing with current or short-term projects originates from operating officials. In such cases where the project is to be turned over to research to conduct, plans are drawn up by research and approved by operating, the work being under the supervision of research but with constant touch and advice from operating officials.

8. Where it becomes advisable to assign a research technician to conduct his work within an operating department (such as chemical control of manufacture, of rubber compounding, of synthetic products, or of engineering work involving machinery for processing), the dividing line does not seem to be

clear in all cases. In some few instances a research man is definitely delegated to supervise the production processes involved; in more numerous instances, the research man temporarily reports to the line official for general supervision but with an understanding that research is to specify and control technical methods and procedures for the conduct of the experiments.

Personnel—Labor Relations

It has been only during the second half of the past decade that noteworthy changes as respects the organization status of those handling personnel management and labor relations have become widespread. The reasons are obvious. Such changes have taken two principal directions:

First, the need for uniform dealing with the national labor unions has required that the personnel department or some similar office be given added functions and added status in respect to collective bargaining. In some cases this has involved the actual bargaining and the writing of contracts at the top level; in other cases it has involved participation by the personnel officer as an observer and counselor; in still other cases the personnel officer has acted as management's adviser and as a coordinator of data and principles to keep uniform the bargaining covering the various divisions of the company to avoid the error of giving one local more than another.

Second, along with the raising of collective bargaining to the top level, has come a decided emphasis on employee participation; on the institution of more carefully planned and conducted suggestion systems; on the improvement of personnel techniques, job-evaluation methods, merit rating, standardization in wage and salary determination, and so on. Perhaps most significantly, there is just now beginning to be put into general practice a conscious development of more systematic and rational interviewing and counseling programs in order to help the individual worker adjust himself to the total situation—both within and outside the plant—which confronts him.

It is increasingly customary to find that the man who handles such work as is indicated in the two preceding paragraphs now reports directly to the chief executive—a major shift in organization in tune with the times.

Miscellaneous Developments Which Merit Attention

1. Quite general decentralization of clerical and service functions; thus each major division of the business has its own office management (with the occasional exception of a central clerical pool, the use of which is optional), its own personnel officer (who must keep in close touch with the company personnel officer), its own mail and files, its own maintenance, and so on.
2. Where a central service unit exists, any other unit of the company is free to utilize the services or not as they choose. In no case does such service unit have control or authority over the activities of any other department, the necessary co-ordination being performed by the chief executive or his "staff" (as defined).

3. The practice of having accounting personnel in outlying subsidiaries report directly to the accounting personnel in the headquarter's office (functional), is followed in some cases, but this practice is decreasing. In most companies the outlying accounting personnel reports to the local manager; the headquarters officials have authority to regulate over-all company procedures as approved by general management.

4. Training activities are outlined by headquarters specialists, but in most cases actual conduct of training is under the jurisdiction of the department head, or of the resident manager of the subsidiary, whose personnel is being trained. In at least one company the personnel manager reports to any one of three co-ordinate manufacturing vice-presidents, according to which group of employees is being dealt with; this personnel manager, furthermore, has a personnel man in each plant, who, under the functional principle, reports direct to him.

5. Quality inspection, of course, is now quite generally removed from the supervision or influence of the man who is immediately responsible for quantity production.

There have thus been outstanding contributions during the past decade to the organization problems of structure, of control, of research, and of personnel relations. Under the fire of the depression, of defense, and then of war, industrial managers have forged a direct and flexible, yet essentially simple structure which combines maximum opportunity for direct action with minimum necessary central control. They have refined and made more responsive that control. They have extended and integrated research—both for war and post-war use. And the field of human relations has been raised in status, and refined in technique.

Real progress has been made toward finding the answers to some of the most perplexing problems which modern conditions have forced upon top administration—the problems of determining sound policy, of minimizing bigness, of the burden on the chief executive, of the two-way flow of information, of permanence and continuity of management, and of striking the balance between decentralized operation and central control.

MANAGEMENT RESEARCH

By Edward H. Hempel

As a function of industrial operation the art of management is now firmly established because of the general acceptance of the fundamentals. The promise of the future is to lead to a higher professional standing through the development of intellectual, societal, and moral attitudes and values.

L. P. ALFORD, 1932.

The Scope of This Report

In mechanical, chemical, or any other branch of engineering it is relatively easy to discern and segregate research from actual work performance or established practice. In management matters this is more difficult since often enough research is made merely a process of thinking up a new method of doing or organizing, which then is immediately applied without much experimental work or scientific description. The good old habit of doing, describing, and publishing research work on management subjects has become much less frequent than it was during previous decades. It seems that the last ten years have been perhaps too hectic and disturbed to induce the composition of an extensive "research" literature on management, and that the progress which has been made expressed itself more in actions and practical work than in treatises on new ideas.

Many who actually do management work do not identify part of it as "management research," although it might fall under this heading. Even definitely new and novel ideas, policies, methods, and applications of management are still merely considered as part of the daily job, as improvements, or routine. They are not especially rated or reported by their authors as scientific achievements, even if they would merit it, and are evolved by quite the same methods of recording, fact finding, analyzing, modifying, and perfecting, exactly as novel ideas are developed in technical research.

Since there is no patent literature on management subjects, and the various contributions to management research are scattered widely and not always discernible or marked as new ideas, this report has been prepared for the very purpose of bringing out the new thoughts which have been added to the science of management. Efforts have been made to consider actually applied but not reported developments as well as those which have been reported in the literature.

In view of the complexity of actual developments, and considering the great number of books and articles published on management subjects during the last ten years, the tracing of the progress in management research has been a sizable task, and, in spite of all efforts, the findings may not be complete. But it is hoped that the following will bring into focus at least the most pertinent developments. Most difficult has it been to draw the line where "economics" ends and "management" begins, or *vice versa*, since the two fields have become much more closely interwoven than ever before.

Government Research

The government, having at its disposal not only millions but billions of dollars year after year, undoubtedly has taken over the lead in economic and management research. As it extended its influences, and later on its activities, from welfare and unemployment-relief programs into labor legislation, then into centrally directed defense production, and now into outright control of most war and many civilian activities, it extended its research facilities far beyond any precedent. Vested with legal powers of inquiry and investigation it could obtain data and information as no other researcher or research institute ever had at his disposal.

The Departments of Labor, Interior, Commerce, Justice, Treasury, Agriculture, alone or together with special Committees (Temporary National Economic Committee, for instance), and quite a few new Administrations (N.R.A., W.P.B., O.P.A., R.F.C., Economic Defense Board, etc.), all have researched extensively in subjects pertaining to the field of management, and to some extent they even have developed management and administrative policies and techniques of their own which should not be overlooked. The War Department, for instance, employing close to one million people in technical or administrative work certainly became the biggest single employer and producer practicing administrative as well as technological management.

A great many of the more recent government activities in the field of management have not been described as yet, and of the research studies made during the depression and recovery years many are predominantly legal or economic in character. But those which clearly deal with management subjects are listed in this section under the proper subject titles.

Industry and Trade Association Research

While even in "normal" times quite a few management problems are being investigated by the associations for the benefit of their members, the subjects added during the last ten-year period were unusually numerous. The main efforts were directed on the economic and legal aspects of management and operation. The occasions to make such studies were caused either by extraordinary economic developments or by new government policies or administrative regulations.

A fairly good survey of what were the main industrial problems and how American Industry proposed to solve them, can be obtained from a study of the "Annual Declaration of Principles" proposed at the Annual Congresses of the National Association of Manufacturers, which are well complemented by the speeches and papers presented at the meetings. They also show how the traditional concepts and practices of industry were gradually assimilated to the new thoughts.

Besides, nearly every one of the many trade associations covered those specific difficulties and problems which were of particular interest to their industries. The Food, Drug, and Cosmetics Act, the N.R.A., O.P.A., Wagner Act, and quite a few other regulations were considered by nearly every association, which has caused a considerable literature of its own. As interesting as some of these presentations are, no effort has been made to incorporate them into this report.

Scientific and Professional Association Research

The Research efforts of most of the scientific and professional institutions have been extended considerably into the economic aspects of management and in general more thorough work and thought has been applied in the various subjects covered than in past decades.

Outstanding in this respect are the publications of the American Academy of Political and Social Science, which has sponsored the investigation of the most important problems of the period and has published the findings in book form. Arranged in chronological sequence they show the following list:

1931   *Insecurity of Industry.*
          The Coming of the Industry to the South.

1933   *Essentials for Prosperity.*
          Social Insurance.

1934   *Social Welfare in the National Recovery Program.*
          Banking and Transportation Problems.
          The Ultimate Consumer; A Study in Economic Illiteracy.

1935   *Pressure Groups and Propaganda.*
          Increasing Government Control in Economic Life.
          Economics of Planning. Principles and Practice.
          Education for Social Control.

1936   *Railroads and the Government.*
          Government Finance in the Modern Economy.
          Progress of Organized Labor.

1937   *Revival of Depressed Industries.*
          Consumers' Coöperation.

1938   *Present International Tensions.*

1939   *Government Expansion in the Economic Sphere.*
          Ownership and Regulation of Public Utilities.
          Refugees.

1940   *When War Ends.*
          Marketing in Our American Economy.

1941   *Billions for Defense.*

The nearest to it in systematic completeness are the publications of the Chamber of Commerce of the United States whose pamphlets and bulletins support and extend the list:

1931   *Distribution in the United States, Trends in Organization and Methods.*

1932   *Banking Legislation.*

1933   *Federal Expenditures* (annually).
          Federal Bankruptcy Legislation, Municipal Insolvencies and Corporate
             Organization.
          Working Periods in Industry.
          Discriminatory Legislation Affecting Retailers.

1934   *New Opportunities for City Planning.*
          Local Code Problems.
          Standardization of Consumers' Goods.
          Federal Budget and Recovery.

1935   *Government's Relation to the Power Industry.*
        Quality Standards and Grade Labeling.
        Federal Taxation (3 Parts.)
1936   *Report of Committee on Employment.*
        Coöperative Business Enterprises Operated by Consumers.
1937   *Surtax on Undistributed Corporate Earnings.*
        Farm Income in the United States.
        Restrictions on Price-Making Methods.
1938   *Special Sales Events.*
1939   *Distribution Services and Costs.*

This is by no means a complete list of publications, and only titles related to management have been given. If tax and financial topics would be considered in this field, the list would be appreciably longer. The publications of the National Industrial Conference Board and similar institutions are given under the specific fields of management to which they refer.

The contributions to management research published by the professional societies are more restricted to the traditional management subjects, as can be seen from the articles contained in the bulletins of the Taylor Society, the Journal of the Society for the Advancement of Management, and in the publications of The American Society of Mechanical Engineers. While there are hundreds of articles they do not reveal any predominant trends. Attention is fairly equally distributed among all phases of enterprise management. Quite a few of the presentations are merely reiterative, old principles are stated differently or applied in a new way; but there is sufficient material which shows the spark of real innovation and progress. To segregate these articles into those which might be called real advancements or progress in management, and into reiterations, has been the most time-consuming part of this study. It might be well for the editors of management publications to either honor the "progress" articles by a star, or by printing them in a special "Progress in Management" Section, of their respective magazines.

Scholastic and Academic Research

Professors and educational institutions established a greater number of courses on Management, and especially time- motion- and method-study courses have come into greater demand than ever. It seems that also Industrial Engineering, which is really a combination of engineering and production management, is coming more into its own since many companies have begun to attempt real savings in the costs of their production.

The many textbooks on scientific industrial organization which were brought out during the period were definitely more voluminous than in past decades, but not all of them represent progress. Some are definitely more academic and lifeless than they ought to be and they fail to inspire a student to think up new ideas beyond those which he needs to solve the "problems" offered in the book.

More recently the tendency to bring out more specialized texts for the various fields of management has been a useful move, *e. g.*:

MAYNARD, H. B.: *Operation Analysis*, 1939.

RAUTENSTRAUCH, W.: *The Design of Manufacturing Enterprises*, 1941.

More of such texts on specific management subjects suited for graduate training, and closer alignment of the subject with actual practice, instead of adherence to generalization and assumed "cases," would be more desirable.

Research in Administrative Organization

In this field relatively little new thought was proposed, because it was very well developed during the previous decade. There was obvious, however, a clear tendency to consolidate the knowledge of management and to extend it, as is proved by many books and articles on this subject. Only a few are listed:

ALFORD, L. P.: *Cost and Production Handbook*. Ronald Press, 1934.

WHITEHEAD, A. C.: *Planning, Estimating, and Rate-Fixing for Productive Engineers and Students*. Pitman, 1933.

PERSON, H. S.: *Technique of Planning. Industry's Contribution to Social-Economic Planning. Taylor Society Bulletin*, No. 1, pp. 29–34. November, 1934.

GESCHELIN, JOSEPH, and YOUNGER, JOHN: *Work Routing-Scheduling and Dispatching in Production*. Revised edition, Ronald Press, 1942.

THOMPSON, S. E.: *Optimum Productivity in the Workshop. S.A.M. Journal*, 4, pp. 39–44. March, 1939.

LANDY, T. M.: *Production Planning and Control of the General Electric Company. S.A.M. Journal*, 1, pp. 3–8. January, 1936.

In actual practice a more definite placing of responsibilities and decentralization of executive functions could be noted and a general desire to co-ordinate the various departments of a company or the sections of a shop into better functioning units. The number of companies using planning systems was increased and planning was adjusted to numerous specialized fields, for instance:

STONE, N. I.: "Systems of Shop Management in the Cotton Garment Industry." *Monthly Labor Review*, Vol. 46, pp. 1299–1320. June, 1938.

THOMPSON, H. L.: "Going Straight Line. Advice out of the Clothing Industry." *Factory Management and Maintenance*, Vol. 97, No. 1, January, 1939.

Research on Procurement and Material Control

Up to 1937 neither the procurement nor the control of materials caused any difficulties. Nor was industry caught with great excess stocks and losses after 1929 as it had been after 1919. The various methods and systems of material control developed by scientific management were well established and successfully applied in most plants.

Only as the various attempts to stimulate recovery failed to succeed convincingly, did the need for better co-ordination of purchasing with actual production requirements and for very close control of this phase become obvious:

ZINK, W. C.: "Purchases Are Tied to Production." *Factory Management and Maintenance,* Vol. 98, No. 3, March, 1940.

LEWIS, H. T.: "Standards of Purchasing Performance. Analysis of Purchasing Expenses." *Harvard Business Review,* No. 4, pp. 480–493, July, 1936.

BRECHIN, C. H.: "Standards for Handling Incoming Materials at Westinghouse Electric and Manufacturing Company." *Factory Management and Maintenance,* Vol. 95, pp. 67–68. September, 1937.

When material scarcities became pronounced with the intensified defense, lend-lease, and war programs, and aggravated by the loss of the Far Eastern material supplies, quite a few new features were introduced into the procurement of materials:

WAR PRODUCTION BOARD, see Priorities Division, Materials Division, and Contract Division publications on Priorities, Subcontracting District Offices, etc. For Scrap Salvage see: W. P. B., Bureau of Industrial Conservation.

A.S.M.E., Committee on Conservation and Reclamation of Materials. A.S.M.E. Annual Meeting, 1941. *Mechanical Engineering,* January, 1942, p. 25.
See also:
"Engineering Aspects of Industrial Scrap Salvage." *Mechanical Engineering,* June, 1942.

SPOONER, W. B.: "Preference Ratings Are Your Job!" *Food Industries,* January, 1942.

EDITORIAL: "Let's Look at Substitutes." *Factory Management and Maintenance,* Vol. 100, February, 1942.

ODLUM, F. B.: "How I Plan to Spread Defense Contracts" (Division of Contract Distribution, Office of Production Management). *Factory Management and Maintenance,* Vol. 99, No. 11, 1941.

VAN VLISSINGEN, ARTHUR: "Farm-Out Plan Adds 67% Capacity." *Factory Management and Maintenance,* Vol. 99, No. 2, February, 1941.

The more recent economic, military, and political aspects of material procurement will be found covered in the following references:

U. S. SENATE, Committee on Military Affairs: Strategic and Critical Materials and Minerals. Hearings, 1941. Superintendent of Documents. (U. S. 77th Congress, 1st Session.)

U. S. TARIFF COMMISSION: "Latin America as a Source of Strategic and Other Essential Materials." Report No. 144, 2nd Series, 1941.

On synthetic rubber and other chemical substitutes *Chemical and Metallurgical Engineering* and *Chemical Industries* have published excellent information.

Research in Job Standardization and Work Simplification

Job standardization and work simplification are also definitely among those subjects which have been done in large scale without having been described much in the literature. Only occasionally do companies or their employees take out time to report on such work for publication.

Also the methodical presentation of the scientific principles involved in this kind of work is still only tentative in character, partly because the field is a very wide one, partly because those developing the subject have not access to sufficient actual shop information, and in school laboratories only some kinds of work simplification can be experimentally developed. Nevertheless, progress has been made through the following contributions:

MAYNARD, HAROLD B., and STEGEMERTEN, G. J.: *Operation Analysis.* McGraw-Hill Book Co., New York, N. Y., 1939.

MOGENSEN, H.: *Work Simplification Conferences, Lake Placid, N. Y.,* and various publications (annual).

WANSKY, S. L.: "Foremen Eat Up This Work-Simplification Course." *Factory Management and Maintenance,* Vol. 99, No. 9, September, 1941.

KOCH, B. C.: "Motion Economy for All." International Business Machines Corporation, *Factory Management and Maintenance,* Vol. 96, pp. 56–57, June, 1938.

KLOPSCH, O. Z.: "Sat Down and Wrote Up the To Do and the Why. Wolverine Job Standards." *Factory Management and Maintenance,* Vol. 96, pp. 59–60, May, 1938.

CARROLL, JR., P.: *Time Study for Cost Control.* McGraw-Hill Book Co., New York, N. Y., 1939.

The techniques necessary for work simplification also have been advanced through new ideas:

BARNES, RALPH M.: Photocell Motion-Study Research. Various articles in *Factory Management and Maintenance,* Vol. 97, No. 1, January, 1939, and subsequent issues.

KOSMA, A. R.: "Motion Analysis in Three Dimensions. Stereoscopic Method." *Factory Management and Maintenance,* Vol. 99, April, 1941.

Research on Cost Control and Budgetary Control

When sales declined during the depression, and especially when they declined to the dwindling point in 1932 and 1933, costs, cost-savings, and cost controls gained in importance. Therefore, cost accounting and budgetary controls which had been, so far, helpful in reducing costs were improved by many organizations. Mostly, however, the traditional methods of analyzing standard setting and budgeting of costs were found to be inadequate. The seriousness of the situation required more direct and truly effective measures.

The first step taken was usually a careful *check of the "book costs"* of operation, processes, parts, or products as established by cost-accounting methods. It was found over and over again that even careful allocation or distribution of burden items did not give true actual costs. Furthermore, even if costs appeared to be fairly accurate, they still had to be brought down.

This led to the second step: A careful analysis and *study* of each operation or process *from a technical angle combined with the purpose of reducing costs*. When this approach was found to be truly effective, quite a number of companies which previously had relied on accounting and budgeting controls began to build up industrial-engineering departments and by now the larger companies employ sizable technical staffs which control and try to reduce time costs by time and motion studies and revisions; material costs by trying out substitutes or cheaper materials; machine and tool costs by careful checks, redesign, and control of pertaining charges, etc.

Thus the real cost control has been in many instances passed on from the cost accountants to industrial engineers, and cost engineering has become much more real than it has ever been, at least in the best managed and controlled companies. In the majority of plants, however, accounting cost control still prevails, with or without the use of standard costs and budgets to serve as measuring sticks.

The literature in this field was ample and diversified. The following merely are samples:

BIGELOW, C. M.: "Gone Are the Good Old Days; Suggestions for Reducing Costs." *Factory and Industrial Management*, Vol. 83, pp. 17–19, January, 1932.

DUTTON, H. P.: "How to Install and Operate a Cost Production Department." *Factory and Industrial Management*, Vol. 83, pp. 413–415, November, 1932.

SITTIG, L. P.: "Methods Engineering Will Get the Most Out of Your Plant." *Factory and Industrial Management*, Vol. 81, pp. 966–969, June, 1931.

KNOEPPEL, C. E.: *Profit Engineering*. McGraw-Hill Book Co., New York, N. Y., 1933.

GOROFSKI, I.: *New Developments in Controlling Labor Costs*. N.A.C.A. Bulletin No. 20, pp. 1–11, September, 1938.

GILLESPIE, G. M.: *Accounting Procedure for Standard Costs*. Ronald Press, 1935.

PECK, S. A.: *Managerial Aspects of Controls*. N.A.C.A. Bulletin No. 20, pp. 471–490. December 15, 1939.

CARTER, W. L.: "Industrial Management and Accounting." *Journal of Accounting*, Vol. 60, pp. 345–356. November, 1935.

WARD-BENSON, D.: "Cost Control of the Belt Conveyor. The Department Recovery System." *Mechanical Handling*, Vol. 25, pp. 205–206. July, 1938.

MALLET, L. C.: *Problems in Costing Airplanes*. N.A.C.A. Bulletin 18, pp. 1152–1158. June 15, 1937.

EBERT, G. M.: *Cost Accounting for Airplane Production*. N.A.C.A. Bulletin 19, pp. 1333–1351. August 1, 1938.

KRAFFT, E. H., and KING, H. F.: "Budgeting for Varying Volume." *Factory Management and Maintenance*, Vol. 99, June, 1941.

MERRILL, A. A.: "The ABC of the Variable Budget." *Factory Management and Maintenance*, Vol. 98, April, 1940.

Research on Industrial Marketing

The most satisfactory features in the scientific progress made in this field are two: (1) A great deal of the superficialities and easy success philosophies which prevailed before the depression were abandoned under the convincing weight of actualities, and (2) More careful and detailed research was given to all those phases of industrial marketing, which were found worthy and useful of development under the more severe sales conditions.

While at first the difficulties encountered in selling were exclusively economic in character, gradually also government regulations were introduced prohibiting below-cost selling (N.R.A.), later on came price supervision, and finally O.P.A.'s War Price and Rationing Boards. The simultaneous co-ordination of all sales efforts to war demands and an ever-increasing amount of restrictions on the manufacture of certain civilian goods created quite difficult sales conditions in some industries.

Since also the consumer, consumer organization, the coöperatives, the development of supermarkets, product research, forecasting, and the dependence of sales and selling on economic conditions were taken up as special research fields, a multitude of new thoughts were contributed in this field. The literature is so numerous that only samples can be offered:

GARLAND, C. M.: *Depressions and Their Solutions.* Guilford Press, 1936.

DULLES, E. L.: *Depression and Reconstruction.* University of Pennsylvania Press, 1936.

HART, A. G.: "Failure and Fulfillment of Expectations in Business Fluctuations." Record of Economic Statistics, Vol. 19, pp. 69–78, May, 1937.

FREY, A. W.: *Manufacturers' Product, Package and Price Policies, Modern Merchandise Management.* Ronald Press, 1940.

STIDSTONE, G. W.: "Field of the Industrial Engineer in Merchandising." *S.A.M. Journal,* Vol. 1, pp. 78–81, May, 1938.

COWAN, D. R. G.: "How Sales Effort Can Be Audited." *Advertising and Selling,* Vol. 32, pp. 41–43, June, 1939.

FOX, W. M.: *Profitable Control of Salesmen's Activities.* McGraw-Hill Book Co., New York, N. Y., 1937.

COWAN, D. R. G.: "Improved Standards of Sales Performance." *American Statistical Society Journal,* Vol. 32, pp. 75–82, March, 1937.

HOLLERAN, O. C.: *Check Sheet, Introduction of New Consumer Products, With List of Government Sources of Market Research Material.* U. S. Dept. of Commerce, Superintendent of Documents, June, 1935.

HENDERSON, LEON: *Consumer and Competition*. Annals. P. 363.

MANN, W.: "Do You Favor Consumer Research?" The Sales Executives' Forum. *Sales Management*, Vol. 36, pp. 166–167, February 1, 1935.

AGRICULTURAL ADJUSTMENT ADMINISTRATION, Consumers Counsel Division:
> Consumers' Guide, published semimonthly.
> Consumers' Market Service, published semimonthly.
> Consumer Services of Government Agencies, 1936, 1937, 1938.

U. S. NATIONAL RECOVERY ADMINISTRATION, Division of Review: Legal Aspects of Price Control. February, 1936.

Ibid: The Control of Geographic Price Relations Under Codes of Fair Competition. March, 1936.

Ibid: Minimum Price Regulations Under Codes of Fair Competition. March, 1936.

Ibid: Price Filing Under NRA Codes. March, 1936.

U. S. CONGRESS, TEMPORARY NATIONAL ECONOMIC COMMITTEE: Hearings. During these hearings the sales and price policies and methods of quite a few industries were investigated and a great number of other management subjects were probed. Among the references frequently referred to were:
> MEANS, GARDINER C.: Industrial Prices and Their Relative Inflexibility. 74th Congress, 1st Session, Document No. 13.
> NOURSE, E. G., and DRURY, H.: Industrial Price Policies and Economic Progress. Brookings Institute. No. 76, 1940.
> HAMILTON, W. H.: *Price and Price Policies*. McGraw-Hill Book Co., New York, N. Y., 1938.
> DENNISON, H. S., and GALBRAITH, J. K.: *Modern Competition and Business Policy*. Oxford University Press, New York, N. Y., 1938.

Many new thoughts were expressed in these texts and they were used to some extent as a basis for argumentation on the government's side.

The hearings were held for the "Investigation of Concentration of Economic Power" and they were published in 31 parts. Of special interest are the following:

Part	1	Economic Prologue
"	2, 3	Patents
"	5	Monopolistic Practices (5 and 5A)
"	6	Liquor Industry
"	7	Milk and Poultry Industries
"	8	Problems of the Consumer
"	11	Construction Industry
"	14–17A	Petroleum Industry
"	18–20	Iron and Steel Industry
"	21	War and Prices
"	25	Cartels

Part 26, 27   Iron and Steel Industry
" 30   Technology and Concentration of Economic Power
" 31   Investments, Profits, and Rates of Return for Selected Industries
" 31 A   Supplemental Data
Recovery Plans. TNEC Monograph No. 25, 1940.

Research in Job Analysis, Job Rating, Employee Merit Rating and Wages

While in past years these subjects were still in their development stages, mostly theory, and considered as separate fields, during the period under review a considerable number of companies introduced all of these methods into their activities and daily practice. Tying them together and adjusting them to their specific needs, they began to investigate in fine detail the relationships between the characteristics of all jobs, then they established definite ratings for the jobs as well as for those doing them, and finally they began to establish wage rates in line with the findings. In this manner they arrived at truly scientific evaluation practices and solidly founded wage and reward policies.

The main reason for this intensified scientific approach to job rating and wage problems was the ever-increasing pressure of the unions to obtain higher wages for any kind of job. These attempts could not be met in any other way but by a better co-ordination of job analysis with all the other problems. Thus the companies are now in a position to prove or check how a wage rate was arrived at and how it is justified by the character of the job. Once a wage structure can be "proved," the unions have little left to attack it, and a most troublesome problem in labor relationship is solved or at least made more satisfactory for all concerned.

While a truly impressive amount of work has been done by the companies, the unions, and also by federal agencies (Federal Security Agency—Employment Service Division), the literature contains little evidence of this research. The nearest to it are:

U. S. EMPLOYMENT SERVICE: *Directory of Occupational Titles*, Part I: Definitions of Titles, Part 2: Job Families. Washington, D. C.: Superintendent of Documents.

KRESS, A. L.: "How to Rate Jobs and Men." *Factory Management and Maintenance*, Vol. 97, October, 1939. (Discusses National Metal Trades Association Rating Plan.)

MILLS, N. G.: "A Point Plan for Rating Jobs." *Factory Management and Maintenance*, Vol. 98, December, 1940.

CLARKE, W. V.: "Rating Employees." *Personnel Journal*, Vol. 15, pp. 100–104. September, 1936.

NATIONAL INDUSTRIAL CONFERENCE BOARD: *Plans for Rating Employees*. Studies No. 8, 1938.

RIEGEL, J. W.: *Wage Determination*. University of Michigan. Bureau of Industrial Relations, No. 138, 1937.

Research on Personnel and Employment Practices

(A) WHITE COLLAR PERSONNEL

The executive, his responsibilities and functional duties, came up for special study, and during the decade it was his performance which counted rather than his "superpersonality." New light also was cast on the role which the foreman ought to play in a good organization.

SACKSTEDER, O.: "Putting It Up to Department Heads to Swim or Sink." *Printers Ink,* Vol. 156, pp. 98 ff., July 31, 1931.

BARNARD, C. J.: *Functions of an Executive,* 1935.

METROPOLITAN LIFE INSURANCE CO.:

Functions of the Production Executives, 1935.

Functions of the Controller, 1935.

EDDY, H. P.: "What an Employer Looks for in a Young Engineer." *Civil Engineering,* Vol. 6, p. 832, December, 1936.

LENZ, A.: "Foreman Has Key Role in Maintaining Harmonious Relations With Employees." Chevrolet Foundries. *Automotive Industries.* January 12, 1935.

TINSLEY, J. F.: "Foremen Invested With Responsibility Are Keymen to Success of Industry." *Steel,* Vol. 95, p. 38, December 10, 1934.

KRESS, A. L.: "Foremanship Fundamentals." *Factory Management and Maintenance,* Vol. 99, No. 10, October 1941, and

Ibid.: "The Foreman on His Job." *Factory Management and Maintenance,* Vol. 99, No. 10, October, 1941.

(B) WORKERS

Hiring. While during the depression dismissals prevailed, the requirements and standards for those to be hired were raised and actual skill was desired and tested for by the companies. They were not any longer satisfied with the mere fact that a man had "experience." The unskilled or less skilled men were gradually absorbed by Works Provision Administration projects, or had to remain on relief.

On this aspect of employment practices quite some literature of a social-economic nature was produced, but little was published treating this phase from the management angle.

Aptitude Tests. With the defense program and its final evolution into full-fledged war production, the necessity arose to select a great number of workers from the as yet untrained or only semitrained applicants. In order to avoid too great mistakes the "aptitude tests" previously developed were revived and new tests were developed to suit specific company or job needs. In most instances tests like those used in Army aptitude testing were applied. More specific testing methods were described by:

GILLETTE, ROBERT W.: "Help for the Hirer." *Factory Management and Maintenance,* Vol. 98, No. 3, March, 1940.

GILLETTE, ROBERT W.: "Tests Help You Hire Right." *Factory Management and Maintenance*, Vol. 99, No. 10, October, 1941.

EDITORIAL: "General Electric Tests and Trains Meter Makers." *Factory Management and Maintenance*, Vol. 98, No. 7, July, 1940.

TAYLOR, HAROLD C.: "The Selection of Subordinate Personnel." *Mechanical Engineering*, November, 1941, pp. 807–810.

Women in Industry. When the draft took many men from industry and prevented the availability of sufficient men as required in the rapidly expanding war industries, women had to be hired, at first only for light work in the aircraft industries and later on also for heavier work in mechanical shops. When women were paid the same wages as would have been paid to men, the results were considered as satisfactory.

EDITORIAL: "What Women Are Doing in Industry." *Factory Management and Maintenance*, Vol. 100, March, 1942.

EDITORIAL: "Enter Women—to Do Men's Work." *Factory Management and Maintenance*, Vol. 100, April, 1942.

Prevention of Seasonal Unemployment. Among the most noteworthy innovations in employment practices is the as yet limited tendency among employers to plan and provide for an exchange or shifting of employees from one company to others, so as to provide employment for the workers in off-seasons or seasonal slow-downs. More research and wider application of this practice with a view to postwar conditions are highly desirable. References so far known are:

EDITORIAL: "Big Firms Interchange Workers in Chicago to Fit Each Other's Busy Season." *Business Week,* January 28, 1939.

LUM, M.: "Swapping Workers in Seasonal Slacks." *Nations Business*, Vol. 27, p. 44, September, 1939.

U. S. Government Agencies for Employment. Another very important feature in personnel administration is the establishment of various government agencies for the purpose of recording and using the manpower of the country to best advantage. The most important of them are:

NATIONAL RESOURCES PLANNING BOARD, National Roster of Scientific and Specialized Personnel, Washington, D. C.

U. S. EMPLOYMENT OFFICES, established throughout the country to assist in finding and placing workers, and

U. S. MANPOWER COMMISSION, WASHINGTON, D. C.

Research on Labor Practices

This field was considerably reformed by government action. New laws and regulations were put into effect, discussed, and management had to be adjusted to them. A complete review is impossible but the following references should help in revealing the new developments during the period.

U. S. Dept. of Labor: Annual Reports.

U. S. National Recovery Administration, Division of Review, Labor Studies Section: *The Labor Program under the N. I. R. A.*, 5 parts, March, 1936.

U. S. Works Projects Administration: *National Research Project on Re-employment Opportunities and Recent Change in Industrial Techniques* (Productivity of Labor, etc.). Various volumes 1939, 1940.

Appraisal of Results of W. P. A. December, 1938 (Works Progress Administration).

U. S. National Labor Relations Board: *Functions and Relations to Other Boards.* Activities, etc. July 9, 1934, October, 1934, and later.

Decisions and Orders (Annually since 1936).

Annual Reports (since 1936).

U. S. Department of Labor, Labor Standards Division: Digests of Labor Bills, Investigations, Health and Safety Regulations (Since 1935).

U. S. Department of Labor, Labor Statistics Bureau. Studies on Unemployment Insurance, Employment, Payrolls, Employment Office Service, Labor Standards in Government Contracts, Co-operative Movement, Union Progress. 1934 and later.

   See especially:

Labor Unions, Characteristics of Company Unions, 1938.

Fair Labor Standards Act. Interpretive Bulletins on Methods of Payment, Maximum Hours, etc., 1938.

Labor Research Association: *Labor Fact Book.* International Publishers. 1941.

McNaughton, W. L.: *The Development of the Labor Relations Law.* Complete Bibliography. pp. 182–193, 1941.

Slichter, S. H.: *Union Policies and Industrial Management.* Brookings Institute, 1941.

Twentieth Century Fund: *Labor and National Defense.* 1941.

Balderston, C. C.: *Industrial Relations.* (Misnomer) *Executive Guidance of Industrial Relations.* University of Pennsylvania. 1935.

Westbrook Pegler was the most outspoken critic of labor practices and especially of union policies. His editorials were published by the *World Telegram* and many other newspapers.

Increase of Adaptability of People to Industry (Training)

A great deal of effort and research was extended to the training of workers, foremen, and junior personnel, and excellent methods were developed by official as well as by private initiative. The Division for Training Within Industry (War Production Board) established a nationwide organization to assist employers in their job-training efforts by providing training-course outlines, instructors, and material. While this work was exceptionally successful, hardly anything has been published as yet about it or the methods used.

During the recovery period, and more recently, quite a few companies, and in same industries (aircraft, steel) nearly all of them, developed systematic training, ranging from fundamental job operations to complete training programs on technical and management subjects. The following references are helpful in tracing at least the main developments:

CHENEY, A. S.: "Workers' Education in the U. S. A." *International Labor Office Review*, Vol. 32, pp. 39–59, July, 1935.

DILDINE, P. L.: "They All Go to School." Goodrich offers every worker an opportunity to get more education. *Factory Management and Maintenance,* Vol. 93, pp. 159–160, April, 1935.

EDITORIAL: "Four Out of Five Industrial Companies Training Employees." *Steel,* Vol. 101, p. 30, September 6, 1937.

EDITORIAL: "America Trains Her Industrial Army." *Factory Management and Maintenance,* Vol. 98, November, 1940.

IRWIN, R. R.: "Quick Training Gives Lockheed the Men It Needs." *Factory Management and Maintenance,* Vol. 98, December, 1940.

WOOD, T.: "Training Operatives for Conveyor Production." *Mechanical Handling,* Vol. 25, p. 268 ff., September, 1938.

STEPHENSON, A.: "Training of Unskilled Labor." *Engineering,* Vol. 145, pp. 347 ff., April 1, 1938.

VANDEN BOSCH, J. W.: "Training People for Factory Work." *Factory Management and Maintenance,* Vol. 98, September, 1940.

The training of college- and subcollege-type employees by companies, too, was intensified considerably and quite novel features were developed as may be seen from the following articles:

A.S.M.E., Survey of Training for National Defense—Government, Civil Service Commission, Navy Training, Aeronautics Industries, etc. (Excellent). *Mechanical Engineering.* March, 1941, pp. 183–194.

STEVENSON, JR., A. R., and HOWARD, A.: "General Electric Company's Advanced Course in Engineering." *Electrical Engineering,* Vol. 54, pp. 265–268. March, 1935.

KIRBY, F. B.: "Study Clubs for Employees. Abbott Laboratories." *Nations Business,* Vol. 26, pp. 108–109. April, 1938.

EDITORIAL: "50 Per Cent of Tuition Fee Paid." *System,* Vol. 64, p. 20. March, 1935.

DAVIS, E.: "Educational Refunds in Industry." Princeton University, Industrial Relations Section, 1935.

FREUND, C. J.: "College Crop. Fitting Engineering Graduates to Their First Jobs." *American Machinist,* Vol. 79, pp. 520–521. July 17, 1935.

TEICHROEW, H. W.: "Trade School Crop Vs. College Crop." *American Machinist,* Vol. 79, pp. 796 ff., October, 1935.

*Research on Management's Attitudes and Industry's Relations
with Federal Government*

In view of the ever-growing importance of government policies giving a new background to industrial management, quite some literature evolved dealing with the new kind of relationship. As indicative presentations on this subject may be considered:

CLARK, J. M.: *Social Control of Business.* McGraw-Hill Book Co., New York, N. Y., 1939. Second edition.

DYKSTRA, G. O.: *Textbook on Government and Business.* Callaghan, 1939.

FORTUNE MAGAZINE: Business and Government. March to October, 1938.

LEE, M. G.: *Government's Hand in Business.* Baker Voorhis & Co., 1937.

BURNHAM, JAMES: *Managerial Revolution.* John Day, 1941.

U. S. NATIONAL RECOVERY ADMINISTRATION: *557 Codes of Fair Competition, Supplements, Amendments, Executive and Administrative Orders.* For detailed information see U. S. Government Catalog of the Public Documents 1933–1934, pp. 488 to 575.

PHILLIPS, C. F. and GARLAND, J. V.: *Government Spending and Economic Recovery.* Wilson 1939.

KIMMEL, L. H.: *Cost of Government in the U.S.*, National Industrial Conference Board, 1938.

The Management Problems of the Future

Which problems will be in need of special investigation and research in the years to come is as yet difficult to state. Management's problems and character will undoubtedly be finally formed by the present war, and following it by the prevailing government attitudes, but there are certain trends and indications, which allow one to discern a few pertinent facts:

The high taxation on corporate and personal incomes is bound to remain in effect for so many years to come that it will require lowest cost production and further research toward that end in all management branches pertaining to it.

Organized labor and legislation on the rights of labor have become such strong factors in the industrial pattern that research will have to find better than present methods of reconciling labor's and management's interests. Scientific management should prove itself superior to the policies and attitudes now in vogue.

Considerable changes in materials and material supply will become permanent features and will involve not only technical problems, material and product research but will evolve also new methods of supply planning, expressing themselves in novel methods of purchasing and more improved stockroom management.

The systematic co-ordination of production of entire industries achieved by now on an unprecedented and never-expected centralized scale will probably be modified, but its advantageous features will be maintained and novel schemes of industrial co-ordination may be expected.

The art of selling and methods of distribution, deprived by now of much of their previous expensiveness, will have to be simplified further, and greater effectiveness and directness will be favorite subjects of research.

Price controls and price ceilings are not popular in peacetime and will probably be abandoned; but determination of true costs, price setting, and pricing policies will be restudied and the voluntary achievement of price stability will become more general policy as soon as it becomes better recognized as one basic prerequisite for better planning.

Military service—and especially the air-force training—now given to millions of young men, enabling these same young men to become specialists in many new technical subjects and in their application under most difficult conditions, training them in teamwork, discipline and human co-ordination— all of this is bound to make a deep imprint on the management of tomorrow.

Only time can and will point out more clearly the specific problems and detail tasks which will have to be investigated for new solutions.

MANAGEMENT ATTITUDES
By Erwin Haskell Schell [4]

Some psychologists maintain that attitudes are much more the product of our surrounding culture than of our personal experience. I believe the attitudes of the manager are an exception to this rule. It is not what people say to him, but what the world does to him that orders his temper of mind. And when we examine his environment during the past ten years, what an extraordinary kaleidoscope of change lies before us.

We first find our industrial economy in company with that of almost every other nation spiraling close to the bottom of a deep pit of international depression. And today, at the end of these ten years, we are well on the way to the greatest industrial output we have ever known. With such a spectrum of change before us, it is to be expected that management attitudes should reflect important adjustments. To say that these trends have, on the whole, marked progress is to make a bolder statement, for there are those who question if our standards of life have increased during this decade, even though standards of living in the United States have shown clear advance.

There has been one fundamental attitude which has revealed little variance during these years. It is management's ever-present temper of extreme concern over the health and continuance of the individual business. In its highest manifestation, this is an attitude of responsibility; in its primitive form, it is an expression of self-

[4] Former Head of the Department of Business and Engineering Administration, Massachusetts Institute of Technology, Member, American Society of Mechanical Engineers.

preservation. In either instance it is the product of the precarious state in which business and industry have found themselves. Even in normal times, as everyone knows, it is the exceptional establishment which weathers the pressures of competition. During this decade, the casualties have been unusually high, and the number of enterprises in this country, whose corporate life has for months or years literally hung by a thread, are numbered in the thousands. This basic fact has had little advertising value, and therefore has not been granted the weight that it deserves in explaining the attitude of industrial managers during these difficult years. The psychologists again tell us that people have public attitudes and private attitudes. When management appears at times to strike out unreasoningly at whatever obstacle confronts it, we may be sure that the irritability displayed is due to a deeper concern which the manager bears for those whose welfare is in his charge.

Yet we must admit that with the increasing waves of change which are sweeping across our country, we are witnessing two different managerial attitudes emerge. On the one hand, there are those reaching forward boldly and even eagerly to ride upon these wave-crests and to travel with them to the new. Others are turning and seeking the sand beneath their feet so that they may run for the shore. As this report is a component part of a larger survey of progress in management, we feel that we may properly deal only with the attitudes of those fighting folk who see in change an opportunity rather than a difficulty.

Needless to say, managerial attitudes have been infinite in number and variety, for they spring into being with every individual response to every managerial situation. To detail any fragment of these attitudes, therefore, is to open oneself to the inevitable criticism of omission or under-emphasis. Conversely, a commentator has the advantage of presenting his own viewpoint without fear of serious challenge, inasmuch as no objective measurement via attitude polls has, during this period, acquired sufficient reliability or validity to be scientifically dependable. As the advent of war during the last year has introduced the most radical changes in managerial attitudes occurring during the decade, it will be reserved for the final topic in this presentation.

Methods

The beginning of the ten-year period saw the end of the rapidly waning opposition to the advent of science in management. Again, almost the last barriers of secrecy in methods had disappeared, the final stand being in the areas of new product development. Managers increasingly turned with favor to methods or procedures which could be mechanized and almost automatically operated. An extraordinary growth in clerical machinery and in control mechanisms reveals the readiness with which management has accepted the benefit of these devices. There has also been a change of attitude toward methods of maintaining quality. Originally, quality was viewed largely as a disciplinary problem. More recently, emphasis is being laid upon technical improvements in fabrication and in quality measurement as roads to improvement. As the period advanced, the presence of standards was no longer viewed as an innovation but as a necessity in the same category as machinery or cash. In the Midwest, a whole new methodology has developed around the refinements of flow production, and a technique has been perfected which permits adjustment to demands for variations in product as well as rates of output. Perhaps the most dramatic change in managerial attitudes toward methods has been the accelerated acceptance on the part of industrialists of work simplification applied through the medium of foreman and employee training.

Facilities

Here, the greatest fundamental change in attitude has been the growing acceptance of process as the dominant element around which facilities are to be arranged. In many plants at the beginning of the decade, to move a machine required almost the same mental wrench as to move a tombstone. Today, flexibility of equipment and versatility in arrangement is sought by many aggressive managers. In the last analysis, the pivot upon which the enterprise turns in capitalizing upon the winds of change is now the resource of managerial and technical skill. Managers hold that facilities, materials, and products should be readily shifted and altered in order that these fundamental resources may be applied most directly and efficiently.

In no previous decade has there been greater change and overturn of orthodox methods of fabrication than in this. Flame-cutting, welding, die-casting, powder metallurgy, and the advent of the synthetics have revolutionized many processes which, for over a hundred years, have held their position in our industries. These developments have called for a much more open-minded attitude on the part of managers than hitherto, a point of view easiest accepted by those who are familiar with the humilities of the scientific spirit.

Personnel

In no field has the manager found it necessary so radically to vary his attitudes as in that of personnel. The economic holocaust which swept across the world in the early '30's revealed to everyone that neither the individual establishment, nor the industry, nor the combined abilities of a nation were sufficient to prevent unemployment. With perhaps 15,000,000 men without a place to work as our era begins, it was clear that marked changes in employee as well as employer attitudes must inevitably result. Out of the maelstrom of conflicting opinion, confusion, and dismay, there have arisen certain constructive attitudes which merit mention. The first is the growth in awareness of the dignity and importance of simple human relationships. At the height of the turmoil, one manager remarked,

> We have no idea how things are coming out. But one resolution we have made.
> It is that when the dust has settled, we shall have retained our personal friendships with our employees, which we have built up over so many years.

A second change of attitude is the increase in managerial interest in relation to the individual. As one executive put it,

Ten years ago, my foremen knew their employees by numbers; five years ago they began to call their men by their last names; then we swung to a first-name basis, and today (prewar) my supervisors are trying to know the members of the family as well.

Managerial attitudes have given new emphasis to the maintenance of employee good-will. Complaints are viewed with greater concern; inequalities of basic wage have been the cause of extensive analyses in many plants, and the techniques of evolving mutually satisfactory working relationships between management and labor have been given far greater weight than in previous years. To a growing extent, management is looking at personnel as co-managers, rather than as employees, inasmuch as the manager of a machine is in many regards an executive in his own right, although his control is not over human stuff.

Supervision

At the beginning of our period the importance of the supervisor was rapidly growing in the eyes of management. Yet the depression years forced many companies to skeletonize their organizations, and improvement in this sector resulted as much from the removal of mediocrity in supervisory personnel as from foreman training. With the rapid acceleration in the growth of labor organizations, new problems of such severity developed that in many establishments management short-circuited the supervisor in an attempt to allay difficulties. The ineffectiveness of this procedure was soon recognized, and as our period draws to a close it is the growing attitude of management that to the greatest extent possible the supervisor should be trained to fulfill his new role of company representative in dealing with labor's appointed departmental spokesman.

A second curious error developed during this interval. In management's anxiety fully to prepare the supervisor for his new duties, his loyalties to the company were so strengthened that his relationships with the men were somewhat weakened and the principle that a good foreman believes in his company but stands for his men was overlooked. This condition was quickly corrected, and today in our progressive establishments we find management hoping that their first-line executives will be men whose heads are with the company and whose hearts are with the employees.

Vendors

An interesting change of attitude is found here. During the ten years, vendors have been viewed less as adversaries in negotiation and more as partners in production. Indeed, one organization has required that its sources of supply be known as its resources. The mutuality of interests between vendor and customer has been more widely explored, and agreements upon inspection methods and other technical details effected. Back of this change of attitude is the realization by management that the extreme fluctuations in the business world when shifts from a buyer's to a seller's market occur almost overnight, make it necessary that beneath commercial relationships there should be constructed a stratum of fundamental goodwill and friendship. To maintain a lively competitive spirit has been found entirely possible without the corrosion of mutual personal regard and respect. These trends are reflected in the modern purchasing installations which give increased attention to the convenience of sales representatives and economy in their expenditure of time.

Stockholders

It is a truism that in times of peril all animate life seeks protection through closer relationships with its kind. The long depression followed by growing international uncertainties has doubtless been a contributory factor in the change of attitude on the part of management with respect to stockholders. At the beginning of our period the stockholder was a name in a big book. At the close of the decade he is a person who, management sincerely hopes, may become interested in the welfare of the business of which he is a part. Early in the decade when it became clear that management had lost the vote, there were sporadic efforts made by some executives to awaken sudden interest on the part of stockholders. This was but a surface phenomena however, and a deeper and more hopeful change of attitude has been the tendency throughout the country to provide the stockholder with such facts about the business as will reflect the situation truly and yet simply. The problem has not been an easy one, inasmuch as the growing tendency of the American buyer has been to measure his purchases solely by results with less interest in the methods by which these results are obtained.

The Public

Despite sporadic evidences to the contrary, management's attitude toward the public has rarely been antagonistic. The physical nature of manufacturing processes with their screen of buildings and property have naturally insulated production from the community and the public. That there was any reason for closer mutual understanding and familiarity was little realized. But when it became clear that without such relationships industry might find itself in a weak strategic position, a wave of concern developed in these areas. Little by little it became clear that it was not only the privilege but the responsibility of management to make its activities an acceptable and understood part of the community. Applying the common principles of hospitality, management found it sound practice to "put the house in order before the guests are invited." Frequently these preparatory activities took longer than was anticipated. As our period drew to a close many managers throughout the country were reflecting attitudes of satisfaction that such constructive steps had been taken and that such responsibilities had been shouldered. In some instances definite resources of immediate practical benefit to the company had been disclosed; in others potential gains are in the offing. Chief among the changes in attitude, however, was the realization that the industrial establishment may wisely view its market as only a fragment of the public with whom it should be on close and friendly terms.

Government

When it became clear that the depression suffered in the United States was common to practically every other industrial nation, it became equally patent that our country as a unit must inevitably assume new responsibilities, undertake new activities, and develop new relationships with its people. Later when the fire of war began sweeping over the planet, it was doubly obvious that our unity as a nation must be given new significance, dignity, and implementation. Management's attitude toward government during the past decade has been colored by the complete spectrum of human emotions. At one end of the scale we find intense antagonism and now at the other we find the height of loyalty and support. Over the period two simple facts have come to light widely affecting management attitudes. The first is that government has become the largest business in the country and that it is carried on by human beings who live and breathe as do managers. Indeed, many of these individuals are themselves managers in but a slightly different field of endeavor.

The second fact is that management increasingly has had need of government in view of the heightening world conflagration. These two certainties have gone far to lessen the pain of limitation which governmental action has inevitably found it necessary to throw about American business and administration. Managers and government officials are getting to know each other better, and attitudes of uncertainty and suspicion are changing to those of familiarity and mutual understanding. As the nation entered the war there was no question but that the trend of management attitude toward government was definitely in the direction of increased co-ordination, co-operation, and harmony.

Wartime Attitudes

While our so-called defense period served to usher the nation into a war-time economy under somewhat more gradual auspices than would otherwise have been the case, yet it is true that with Pearl Harbor there came a sudden, and in some instances, drastic change of attitude on the part of management. Still in a state of flux, these points of view are yet plastic in terms of current changes, and may be only incompletely discerned. Their apparent contour as revealed by recent contacts with several hundred wartime establishments may, however, be highlighted. Wartime attitudes toward method have fortunately responded promptly to the revolutionary point of view which the emergency made essential. During the initial stages, all thoughts of cost or efficiency had to become secondary to the objectives of sheer quantitative output. Where conversions were most severe, and where great expansion was called for, intelligent management sought effective production first and qualitative cost or economy values second. Already many firms are rapidly swinging to the intensive cultivation of qualitative manufacturing methods which will markedly enhance production without commensurate increases in expenditures.

Wartime facilities proved an initial point of constriction. Once more management attitudes swung from costs to output as the dominant objective, with the ensuing refurbishment of old machines, conversion of existing facilities and building by company establishments of their own new equipment. The wartime attitude is "any machine is better than none."

A new note has been sounded in personnel relations which has been expressed by an able commentator as follows:

> In France, the nation collapsed in important part, because labor's spirit had been broken; because workers didn't see much for which to fight; in England, the nation rallied in important part, because labor had a real stake in government; because workers felt that they did have a reason to fight; in Russia, the resistance exceeded all expectations because the people felt that they had a stake in winning; because they had a reason to fight.
>
> Here nothing should be done to discourage workers, to give them the idea that there is little to defend. Everything should be done to give labor a big stake for which to show an interest and for which to fight.[5]

Here is the underlying philosophy which is basing all decisions of personnel policy and which dominantly colors the attitude of constructive management.

In the field of supervision, a new spirit has arisen. Supervisors increasingly take the attitude that they are working *with* their men *for* their country. A new quality of morale, not to say devotion, results from this feeling and we may anticipate an even closer bond of camaraderie between the rank and file of our industry, as labor-management committees continue to grow in numbers.

Never before have vendors attained so high a position of eminence in the eyes of the industrial buyer. The attitude of management is one of prayerful thankfulness they have been able to build any residue of goodwill which now may be capitalized in these relationships. Unquestionably, this new mutuality of interests the war has brought will go far toward effecting stronger and more creative opportunities for closer productive co-ordination between buyer and seller when the hostilities come to a close.

As Army and Navy pennants are awarded and as trade literature reveals the efforts companies are making in the interest of the Nation, an unusual surge of support and enthusiasm has come from stockholders who now feel themselves, in part at least, related to the war effort of the industries whose securities they hold. There is little question but that here the war is bringing stronger bases for close affiliation than have been enjoyed in many years.

Never has industry been so inextricably involved in the concerns of the community as in this wartime period. The recruiting of our vast army has involved mutual sacrifices on the part of both to which each has cheerfully responded. Community and company have stood shoulder to shoulder facing the inevitable losses of industrial manpower which mobilization has demanded. At this writing, management is in the process of turning to the sisters and mothers of these young men for their assistance in manning machines and work places. New sociological relationships between indus-

[5] *United States News,* Vol. 2, Aug. 2, 1941.

try and community are an inevitable outcome of these activities and closer contacts will continue to strengthen mutual understanding and regard.

With respect to management's attitudes toward government, the wartime temper can best be reflected by a distinguished manufacturer who recently said, "Yesterday the man in the White House was my President; today he is my Commander in Chief." To offer unselfishly, unfalteringly, and unreservedly the services of management to those in whose hands the conduct of the war rests is the kind of attitude upon which ultimate victory for the Nation depends. Its wide prevalence throughout our land holds high promise for victory.

Ten Years' Progress in Management, 1943-1952*

and

Panel Discussion

1953

Within the four decades of the Progress Reports, the Science
of Managing expanded to international dimensions with applications in industry, government, agriculture, the home—
in brief, it encompassed more and more of the spheres of
human activities.

There were healthy and honest divergencies of opinions
reflected in the Discussions which followed the Report. But
from this open exchange of ideas and the dissemination of
information—which had been urged by Henry Towne in
1886—the Science of Managing has continued to grow and
exert its dynamic influence on the industrial processes and
on the Society in which they function.

* "Ten Years' Progress in Management." Contributed by the Management Division and presented at the Annual Meeting, New York, N. Y.,
November 30–December 5, 1952, of The American Society of Mechanical
Engineers. *Transactions*, Vol. 75, 1953. Permission to excerpt by courtesy
of the Society.

TEN YEARS' PROGRESS IN MANAGEMENT, 1943–1952
and
PANEL DISCUSSION

Foreword by Lillian M. Gilbreth [1]

THE FIRST MANAGEMENT PROGRESS REPORT,[2] entitled "The Present State of the Art of Industrial Management," was presented by a committee of which James M. Dodge was chairman and L. P. Alford, secretary. The committee submitted questions on management to various experts, assembled their replies, and deduced from them the contents of the report. It presents what was being done, the advocates and opponents of scientific management, and the important emphases. These include not only techniques of production, but aspects of human relations, calling attention to the importance of skill, of motivation, and of attitudes. Mr. Dodge, a satisfied user of scientific management, was president of the Link Belt Company; most of the other members of the committee were also manufacturers. The report is supplemented by a list of the important papers on scientific management printed by this Society, sixteen—written by ten authors. There is also a minority report, signed by one member of the committee, stressing the art of management as more important than the science. Dr. Alford did his usual fine objective job as editor, and the reports evoked much worth-while discussion.

In 1919 Dr. Alford wrote what he considered a supplementary management report, called "The Status of Industrial Relations."[3] This is not considered one of the "Ten-Year" reports, but is important in that it stresses the increasing emphasis on human relations. "Principles, practice, and law" are all considered and the main topics of interest listed and discussed. A bibliography follows. Again, the discussion is excellent.

The 1922 report is entitled "Ten Year's Progress in Management"[4] and is writ-

---

[1] President, Gilbreth, Inc. Honorary Member, American Society of Mechanical Engineers.

[2] Majority Report of Sub-Committee on Administration, *Transactions*, American Society of Mechanical Engineers, Vol. 34, 1912, p. 1131.

[3] Prepared at the request of the Committee on Meetings and Programs, *Transactions*, American Society of Mechanical Engineers, Vol. 41, 1919, p. 163.

[4] Prepared by request and presented during Management Week, October 16-21, 1922, and the Annual Meeting of that year, *Transactions*, American Society of Mechanical Engineers, Vol. 44, 1922, p. 1243.

ten by Dr. Alford as author, with no committee assistance. He was recognized as the most fitting person to evaluate the decade. He stresses that progress has largely to do with the human element—adding to the 1912 criteria the motive of service, and concluding, "Management is the agency by which community, state, and nation shall endure." An appendix contains accounts of management societies in existence at the time. Engineering schools which have management courses are listed, as among the evidences that management activities have broadened. The discussion is as interesting as the report.

The 1932 report, also by Dr. Alford, presents steady progress.[5] This includes more effective technical procedure, and better human relations as well as wider public service, mentioning national planning; also more courses in engineering colleges. The discussion, though short, is stimulating.

The 1942 report [6] was planned by Dr. Alford, who was assembling his material when he died. It was completed under the sponsorship of a special committee of the Management Division, by the devoted effort of George Hagemann, the vice-chairman of this committee who had worked with Dr. Alford. It is dedicated to Dr. Alford, and includes summaries of the 1919, 1922, and 1932 reports. It covers sections on the various aspects of scientific management. These had been assigned to various authorities in the field whose articles were combined into a report that reflects the thinking of the decade.

The 1952 report follows the pattern of the 1942, but with more participation of the Management Division Committee who discussed the plan of the report, the fields of interest, the assignments, and the procedure, in detail. Various authorities in the field of management have been asked to present and evaluate what has happened in the decade, and the reader will see for himself the expansion of the field and the problems and prospects it presents.

On the whole we have a challenging picture. Scientific management has expanded in its geographical application and in its application not only to industry and business but to government, to agriculture, to the home, to libraries, to hospitals, and to work with the physically disabled. Technical adequacy has not diminished, though the continued need for research is evident. Emphasis on human relations has increased, with both courses and work carried on in physical, mental, emotional, and social adequacy, and with a new emphasis on the art of communication. Local, regional, and national groups are united in a National Management Council which is a part of the CIOS, the international management group. The programs of the nine International Management Congresses so far held, beginning with the 1924 Congress in Prague, offer evidence of the expanding field, as do preliminary plans for the program of the tenth Congress, to be held in Brazil in February, 1954. To be noted also

[5] "Ten Years' Progress in Management—1923–1932," contributed by the Management Division and presented at the Annual Meeting. *Transactions*, American Society of Mechanical Engineers, Vol. 55, 1933, Man. 55-2, p. 7.
[6] "Ten Years' Progress in Management," presented at the Annual Meeting 1942. *Transactions*, American Society of Mechanical Engineers, Vol. 65, 1943, p. 213.

are the closer relations of industrial engineering with industrial medicine, psychology, psychiatry, and so on. This is evidenced in curricula of colleges, in programs of management meetings, but especially in research, both fundamental and applied.

Our chief problem seems to be to enable more people to have work that will produce not only necessary goods, but satisfaction to them and to everyone. We look forward to a future of effort, and of service.

MANAGEMENT DIVISION

The Management Division, in planning this 1952 Report, has tried to clearly continue the form and purpose of 1912, 1922, 1932, and 1942 reports. We believe that each paper represents an important area of management, and that the pattern of this report will be of assistance to our Division in preparing the 1962 report, which will record the first 50 years of Scientific Management.

We extend our sincere thanks and appreciation to the authors who have unselfishly contributed their knowledge and valuable time in preparing this report.

ARTHUR M. PERRIN, *Chairman,*
Ten Years' Progress in Management Committee
and *Editor* of Report

ERCOLE ROSA, JR., *Co-Editor*

Management Division, *Executive Committee,* 1953

E. H. MacNIECE, *chairman*   W. A. MacCREHAN, *secretary*
A. M. PERRIN, *vice-chairman*   ERCOLE ROSA, JR., *assistant secretary*
T. A. MARSHALL, JR.   PHIL CARROLL

E. STOKES TOMLIN, JR.

THE THEORY OF ORGANIZATION AND MANAGEMENT

By Robert T. Livingston [7]

This paper is intended to set the framework for the study of progress in management from 1942 to 1952. Our main thesis submits that great though the progress has been in management mechanisms, much less has been achieved in developing a true science of management. It is suggested that what we have witnessed is largely a continuously branching specialization and intensification of detail with very little feedback into the basic stream of theory. It proposes a return to Taylor.

A progress report is intended to answer three principal questions:

1. Where are we?
2. How did we get there?
3. Where are we going?

[7] Professor of Industrial Engineering, Columbia University, Member, American Society of Mechanical Engineers.

The year 1952 is a particularly apt one in which to do all three for it is apparent that management today is faced with increasingly new and increasingly difficult problems. In many ways the situation is not unlike what it was in 1912, and it seems wise in this paper, rather than merely to catalog the many unusual and indeed dramatic occurrences of the past 10 years, to look back further and in rather fundamental terms assess where we are now, where we were then, and how we got from there to here. Perhaps in the light of these 40 years of experience, we can, in some measure, assess the probabilities of the future.

Management an Engineering Problem

Men have managed men since prehistory, yet even to this day the current operations of an enterprise continue to present new and different problems to the manager. By *prévoyance*, planning, and preparation the solution of many problems may be routinized and presolved but because of changes in technology, changes in the institutions and goals of society, because man, as Gillespie has it, is purposive, we will never "solve" the problem of management. However, it is believed that it is possible to evolve a rational theory or system of management.

In the 1913 *Transactions* of this Society is a definition of "management" which today stands equally valid:

> Management is the art and science of preparing, organizing and directing human effort applied to control the forces and utilize the material of nature for the benefit of man.

Here is a description and a value system. The engineer is not to be a mere scientist seeking truth; he is dedicated to the benefit of man. And we hold with Taylor's definition of scientific management written 40 years ago:

> Scientific management, in its essence, consists of a certain philosophy which results . . . in a combination of the four great underlying principles of Management:
> Development of a true science;
> Scientific selection of the worker;
> His scientific education and development;
> Intimate, friendly and co-operative relations between management and men.

It is the premise of the paper that regardless of how much the three last principles have been applied, developed, and used, that far less progress has been made in the first and the most important of all, namely, "the development of a true science of management."

Our central theme is, that for the peace of the world to come, management, and the engineer especially, must accept an increasingly greater responsibility for the operation of our society. It is maintained that we have, or science will give us, assets and resources in plenty but that the really great potential of society is the creative abilities of the people. While the nuclear scientist has unlocked the hitherto untapped energies of the atom, the great potentialities of man's brains, ingenuity, and genius remain only partially utilized.

Progress in Management. Progress is a difficult thing to assess, since progress is not synonymous with change. The scientific-management movement, which formally is only just over 40 years old, has had a deep and profound effect upon our society and there is no doubt that its importance grows daily. Its use is not restricted to capitalism; on the contrary, a recent, quite important book came out of Russia called *Industrial Management in the U.S.S.R.* which is a very interesting history of how the Soviets have tried to take what they thought was good from scientific management and put it to their own use, always, of course claiming that Marx, Lenin, or Stalin originally set it forth.

Any categorization is necessarily subjective and is always an adjustment between the desire to simplify and the wish to specify. But in considering the question of management, and especially its history, one is forced to categorize in some manner. The four categories, which are set up in the following, differ from Taylor's but perhaps the 40 years will account for the difference:

1. Procedural and process evolution;
2. Change of attitude about the worker;
3. Evolution of a rational process of decision making;
4. Development of a science of management.

Number four was Taylor's No. 1. Number two will comprehend the three others. It is possible to say that procedural and process evolution was implicit in his thinking and finally that progress in management may best be measured in terms of the evolution of a rational process of decision making.

Management is the taking of action to answer stimuli; in a word, it is a solving of problems, problems which change in time. Thus it is maintained that "progress" in management can only be assessed intelligently in the light of the problems that management is called upon to solve. These problems are in the fabric of the social and economic structure, are indeed the dynamics of society.

Fields of Application. While engineers have contributed greatly to the development of a theory of management, as designers they organize, and as operators they administer, it is obvious that all managers are not engineers. There are many fields of management:

1. Public and Institutional: The government and public institutions such as the schools and hospitals.
2. Private Institutions: Industrial and business associations, labor, and other associations.

While these are distinctly different as to the fields in which they operate and the goals they seek, yet there are certain common characteristics which make it possible to study them all together. The common denominator is that they all are dealing with men, in a goal-seeking association, expressed usually in some kind of a process dealing with some kind of material, existing with a social matrix, and interacting with other institutions while serving society.

The Climate Within Which Management Has and Must Function

The function of management is omnipresent. It exists in government as well as in industrial associations, and it exists in organized labor. However, while we maintain this, our accent in this paper is on the management of industrial enterprises. While there are many factors that influence management insofar as its decisions are concerned, we will first set forth six classes of influences:

1. The industrial institution known as the corporation;
2. Supplier of capital;
3. Labor, not as a supply but as a most important factor in production and society;
4. The State, Federal and local, as an institution;
5. The state of science and technology;
6. The social matrix—all those forces which determine the demand for the industrial institution's existence, but also those forces which influence and make demands upon the managers.

The making of decisions is regulated by the location of major power or by the relative weakness of the contenders. Therefore much can be learned about management by studying the relative power positions of those who bring pressures to bear upon management.

Management makes decisions and attempts to implement them, decisions about the goals of the institution which it is operating. Since different institutions have different goals, so different kinds of management will make different kinds of decisions but the process of decision making is universal. Decisions are made involving other people, men, machines, and process. Thus decisions are limited and are not free.

Throughout history there have always been rulers, people who possessed authority, made decisions, and exercised power. There has not always been calm acceptance of this power, and the early idea of ultimate and absolute power over all facets of life has been discarded completely in western civilization; in a word, power is divided. As power became divided and because so many of man's activities overlap, there is a natural conflict as to the relative division of this power.

The Industrial Association

Let us assume that an "industrial association" is an entity existing at a point of time in a force field which we will call the "social matrix." The industrial association is one kind of institution within that matrix—there are others.

Consider an association as an entity which has been formed in some manner. It interacts with the social matrix. It establishes routine channels of communication with other institutions, and it adjusts its internal structure, perhaps according to the principle of least effort. But certainly an association, at any instant, can be considered in a sort of "steady state" in the thermodynamic sense. It receives communications of various kinds, it carries on its process, it grows or decays—constantly readjusting within certain limits—and it emits communication.

The corporation is an important institution, worthy of far more thought than can be here devoted to it; it is old but its use for production is but little over 100 years old, and its public use almost exactly 100 years old. Its adoption was seized upon avidly and used widely and quite naturally there were abuses. As the abuses increased and the advantages gave unusual power to individuals and groups, quite naturally antithesis arose—the ICC, the Sherman Act, and so on.

The corporation of 1892 was predatory and exploitive; the corporation of 1952 is almost entirely concerned, as Peter Drucker has it, with self-perpetuation. It has, in effect, become a member of society with all the rights and responsibilities which accrue thereto.

The Supplier of Capital. Out of the same social matrix we shall abstract the supplier of capital as another directing force. Regardless of the kind of society, funds must flow, plants must be built, assets must be available. The problem then revolves about how this capital will be formed and the influence that the contributors of the capital will have upon the decision-making manager.

Time was when the venturer was the owner and usually the manager—but by the end of the nineteenth century there was already a distinct differentiation between the operative manager and the supplier of funds. The supplier of funds was a person who dealt in relatively large sums of money and management's decisions were slanted toward that person with money; ownership was important. The archetype of American Society was the successful individual entrepreneur.

Came the first World War and the "Baby Bond," followed by no-par-value stock. As more and more people went into the market, ownership became diffused until it was no longer an important individual controller. We had a new economic era; the American industrial corporation was no longer bound by the old economic laws. Employees owned stock, customers owned stock, everybody owned stock. Competition [8] was the great controller of our society. There were vague rumblings of discontent it is true, and there was a "farm problem," but finance and "Wall Street" were in the saddle.

Then 1929!! Since there had to be a scapegoat, the fingers pointed at the "banker." Banks were closed and at last money came to mean what it was designed to be, a medium of exchange, and the banker what he really is—a man performing a useful service for society. But who was to assume leadership? The banker was out, the industrialist was not yet ready to assume the onus—only the state remained, so, fumblingly at first but then with great confidence, government took over. . . . the "New

---

[8] Except in the public-utility field where the industrial mergers of a generation ago were being duplicated.

Deal," national planning, the good of society, the allocation of raw materials. . . . As World War II came, government assumed an increasingly important part in our economy and was increasingly a determinant in management's ability to make decisions. Regulative and administrative agencies entered into all the many facets of industrial and corporate life.

Furthermore, with a war upon us, government became a big customer—in many cases, the largest single customer. As such, government was in a position to exercise pressures upon management in a new direction—it could regulate as government but it also could control as the single most important customer. Now the state began to assume the dominant position in decision making that previously had been exercised by ownership, and the compass of management's valuation was turned from distribution of profits to the shareholders to operating within the limits of government restrictions.

Labor

Meanwhile labor, as an institution, has had its tides, its rises and falls. In actual fact, in the broad sweep, it was not until 1942 that there was any power-sharing with labor except in individual cases. At the turn of the century management offered jobs on a take-it-or-leave-it basis, regarding labor very definitely as a commodity to be bought and used. If the domestic market would not supply the labor, then labor was imported. The Sherman Anti-Trust Act and the "Yellow Dog Contracts" tied up labor even more completely; under them, when the job was taken, it had to be kept and labor became even more of a commodity, bought and contracted for, with the contract regarded as a most sacred thing. The 1920's did not improve labor's position greatly although it did lay the ground for many of the later gains. This "era of good will" was a time of prosperity when wages could be raised without too much trouble since it is more important not to have a work stoppage. From 1932 to 1942 many of the problems of labor organization were worked out; the pattern of the relations of labor to government and to management were explored and the groundwork was laid for many events which have left labor, at the opening of 1952, in a new position—a third contender for power in society.

While the "top" management of labor learned and grew to power in a struggle for recognition and power, and quite naturally, thinks in terms of immediate goals and fundamental differences, the younger men have experienced a period in which their right was recognized. Their problems have been problems of adjustment to situations of permanency rather than of emergency. It is believed that the next ten years will see a change in labor leadership of great importance which may well make possible great technological advances. As the unit cost of labor rises, management must increase productivity per labor unit and this can be done only by increased mechanization and increased participation by labor in labor- and waste-saving. If the demands of labor for continuity of employment are to be met, then labor in turn must guarantee against stoppage of production while disputes (and there always will be disputes) are going on, but management in turn must learn to control production and this has many curious implications.

The State

The state is one of man's earliest institutions but the American State of 1952, or the monolithic Russian State is a far different thing than the police-power state of, say, 1892. Here is a complete change of thinking in sixty short years. The ambit of the state's activity has increased to a point that no industrial decision today can be made without consideration of the State. In the early days, regulation and control were largely *ex post facto;* most regulative agencies were local as indeed were most enterprises.

The property of municipal administration was finally recognized in the growth of the city manager. The over-all need for forethought was reflected in the growth of planning agencies at all levels and the need for control gave rise to the regulative agency.

At the same time, administration within the state was changing drastically, both in kind and degree. The change in quantity is well known but there has been a great change in character as well, a professionalization of public administration and an examination of quality.

The Social Matrix. Next there is a set of what engineers may call imponderables but which we here name the "social matrix." None of us, nor our institutions, exists in a vacuum. On the contrary, there is an "N" dimensional sea of social forces that impinge on all of us and upon our institutions, forces which create our system of value judgments. For example, what was accepted as merely shrewd in 1892, may be criminal today, and what was once supposed to be a local responsibility is today a federal charge.

This thinking permeates our whole life and is, in this particular case, reflected in the position of the manager. A generation ago the profession of public-relations councilor was unknown, and few people formally consulted public opinion. Today most companies have public-relations councilors and public polls are avidly followed.

Interpersonal Relations. In the "good olde days" there was a very intimate relation between the manager (who was the owner) and the worker. For better or worse, good or bad, it was a direct and personal one, and man, it seems, craves personal relations. It is probably psychologically better to be browbeaten and kicked than to be ignored. While prior to 1892 there were large aggregations of labor, such aggregations were the exception rather than the rule. However, as aggregations grew, and this was not a rapid process, absentee ownership and professional management grew, and interpersonal relationships became increasingly impersonal.

True it was that there were many owners and managers who were humanitarians and who were interested in the "lot" of the worker, and who tried to "improve" matters—Pullman, Hershey, Kohler, and others, and it is a false stereotype to think of owners and managers deliberately "grinding the face of the worker into the ground."

416

There were abuses, but they were faults of omission rather than commission. Humanitarianism, however, did not, could not, will never work, because it is a gift from above as a favor and a favor may always (or, at least it is feared) be withdrawn. It is somewhat like the difference between the United States and the USSR Bill of Rights. That which is a "right of the people" is very different from that which is a "privilege" granted by a superior authority.

It has been said that there is a profound difference in the working force of 1952 and of the working forces of, say, 1942 and 1912, in large part resulting from the increasing educational age of the worker. This, in effect, means that there is a contraction of the difference of formal education between the manager and the person managed. This is important but can we say casually that the average increased educational age is advantageous? There are problems of adjustment and more additional years of formal education and especially modern education do not of necessity mean increasing ability to assume responsibility. The individual has greater rights and privileges, but is that reflected in greater assumption of social responsibility? People today are increasingly aware of their rights, but are they similarly aware of their responsibilities? This must be learned and the learning process is slow.

The State of Technology. A Newtonian physics yields very different results from a quantum theory, and the difference between Aristotelian and non-Aristotelian thinking is even greater. But we, in our pseudosophistication must not forget that there is a lag between the knowing and the general acceptance of the knowing.

Changes occur only in answer to stimuli. A useful means or mechanism may exist unused until there occurs a "reason" for its adoption and continuance. It may be adopted in isolated cases because of efforts of one man and acceptance by another. It may continue in isolation if the pressures which cause it to be accepted are maintained, but it will not gain widespread acceptance until and unless a "need" arises. By need is meant that its acceptance solves a recognized problem better than the way that problem is at present being solved.

Procedural and Process Evolution. It is in terms of the evolution in procedure and process that management progress has most commonly been considered. Procedure, that is to say, record keeping, and the like, and process: all those matters which are related to, or spring from, production engineering.

It is important to consider all the implications contained in the early Taylor work, for it included not only a small break with tradition, but a rather complete break: The worker was to be trained to do a specific job, not a total or general skill, but a specific job. That job was to be analyzed and the tool redesigned as requisite.

"The Art of Cutting Metal" is also equally provocative, for here is an illustration of solving a problem by a head-on attack. This had implications far beyond its particular field and may indeed be considered the basis to take off from the building of a rational theory of decision making.

The work of the Gilbreths, though independent, was a natural development. The job was still further analyzed into basic components (described as therbligs), the work place was studied, the positioning of the work was considered so that the worker could be taught to do the job in the most effective way.

From time and motion study to "simo-motion" chart and process charts, from work analysis to plant layout and materials handling, inventory control, location of toolrooms and economic lot size, the derivation is obvious. Routing, scheduling, and dispatching, man and machine loading, and the assembly line, lead inevitably to the completely automatic factory which is now a possibility.

The Streams of Management Theory and Their Contributions

Management has been said to consist of two related functions, "organization" which is "design," and "administration" which is "operation." The history of management may be viewed usefully from the point of view of the various schools of thought which have considered either the problem of organization or of administration. The problem of management for the future is to adapt the findings of these schools to practice and to set problems for these schools to study. In a word, it is said that research is essential and that it is the duty of modern management to encourage, aid, and abet research.

We will study the problem in terms of the following:

1. Knowledge of individual behavior;
2. The theory of groups;
3. The theory of communication;
4. A rational basis of decision making.

It is important, however, to realize that in any such approach we are abstracting from the whole. Any study must comprehend the "gestalt"—the physiological, the biological, the psychological, the sociological, the anthropological man, and indeed the spiritual man. It must not be forgotten that he is simultaneously all of these. In a somewhat similar manner while we have arbitrarily, perhaps, divided this section into four parts it must not be forgotten that they are all parts of a greater whole.

While the origin of much of the formal thinking about management was undoubtedly in the engineering field, yet management basically deals with human beings. Not unnaturally the psychologists have made important contributions.

Munsterberg's writings went largely unrecognized. It was the psychological tests of World War I that first gained recognition for the psychologist in the field of management. Here for the first time were tests applied to a large adult population. Management, always avid for help, believed that psychological tests were the answer to all their problems. Tests were applied widely; the round peg was fitted to the round hole. Unfortunately, it was found that both peg and hole reacted to each other and to time, and the perfectly fitting peg today will not necessarily fit tomorrow.

But psychology had much more to offer. Gillespie in England set forth that the task of management was to deal with inerts, dynamics, and purposives, by which he meant materials, machines, and men. He pointed out that men had aims, ideals, needs, and wants apart from the work association and that conflict and frustration arose within the individual which would be reflected in his work attitude. Lecky, a Columbia psychologist, while working for the Long Island Lighting Company, set forth a useful similar theory—the theory of self-consistency. This theory said that each individual was the center of his own particular universe and that all of life had to be consistent with his concept. In a word, Lecky explained the remark so often made in exasperation, "Who does he think he is?" for Lecky maintained that a person behaves in the manner of the person he thinks himself to be.

But it is not alone from the psychologist that insights are to be gained. The biologist and especially the mathematician-biologist, Rasheffsky at Chicago, and Von Bertelanfy at Toronto, seem to have much to offer. The biologist, of necessity, has developed considerable skill at taxonomy and is concerned with organization and adjustment.

Group Theory. Important though as understanding of the individual may be, industry is as much concerned with the behavior of people in groups. Basically this is the field of sociology but it is also the field of anthropology. It is only recently that the sociologist has moved out of studies of the family and similar institutions and that the anthropologist ran out of island and isolated cultures, and that both of them have looked at man in the work situation. The engineer has been doing the same for years. But the sociologist and the anthropologist bring new techniques and new ways of thinking to bear on an old problem. There is no doubt that an understanding of their theories can be of great importance to men charged with the responsibility of organizing and administering.

Group Dynamics. Group dynamics is intimately associated with the name of Kurt Lewin. In this country, after sampling many climates, he settled at the Massachusetts Institute of Technology, but his followers split up and now Michigan as well as M.I.T. inherit the mantle. Lewin's concept was a "field theory." The importance of his concepts are in the suggestions rather than in the concepts themselves. Lewin's topology and Bavelas' development of hodology remain nonoperational but highly suggestive.

Among others the sociologists have another school which for want of a better name may be called the "psychosociometric" school. What is, is, they say, and as you are so will you behave. Moreno and his group say, in effect, that a person's likes and dislikes are important, that you can measure the success of an association (or an organization) in terms of the satisfaction that the person within the association gets. They measure this in terms of whom do you like, whom do you talk with, whom do you like to be with, and so on. The psychodramatist's concept is based upon some hitherto unrecognized inspiration of Emma Sheriden Fry, a great actress of a generation ago.

Shartle, on the other hand, is distinctly different. His statistical mechanisms lead to the consideration of many factors—factor analysis—and the production of profiles. Will this man fit this job and how well? A courageous attempt to predict in a field where many doubt if it is possible.

Communication

When history has finally been written it may well be that the present period will be known as the period of "communication theory." It is important to realize what communication really means. It does not, for example, merely mean the ability to interchange messages—it is much deeper and much more important than that. It means the ability to interchange information and perhaps in the end the religious idea of "being in communion." At least, it has been recognized that most opposition arises not from fundamental differences, but because people do not understand one another. Perhaps the first in this area are Mayo, Roethlisberger, and, in general, the Harvard School of Business Administration which, by the case system, first investigated such individual situations. In spite of the obviously justifiable criticism of the case system there is no doubt of the great contribution which the school has made.

The case method has been followed by the interaction theory so ably set forth by Arensberg, Bales, Chapple, Homans, and Whyte. Here, with the exception of Bales and Homans, is an attempt to measure, without content, the interaction of people, of people in groups, and to educe scientific laws therefrom. Bales, with a system of twelve categories, attempts to measure intent in part as well as interaction.

The sociopsychologists and the psychiatrists by means of depth interviews, critical situation analysis, and similar techniques, attempt to get behind the obvious interactions that the interactionists measure and explain as well as express what is going on.

A Theory of Decisioning. It is the thesis of this paper that, in the end, the progress of management will be traced in terms of the emergence of a rational basis of decision-making.

In this aspect we can recognize a series of sequential and temporal steps in the history of management:

1. Importance of use of facts and data;
2. Rise of early statistical and graphical mechanisms;
3. Idea of partial goal setting and realization;
4. Control of quality, as well as quantity;
5. Information and communication theory, feedback, and cybernetics;
6. Operational analysis;
7. Process of decisioning.

1. The 1912 Report spent much time discussing the importance of making decisions based on facts and data rather than on hunch and judgments. Also, the idea of both internal and external facts: that means comparison. It seems hard to believe today that that should have needed to be discussed.

2. It was the interim report of 1919 that first widely introduced to engineers the statistical and graphical methods. Of course, part of the work of Gantt was graphical. However, the need of statistics arose as soon as the desirability of using data

and facts was accepted. The more facts and data were collected the less the human mind could comprehend, evaluate, and understand them. Statistics serve two major purposes:

  a. To reduce a mass of data to the number of numbers for which a person can comprehend the interrelations—five perhaps conveniently, and these five are

$$N, X, \sigma, \beta_1, \beta_2$$

  b. To discern interrelations—that is

  (1) Curve fitting $y = \phi X$
  (2) Correlating $y = \phi (XYZ \ldots \ldots)$

3. The first World War impressed upon management the concept of goal setting in time and the idea of partial goals and control; that is to say, measuring partial accomplishment *versus* partial goal and the necessity of expediting.

4. *Quality control:* While there was physical interchangeability during World War I, it was not as good as needed. Complete inspection schemes were expensive and some inspection is necessarily destructive. Between 1924 and 1932, Shewhart and others developed quality control and sampling. This was an extension of the control theory in part, but it was also a bridge to the concept of decision making. Statistical quality control inserted uncertainty into inspection—risk; consumers' risk and producers' risk. Before it had been a rather Aristotelian process—you knew or you didn't know. Now it was possible to evaluate the state of knowing or of not knowing, and to make decisions as to (*a*) rejection or acceptance; (*b*) changing or not changing.

5. *Information and communication theory; feedback and cybernetics:* Norbert Wiener and his cybernetics give us promise of the automatic factory which now is practical as well as possible, and Shannon and Weaver in the field of electrical communication have given us many useful ideas that will soon be embraced by the emergent theory of management. It may well be said that the future will not be so much concerned with gathering new data as it will be concerned with judging the pertinence and relevance of the information that it has available, its accuracy, and its usefulness.

6. *Operations research:* Operations research is a relatively new type of application of scientific thinking to certain kinds of management problems. It was developed extensively for quantitative study of military operations in the British and American forces during World War II. Obviously, not limited to the military, it is strongly analogous to the best work in scientific management. (For example, a good deal of Taylor's studies could be classified under this heading.)

This development, in which scientists of many disciplines contributed to the solution of many complex military problems, is now being extended to industry. Advanced techniques of quantitative analysis along with probability theory and statistics are being used to obtain answers to production, organization, and control problems. For example, the optimum number of maintenance personnel in a large transportation industry, the control of sales in a retailing operation, the development of sampling techniques in accounting are among the areas in which scientific team-work has been found to be fruitful. Development of new measurements of effectiveness in many fields such as scheduling optimal utilization of plant facilities, routing and control of traffic, or the conduct of a sales campaign can provide managers with a sound quantitative basis for decision. In such roles, operations research is an important achievement of the last decade and is destined to leave a profound influence on scientific management of the future.

7. *Process of decisioning:* If we expand the concept of decision making to include, on the one hand, the process by which the decision is arrived at, and on the other hand, to include the process by which we implement or make the decision "work," and if we further recognize that this is a continuing, dynamic process rather than an occasional event, then decisioning means something quite different than heretofore and becomes the basis of all managerial action.

The Future of Management—1952–1962

The year 1962 will mark the golden jubilee of the Scientific Management movement. What progress will be noted as we look back toward 1912, to what extent will we have moved from what was set forth in Taylor's monumental work? To what extent will we be able to say we have extended the concepts of those pioneers who founded the first management society? It is important that we be able to say that we have progressed, for the real problem of tomorrow, as it is of today, is "management." We must develop our knowledge of management, for in the end we must apply the principles of scientific management to the world or we will at least retrogress, or perish at the worst.

There will be a wider understanding of the fact that any association is dynamic and must be in a constant state of change. That is to say, the function of routine production will become widely differentiated, as it is in some companies, from the function of organization and analysis. It will be recognized increasingly that here is a continuous problem which requires continuous attention. The problem of long-time self-preservation is not identical with the problem of short-time profit-seeking. It is believed that these ten years ahead will see the development of a valid, operationally verifiable theory of management. There will have been a sufficient number of experimental tests in "on-going" situations to demonstrate its great potentialities and there will be widespread acceptance that management is, in part at least, a science, which will in no way deny that there may be an administrative art. Science may never produce genius, but it will help to avoid the little errors and mistakes which by compounding one another can build up into catastrophe.

Organization, as Alvin Brown understands it, will come into its own but not in a mechanistic sense. Synthesis will show how the findings of the social scientists, the anthropologists, the sociologists, and psychologists are related to, and modify the purely mechanistic approach of Gracuinas and Davis, and research will discover the functional form, as well as the design factors which will be used in producing more flexible productive structures.

The function of management, as suggested nearly a generation ago by Burnan, will become widely recognized but on a somewhat different level. The manager will increasingly become a catalyst, rather than a carrier of authority, a problem stater rather than a problem solver. Not so much because the problems are of increasingly greater difficulty, or because of their complexity, but because of the sheer number of people who will be involved by a single decision, and the need for their acceptance of the decision. Thus a decision accepted by a group does not need implementation and while the decision theoretically may not be as good as another, yet its acceptance may make it, on the one hand, more effective, and on the other hand, may build a bridge of acceptance to the total goal at a later date.

The average executive of today has far too much information—he knows too much about too many things and his time is far too much occupied with the consideration of unimportant things—"administrivia" as some unknown genius has phrased it. It is forecast that the next era of advancement will be in the evaluation of the pertinence and relevance of information, a field which is almost virgin. How much information is required to make a "good decision"? That, of course, depends upon the importance of the consequences of the decision. It is conceivable that a single piece of information might contain, say, 80 per cent of the relevant data and that a decision based upon that single piece of information might have a probability of being 0.8 successful. As additional information is received it does not follow that the decision made on the basis of the additional information will be successively better, but it does follow that the decision will be successively delayed, and that may be important. Thus an 80 per cent decision made today may be better than an 85 per cent decision made a week from today. All of this seems important but it is a matter which cannot be explored within the framework of this progress report but which is of great importance insofar as a theory of management is concerned.

We will increasingly use the available knowledge of the individual and of the group as our knowledge of communication and information theory grow, and most particularly we will gradually learn how to release the creative ability of the individual—the great potential of the future.

Conclusion

This paper appears under the name of Robert Teviot Livingston, the executive officer of the Department of Industrial Engineering at Columbia University, but a report such as this is never written by one man. In actual fact, every member of the staff of the Department made some distinct contribution, as, indeed, did the students. More especially is credit to be attributed to a research team under the direction of the author's graduate assistant—Mrs. Gene Weeks. This team consisted of Benedict

Wengler, Sociology; William S. Sachs, Economics; Richard S. Moore, Public Administration, who collected a mass of material from which this report is abstracted. My thanks are due them, and it is freely and gratefully offered.

In closing, however, may the author add that he feels very humble in the attempt to do justice, in these few words, to what is, he believes, one of the important movements of our modern world. The Greeks had a word for almost anything and while inadequate is not a Greek word, we will close on that accent.

INTERNATIONAL CO-OPERATION

Harold B. Maynard [9]

The latter half of the past decade has seen a tremendous growth in the exchange of scientific-management information among most of the industrial countries of the world. During World War II, the United States had demonstrated to the world that it could produce far greater quantities of materials than anyone had believed possible before. Communications among countries were difficult, however, and the methods by which this production was achieved were little known outside our own country.

Consequently, when the war came to an end and people in the war-devastated countries were faced with the need for the immediate production in large quantities of the many things that were required to restore a normal way of living, they turned to the United States eagerly for information on how to increase productivity. This eagerness for information had its impact on individuals, on management societies, and on governments, and stimulated an interest in American management know-how that was unprecedented.

Barriers to Individual Activity

Normally, a good deal of the demand for management know-how would have been satisfied by individual initiative. Industrial firms in various countries, for example, have long had arrangements for obtaining patents, licenses of various types, management know-how, and the like, from one another. American management consultants have worked in countries around the world introducing American methods and techniques. After the war, however, the difficulties of making working arrangements of this type with American firms or consultants were greatly increased by currency-exchange barriers. It was difficult for Americans to receive payment for services in dollars, and since foreign currencies were spendable only in the countries in which they were issued, there was not much desire to accept payment in local money.

In spite of these difficulties, there has been a good deal of international co-operation on an individual basis. Such arrangements have been most effective and

[9] President, Methods Engineering Council, Member, American Society of Mechanical Engineers.

have made up in quality what they have lacked in quantity. When and if currency-exchange barriers are removed, an immediate upsurge in co-operative arrangements among individuals in various countries unquestionably will result.

Management-Society Activities

The management societies in various countries have been co-operating in the exchange of management know-how on a tremendously increased basis since the end of the war. As soon as hostilities ceased and communications were restored, the national management societies in various countries through CIOS, the International Committee on Scientific Management, began to plan for the Eighth International Management Congress. Because of the war, no Congress had been held since the Washington Congress in 1938. Therefore there was a great interest in Europe in organizing a Congress as quickly as possible and in securing American papers for it in all management areas to fill the gap in communications caused by the war.

The Eighth Congress was held in Stockholm in July, 1947. Over a hundred American delegates attended, for the most part traveling to and from the Congress in a group on the steamship *Drotningholm*. On the voyage over, the delegates held a series of preparatory meetings during which they discussed not only the management information in which it was felt the other countries would be most interested but also how to present this information in a way which would be likely to gain its acceptance.

The Congress itself was ably organized by the Swedish National Committee. The papers and the sessions at which they were discussed provided the opportunity for the exchange of information on a formal basis. The social occasions—of which there were many, all excellently planned and executed—permitted the exchange of information on an informal basis. The informal exchanges were at least as valuable as the more formal sessions. They enabled individuals from different countries to become well acquainted and resulted in the formation of a number of international friendships. Many of these have endured ever since and have helped to keep the channels of international management communications open.

At the business sessions of the Congress it was agreed unanimously that CIOS had a vital function to perform in the postwar world in encouraging the free exchange of management information among its member national committees. It was voted to establish a permanent paid secretariat and to provide funds for operation which would permit CIOS to function between international Congresses.

Growth of the National Management Council

The body representing the United States in international management affairs is the National Management Council. It was formed at the beginning of the preceding decade, namely, in 1933. Up to that time international co-operation in management affairs had been somewhat sporadic. It started off auspiciously enough in 1923 when the government of the newly created republic of Czechoslovakia under the leadership of its scientist-president Masaryk, invited a number of countries to participate in a meeting for the exchange of ideas and experience in the field of industrial management. At the Congress which was held in Prague in July, 1924, each meeting was presided over by two officers, one representing Czechoslovakia and one the United States. This Congress resulted in the creation of CIOS and the beginning of permanent international co-operation.

To direct American participation in other Congresses which were held in Brussels in 1925, in Rome in 1927, in Paris in 1929, and in Amsterdam in 1932, an "American Committee on Participation, International Management Congresses" was set up. It functioned on an informal, volunteer basis, without any substantial support from other management groups. Although it succeeded always in having American delegates and papers at the International Management Congresses, the representation from the United States at the Amsterdam Congress was so pitifully inadequate it became evident that some more effective means of fostering international co-operation was necessary.

As a result of subsequent discussion a joint invitation to consider what should be done was extended in December, 1932, to a number of American management groups by the presidents of the American Marketing Society, the National Office Management Association, the Society of Industrial Engineers, and the Taylor Society. A meeting was held on December 20, 1932, which was attended by representatives from these four societies and in addition representatives of the American Committee on Participation, International Management Congresses; American Management Association; The American Society of Mechanical Engineers; Association of Consulting Management Engineers; National Association of Cost Accountants; and Personal Research Federation.

This meeting was addressed by the late Dr. Harry Arthur Hopf. After tracing the development of the management movement both in America and abroad, Dr. Hopf concluded with the following recommendation:

> As a constructive proposal for joint consideration by the management associations and societies represented at this gathering, the president of the American Marketing Society, the president of the National Office Management Association, the president of the Society of Industrial Engineers, and the president of the Taylor Society have the honor to recommend to their colleagues in the management field the formation of a national management council and to invite their participation in such a cooperative undertaking.
>
> In advance of discussion of this proposal, it is hardly appropriate to refer to the practical aspects which will undoubtedly present themselves for consideration. The presidents of the four organizations named deem it fitting, however, to record the view that a national management council, in addition to addressing itself to matters of broad, general concern to the management movement as a whole, will be in a position to strengthen the relations of the constituent bodies to each other,

to further their intensive development, and to provide a basis for group action whenever that may appear desirable.

The National Management Council was formed as a result of this meeting on June 8, 1933. It continued to sponsor United States participation in international congresses, culminating with the organizing of the Seventh International Management Congress which was held at Washington in September, 1938.

The war then intervened, and the National Management Council by mutual agreement remained largely inactive during the war years. When the war ended, it again came to life and organized the American participation in the Stockholm Congress in 1947.

Up to this point the National Management Council had always functioned largely without funds, relying on the voluntary services of interested individuals for getting its work accomplished. When at Stockholm, it was agreed that CIOS should operate on a full-time basis, it was evident that NMC also would have to be organized in a more permanent fashion. In addition, at Stockholm NMC had agreed to give CIOS substantial financial support, although it was itself without funds at the moment.

With new objectives and new commitments, NMC examined itself after the Stockholm Congress and revised its form of organization and its methods of operation. With the generous support of its management society members and with the aid of a loan—since repaid—from the societies, it set up and staffed a permanent office, adopted a new set of by-laws, and secured new members from management societies, commercial and industrial firms, and educational institutions. It co-operated fully with CIOS and with the national committees of other CIOS countries and began to develop channels and methods of international co-operation far more effectively than had been possible in the past. During 1947 to 1949, NMC managed to meet its commitments in full and to develop itself to the point where it was able to accept the unusual opportunity for international co-operation which presently developed.

Government-Sponsored Activities

The need for co-operative assistance to the war-ravaged countries of Europe which was recognized by the Stockholm Congress also was recognized by the governments of the countries concerned. The Anglo-American Council on Productivity was set up presently to facilitate the exchange of management and technical know-how between the United Kingdom and the United States of America. This was followed by the establishing of the Economic Cooperation Administration or the Marshall Plan with a Technical Assistance Division keenly interested in doing all that it could to encourage increased productivity. A little later the program of assistance to underdeveloped countries was proposed by the President of the United States in his famous "Point 4," and another area of co-operation in the field of international management was opened.

The government programs had behind them huge grants of money. They had the funds which the management societies lacked, but they lacked the management know-how which the members of the management societies had. This situation in the United States was quickly recognized by the National Management Council. Early in 1950 an arrangement was worked out between ECA and NMC, whereby the latter placed at the disposal of ECA its assistance in handling the teams of management people which ECA was beginning to bring from other countries in increasing numbers.

During 1950, 1951, and 1952, the National Management Council guided the training of a number of visiting teams. It did not limit its activities to this form of co-operation, however, but took the initiative in finding other ways of giving assistance. In 1951 it developed the mechanism of the management seminar. Under NMC leadership, small teams of American management experts were sent abroad to hold seminars on management subjects in various countries in Europe. The United States teams met with groups of foreign industrialists and technicians in their cities and discussed the application of management principles to their own problems. This seminar activity is continuing at the present time.

Another important event in the field of international co-operation took place in the fall of 1951. Realizing that an understanding of and a desire for increased productivity must permeate all levels of management before any appreciable results can be obtained, NMC recognized the necessity of bringing the story to top-management people in other countries. Working in co-operation with the National Association of Manufacturers and ECA, it organized what came to be known as "Operation Impact." This project brought over 250 top European executives to the United States in November and December, 1951. They were given the opportunity to meet with and talk freely to men of equal rank and with similar interests in this country. The result was that a new area of international co-operation and understanding was opened on a very important management level.

The co-operation between NMC and ECA not only assisted importantly in spreading a knowledge of sound management procedures throughout Western European countries, but it enabled NMC to earn the funds which it needed to meet its primary obligations. Thus it has been able to give increasing support to CIOS. Furthermore, these activities have not interfered with its other major purposes. Throughout 1949, 1950, and 1951, the National Management Council worked on preparations for the Ninth International Management Congress which was held at Brussels, Belgium, in July, 1951.

Ninth International Management Congress and Future Plans

This Congress developed an interesting new method of international co-operation. At previous Congresses the papers which were presented for discussion were prepared by individual authors. This of necessity somewhat limited the viewpoint from which they were presented. It was decided by the Executive Committee of CIOS that the papers for the Ninth Congress would be prepared by committees. The responsibility for the preparation of each paper was assigned to a specific country. This country set up a committee to take the lead in producing the paper. The other countries who were interested in contributing then set up collaborating committees. They worked with the main committee in the lead country, contributing reports which were included in the final report. Thus, in preparing the twelve papers which were presented at the Brussels Congress, over 600 individual management people co-operated.

It may be seen from what has been said that from a rather low prewar level and a period of practically no activity during the war, international co-operation in the field of management has been increasing at an accelerating rate since 1945. There is every reason to believe that it will continue to increase in the foreseeable future barring major dislocations such as war or economic disaster.

The International Management Congresses, for example, will continue to be held. The Tenth Congress is scheduled to be held in São Paulo, Brazil, in February, 1954. The papers will be prepared again by the method of international co-operation just described. In addition, it is planned to subdivide the congress delegates into small groups of twenty-five to fifty so that they will be able to discuss the papers in small, intimate, round-table meetings. This not only will provide the opportunity for freer discussion, but it will enable the delegates to become better acquainted.

The 1957 Congress has already been spoken for by both Australia and Switzerland. Although it probably will be more convenient for the Europeans to hold it in Switzerland, it is interesting to observe the desire of the Australians to play an increasingly active part in international management affairs.

At the moment of writing there are 16 countries who are members of CIOS. Several additional applications for membership are pending. Through the activities of CIOS, the member national committees are being encouraged both to greater efforts to spread scientific management within their own countries and to fuller co-operation with the management committees in other countries.

The stimulus to international co-operation provided by government will continue in the future. The Technical Assistance Division of the Mutual Security Agency—the successor to ECA—is currently greatly interested in stepping up education for productivity in many countries. Its Advisory Group on European Productivity through its Subcommittee on Education for Productivity is making an informal survey of the problems involved which will lead to specific recommendations. This survey is being conducted with the assistance of over a hundred management people in other countries—another evidence of the way international co-operation is increasing.

It is apparent that we are now living in an international world. Problems which formerly were considered as local or national in nature are now being discussed on an international level. Management is no exception. People everywhere in the world are increasingly insisting upon a better way of life. They are demanding more in the way of material things. To be able to have those things it is necessary to increase productivity everywhere. This is obvious not only to the managers of industry but to governments and workers and all people everywhere. Interest in increasing productivity is on the ascendent, and people are looking to America to help them find the answers. American management—although humbly aware that it does not know all that there is to know and anxious to make the exchange of management information a two-way process—has shown a statesman-like recognition of its obligation to help others less fortunate in every way that it can. Since 1945, international co-operation has been more than a mere phrase. It has become a practical reality. It will continue to be practiced on a widening scale in the decade which lies ahead.

PANEL DISCUSSION

AMERICAN SOCIETY OF MECHANICAL ENGINEERS TEN-YEAR PROGRESS REPORT OF THE MANAGEMENT DIVISION

Remarks on "The Changing Structure of Management"

Harold F. Smiddy

We stand in giant footprints here today, trying to find a clear continuation of the path heretofore marked out in these classic "Ten-Year Reports on Management Progress" which Mr. Alford pioneered for American Society of Mechanical Engineers in 1912, 1922 and 1932, and which Mrs. Gilbreth's committee brought forward after his death before 1942.

Our immediate problem is to define this path plainly through the maze of the complex economy and society which have resulted from the dominant influence of hot war and cold war on a global scale during the ensuing decade. And we do this, knowing that the Golden Jubilee of the American Management Movement in 1962 is but a scant ten more years in front of us.

Professor Livingston's "Ten Year Progress Report" is in the Alford tradition. Brevity forces it to be more of a "Balance Sheet" of the status of Management at the end of this decade than a real "Profit and Loss" record of the gains and set-backs during the period. This is not serious, though the need—in the interest of such brevity —to omit a listing of some of the more fundamental *reasons why* the Progress of Management was shaped as it actually evolved, will be more painful to future scholars than to those of us who lived through the Fateful Forties. I have made one brief list of some of those striking forces and would like to note them for the record if time allows during our discussion period.

For the present few moments, I would like, however, to do three things. *First,* stress a basic *"good point"* which hit me as I read the Progress Report. *Second,* comment on what seemed to me to be one fundamental *weakness,* or "bad point," in Professor Livingston's appraisal of the Management Movement. *Third,* propose an approach for developing a true Science of Management, and a teachable, usable

Theory of Management, which might be in harmony with the "good point" and get around the "bad point" in his scholarly Report.

First, therefore, it is a "good point" that the paper stresses boldly the "need for greater progress in developing a true Science of Management," and not merely "progress in management mechanisms."

Again brevity compels over-harsh statement of the case. We cannot seriously agree *entirely* that "progress is largely a continuously branching specialization and intensification of detail, with very little feed-back into the stream of theory." The very growth of American Society of Mechanical Engineers' Management Division, the Society's largest, negates so sweeping a conclusion. So do the parallel and tremendous growths of the membership and programs of all of our other management and professional societies in the last decade; not to mention the development of our business schools to where they have enrollments and curricula undreamed of ten years ago.

The fact that the programs and contributions of all these societies are not adequately integrated or used as yet, in no sense nullifies the tremendous progress they have made; and we should not let this day pass without noting the breadth and significance of such progress.

But having said so, we can agree with Professor Livingston that there is still terrific need for more attention—by men of good minds and of great experience—to developing, to stating and to propagating a fundamental "Theory of Management" which is clearer than any we now have; and which is more in consonance with the over-powering requirements imposed by the size and the complexity of the tremendous operations and institutions which today's Managers are, in fact, called upon to *manage.*

Parenthetically, the current wave of expansion of Management Society efforts to expanded "Management Development" plans and programs in so many individual companies is but further proof of widespread basic awareness of the need for more understanding of the work of Management and of a more scientific approach to the task of rationalizing the nature and understanding of such work.

To express a personal opinion, many such "plans" seem much too limited, in both scope and imagination. Many are only inventories of prospective Executive jobs and personnel requirements. Others are only schemes to prepare a limited few for promotion to higher executive jobs. These are not the basic problems. The root of it is to recognize that *self-development* has to be the foundation and that the need is to raise understanding of Management Theory and Principles, and then connect application to cases, by *all* members of Management.

This broader goal is necessary for these reasons. *First,* continuity of Management of today's very large institutions is a "public must" and this involves the whole body of Managers in all ranks, not alone the few who will be promoted to higher echelons. *Second,* training and helping the whole group to grow will itself be the best insurance of the required supply of men for top-Management posts. *Third,* raising the *whole level* of performance of Management work is deeply essential to the obvious needs,

431

challenges and opportunities of the future Industrial Society which is unfolding before us.

Going to my *second* chore, I am bothered at what seems to me to be an almost fatal weakness in Professor Livingston's appraisal of how to develop a more acceptable Theory of Management. This "bad point" is difficult to isolate and express without reviewing his whole penetrating text. Let me put it two ways:

First, he talks about "Management" taking action or making decisions. We should talk about *Managers.* Only *individuals* are actually endowed with the power to think, reason or decide; definitely not groups as such.

Second, he refers to a "Social Matrix," or whole social environment, as a mixture and source of so-called "*forces* which determine the demand for the Industrial Institution's existence and also those *forces* which influence and make demands upon the Managers." This approach permeates the analysis and must be noted despite parallel recognition that "while the nuclear scientist has unlocked the hitherto untapped energies of the atom the great potentialities of men's brains, ingenuity, genius (and creative abilities) remain only partially utilized."

This is a straight materialistic philosophy and it will not provide a base for a Theory of Management that will be more palatable to the men managed than the inadequate brand causing our present failures. It is at the root of the dilemma of our scientists, and *their* parallel lack of full and wholesome acceptance as yet by the great majority of their fellow men.

The weakness of the philosophy was sharply apparent in the press reports last month of the views of Dr. Harold Urey, Nobel prize-winning nuclear scientist, when he postulated that the Earth originally was "a vast pool of complex chemical compounds" which reacted and interacted to develop, in turn, a complex series of chemical intermediates and then a "protein molecule" and others like it from the pool of raw materials; and, to quote, "eventually, *by chance* (and I emphasize those two key words), the first bacterium, representative of the most elemental form of *life* developed," and spread 'til "plant life flourished and animal life followed inevitably."

This poses the great question, the ultimate question of Mankind—of the men whom Managers must manage. And as Science widens the complex field it covers, the resultant *Disorder* which is inherent in the "by chance" concept multiplies accordingly.

The true search of the *people* of the World is for Order, not chance.

"Management" should be the Science of bringing the kind of Order which nature exhibits all about us; and of doing so by applying a process of rational Organization to the relationships in which men associate. This is our deep need. As individuals we show little or no more capacity or ability or emotional steadiness than the able men among our forebears. Yet unfolding Science brings new complexities. It is the Manager's job to match them with patterns of simplicity among such complexities which will win the comprehension and acceptance of the individual Men being managed.

Both scientific patterns and business patterns, however, have so far failed to win such acceptance to an adequate degree. That is the real reason for the condition, the real nature of the failure, which Professor Livingston discerns. The need of the day, as always, is to seek those kinds of patterns which—like those of the great Religions of the World—have alone had the power to arouse the faith and hold the support of the great body of individual men and women throughout the Ages.

A true "Science of Management," therefore, must rise above, and derive its principles or truths, from a level above what Professor Livingston calls the "Social Matrix" as a force *determinant* of its progress. Until then, as Professor Livingston has so aptly said in another recent paper,

> although well developed practice can develop without a parallel theory and can operate with reasonable satisfaction, yet practice without theory remains in essence an Art, and is not subject to any criterion except the practical one of "Does it work?"

A Theory—or a profession—is obviously needed to explain the *reasons* for the practices of Managers—and to explain *why* they work. Until then there is far too much likelihood that, as Disraeli so sharply said, "A practical man is one who continues to practice the mistakes of his predecessors."

My *third* effort here is to propose an approach for developing a true "Science of Management"; and a teachable, usable "Theory of Management," to meet the needs, and the criteria, so ably developed in Professor Livingston's Progress Report. This approach may be summarized in ten steps, as follows:

1. There is a foundation for a true "Science of Management";
    One which will be invariate and one whose principles derive from a higher level than the changing forces and pressures of the current Social Matrix; and
    One which can be stated, verified, taught and used as a process in which the principles themselves can be applied to mold the results of Management to approach the desired objectives of the Enterprise in spite of the Social pressures impinging.
2. Such a true "Science of Management," however, will have to be rooted in:
    The principles of Liberty, not the principles of Compulsion
    The principles of Reason, not the principles of Force
    The principles of Leadership by Integration of voluntary individual efforts in cooperative teamwork, and not the principles of Leadership by Command, Control or Dictation; and, therefore, in
    The principles of Morality, not the principles of Materialism,
    The principles of Religion, not the principles of Atheism; and finally in,
    The deep belief that, however complex Society and its Social interrelationships may ever become, the natural rights of the Individual as a Person, including the right to acquire and hold property, are of a different *order of priority* than *all* of the other rights in the so-called Social Matrix; and in recognition that if such *other* rights are to have validity or permanency, they

must themselves flow from initial, voluntary agreement of the *Individuals* concerned to modify their maintenance of their *full* personal Liberties mutually for their mutual, or collective, security or benefit.

Any "theory" which looks at the Social Matrix as only a homogeneous bundle or mixture of resultant modified rights, without distinguishing always the *basic rights* of the *individual persons* from their voluntary concessions in the interest of teamwork, is founded on error; and can only continue the confusion which Professor Livingston so vividly depicts in his "Ten-Year Progress Report."

3. Since collective institutions in which many individuals join their efforts are, therefore, basically possible *only* because of such voluntary modification and interchange of their respective individual rights, the principles of a Science of Management must derive from a correct understanding of such fundamental relationships.

4. Basic among the rights of the *individuals* in Society—once we grant that they are separately Men with Reason rather than only peculiar configurations of chemical molecules—is the right to own, and hence to buy and sell, property.

In other words, unless our Social structure—and our Business Economy—are built firmly on the personal right of free choice of the *Customer* in the Marketplace, it is built either on sand which will crumble or on force which will fail.

5. Since *all* members of Society—be they managers, engineers, employees, shareowners, vendors, educators, clergymen, legislators, government officials, or what have you—are *also Customers* as individuals, this fact affords a focal point of *common* interest among them about which Integration of their respective efforts in their *other*—and highly diverse—capacities may be developed.

And more than that, a point about which such diverse interests may be Integrated for their mutual progress, satisfaction and ability to live and work together in a State of Order.

And mark it well, it is a State of *Order* which they all long for, and which is their *real* desire rather than the "Economic Security" which would come *from* such Order; and which political and other leaders so frequently mistake for their deeper and more fundamental yearnings.

6. Building the economy (and the Plans, Policies and Objectives of its enterprises) on the Customer, and hence on the Free Market, gives the Managers of the resultant Enterprises that genuine legitimacy which flows from the *Common Purposes* of the Leaders and the Followers.

The Managers are thus given a valid starting point from which to *Plan*, as the initial sub-functional task of their distinctive—and ultimately their *professional*—work as Managers.

Hence, it lets them go on from *such* initial Planning to develop a valid *Process of Management* which can be preserved despite the impact of varying Social pressures; just because the Principles, or Truths, which guide it have been anchored to a higher level of Order and Reason than such impinging Social forces and compulsions.

7. With the foundation, and the starting point, of the Science of Management thus defined, the rest of its process flows in readily recognizable elements.

These, however much they may be subclassified or regrouped, rest on an over-all concept of Management as Leadership through the following four subfunctional kinds of Managerial work:

a. *Planning*—the initial task, just described, to set objectives and to outline Plans and Policies, or Guides, to attain them.

b. *Organizing*—to describe the total work needed to be done to achieve the designated objectives; to classify that work into a pattern of orderly tasks and relationships; to designate men for such defined tasks; and to delegate to such individual workers, including the Managers themselves, the authority, responsibility and accountability to do the work; then

c. *Integrating*—to blend the efforts of such individual workers by inspiring from each both maximum personal initiative and creative output on his assigned job and place on the team, as well also as good voluntary coöperation, self-discipline and teamwork to achieve optimum flow, pace and synchronism of their mutual and collective tasks and performance to meet objectives, standards and schedules; and finally, *at every stage* of the Management Process,

d. *Measuring*—to get, analyze and use facts, to the end that decisions by all concerned may be on what Harry Hopf liked to call the "Authority of Knowledge" rather than on the authority of rank or force;

And to the end also that as such facts flow from the *Measuring* process, as one of these four basic subfunctions of the *work* of Managing, they are in turn used to "close the loop" of the Management Process by feeding back such information to modify the continuing parallel subfunctions of the work of Management, as Leadership through Planning, through Organizing and through Integrating.

In turn, the process again repeats and goes on to its Measuring phase, so that, over-all, it results in Management to best use the available human and material resources of the Enterprise to attain its designated objectives economically, profitably, competitively and on sound time schedules.

8. In this sense, "Management" becomes truly a profession, built on a genuinely factual and scientific base. It becomes, therefore, a distinct kind of work from the other functional kinds of work of a business, such as research and engineering, manufacturing, marketing, financial and accounting, public and employee relations and legal work.

Yet it is integrated with them to the twin ends that the efforts of all individuals in the Enterprise may be smoothly blended with each other, and also that the Enterprise itself may be integrated harmoniously into the Society of which it is a part.

9. Particularly notable is the fact that such a "Science of Management" *inherently* incorporates the seeds of solution of such other troublesome problems as those of Integrating and blending successfully the efforts, for example, of both Engineers and Managers; of both white-collar and manual workers; of both the leaders and the followers.

10. Finally—but by no means least important looking ahead to our urgent desire to report better fundamental Progress at the 1962 Golden Jubilee of the Management Movement—such a concept of a "Science of Management," and of a teachable Theory of Management, does have within itself great resources for that improved feedback from the field of daily practice to the basic stream of Theory, whose current absence Professor Livingston so rightly deplores.

This is of utmost significance today when one of the critical limitations on the validity, scope and acceptability of Management of the ever-larger Institutions of our complex, technological Society, is so fast being removed.

Reference is intended, of course, to the rapidly-spreading understanding of the new Science of Cybernetics; and of the new methodology of that guiding and fateful handmaiden of Cybernetics which has come to be called "Operations Research."

For these two, used skillfully together, place us on the threshold of a new era in performing the *"Measuring"* subfunction of the work of Professional Management. And it will be an era in which the availability of new data, new data-using techniques and new electronic data-handling machines are fast eliminating past Managerial limitations due to inability to get and use, adequately and promptly, the facts genuinely needed to make sound decisions.

Today, despite the growing size and complexity of our Institutions, such needed facts are becoming available for the Manager to use in selecting objectives and trends, and also in setting good standards of performance, points of reference and patterns of work.

In turn such patterns can increasingly be communicated with clarity and understanding to all concerned. And all concerned can, in their own turn, then proceed creatively and with initiative; understanding both their individual jobs and their relationships as a team in voluntarily planning and regulating their respective efforts to participate in helping to meet the objectives set up for the Enterprise *as a whole.*

From such progress in *Measuring*, and the kind of understandable communication which it facilitates, can come the long-sought ability of Managers to project *"Patterns of Order,"* which can be "candles in the dark" to shed light on our deeper problems of today and of the decade ahead.

Included are such problems as those of solving the mystery of reviving *individual* satisfaction in jobs in Enterprises so complex that division of labor and skills to tasks which are relatively minute, and hard-to-identify with the whole, is essential if the Manager is to bring the over-all job within the capacity of ordinary individuals to perform.

And, finally, included also are even such problems as projecting *Principles of Organization*—and of Order—into the Management not only of our new Big Business enterprises, but also of our new Big Unions, Big Educational Institutions, and Super-big Governments on the international as well as the national scene.

REBUTTAL TO HAROLD F. SMIDDY'S COMMENTS
Robert T. Livingston

Harold Smiddy apparently wishes to trap me into the unenviable position of defending materialism and simultaneously attacking moralism, free enterprise, liberty, reason, justice and the American Way of Life. However, I am sure that this is merely a case which demonstrates the fundamental difficulty of communicating in this field of management where we are concerned not only with a theory, but with a value system.

This discussion will follow Mr. Smiddy's three points. First, as to "progress in the development of a Theory of Management."

That progress has been made in management was not denied in my paper, but the basic theme was that progress in the development of a valid theory of management has not kept pace with the development of means and mechanism, and is, I think, undeniable. It may well be that theory and practice, in any field, proceed in alternate steps, that the implications of certain theoretical concepts take a long time to be explored, developed, applied and evaluated.

That there has been a tremendous increase in students in Management at both Engineering and Business Schools, and that various Management Societies are very active testifies to the growing interest in management, and to the increasing complexities and importance of the problems facing managers, but is *not* testimony to advances in the development of a Theory of Management.

In part, I think that Mr. Smiddy's objections rise in semantic misunderstanding, and also in part because of the necessary brevity of the presentation. I shall not argue with the criticism that "Managers, not Management, make decisions." Nor with certain other misunderstandings, such as thinking that I set forth the thesis that the social matrix was a "homogeneous bundle or mixture of modified rights."

Mr. Smiddy's second point apparently was that a theory of management should "derive its principles" from what, in effect, is a system of ethics or fundamental beliefs about human rights.

An answer to that point is difficult to make without changing misunderstanding. I have a deep and abiding love for my country and have demonstrated my belief in the American Way of Life by my writings. But these writings were not in engineering or scientific journals, nor did I attach any engineering or scientific validity to them. These, I said, are my beliefs.

Mr. Smiddy's otherwise excellent presentation and critique with which I do not disagree as a matter of personal faith, falls down when he fails to distinguish between process and purpose, between theory and application. In a word, Mr. Smiddy proposes the teaching of a faith and a belief as an engineering theory. There are obvious and great dangers in this as has already been demonstrated in the field of genetics, in the U.S.S.R.

J. G. Bennett in his recent book, *The Present Crisis in Human Affairs*, clearly points out the difference which comes in when we introduce human value systems and transcendental knowledge into engineering and scientific problems, and believes that the resolution of the superficially apparent problem between Mr. Smiddy and myself is the really important problem of today.

The theory of management, like the theory of thermodynamics, is equally applicable anywhere and is only applicable, without modification, to "perfect" systems. This, too, is true, for example, in thermo and the law of perfect gases. Such inapplicability and lack of moral judgment is the nature of a theory.

A knife, a gun, atomic energy all have great possibilities of use for the good of the human race, but they also have possibilities of misuse to human disgrace. So, too, with a Theory of Management. If there is such a thing as a Theory of Management, it will apply in Soviet Russia even as it applies in America. But, and this is the profound difference, the purposes to which it is put and the values which are applied, will be the differentiation.

Now what about the third point—a teachable, invariant Theory of Management— deriving from these higher principles and ethics. This thesis is, of course, inherent in any scientific theory and was presumed in my consideration of a theory. However, if Mr. Smiddy criticizes on the one hand that my concept did not include values and morals, and claims on the other that his proposal *is* scientifically valid, and especially as to variance and measurement, then he must permit his presentation to be submitted to the very judgments which he proposes.

If the theory is based upon "higher principles," then we must state those principles in "invariant" and measurable terms. Principles, except perhaps for a very few basic ones, have varied in time, do vary in place, and vary from person to person. They can only be invariant if stated in such broad terms that they cover all but the most fundamental contradictions.

As he says so well, we must measure, and measurement presupposes a scale. Perhaps the questions of morals, the free enterprise system, liberty, and the like can be categorized, but I do not believe that they can be measured—at least at our present state of sophistication. At best, we can measure, in some scale, *accomplishment,* and impute that morals, the American Way of Life, free competition, and the right to own property and to dispose of it, are *the* important determinants of these material, intellectual and other accomplishments.

In closing, may I repeat that I join Mr. Smiddy, *as an individual*, with the liberty of personal judgments, that our country and culture give in an appreciation, love and willingness to fight for the American Way of Life and the System of Individual Opportunity, but I cannot prostitute my professional and scientific ethics by setting forth that this, my *faith*, flows directly from any engineering or scientific laws or theories of which I am presently aware.

SOME FUNDAMENTAL FACTORS AND TRENDS RESPONSIBLE FOR CHANGES IN PROBLEMS OF MANAGEMENT IN LAST TEN YEARS (1942–1952)

Harold F. Smiddy

The best characterization of the changes in the last ten years is probably embodied in Fenton B. Turck's phrase, "The American Explosion"—the accumulated result of three hundred years of an environment of freedom; vitalized by the mixing and freshening of blood-streams, based on the strength and greatness of the individual, living in a climate of "vitality, open-mindedness, individualism, coöperation and ingenuity."

The resultant "explosive" factors and trends had ramifications throughout the whole economy. They were productive of major changes in political, social, economic and spiritual values. Some of the more striking of such factors may be listed under the major categories of (1) War, (2) Government, (3) Science and Technology, (4) Business Organization and Management, and (5) Home and the Individual.

I. WAR

1. The single dominant influence for change and for creation of management problems has been War—either "hot" or "cold" War, but War on a global scale throughout the decade.
2. This War was financed by modern Credit mechanisms but it has not been paid for and is still represented by staggering debts (either outstanding or chaotically repudiated) throughout the World; with convulsive effects and strains on all important individual, national and international relationships.
3. The net effect has been interference with Individual Liberty and with the Free Market which has been cataclysmic in its proportions and repercussions—in all countries.
4. The necessity to marshall military Force, and weapons, of unprecedented scope has given terrific favorable impulse to the advancement of Research and Science; and has aroused the minds of men to think deeply on ultimate questions of Liberty or Freedom *versus* Force or Compulsion.

II. GOVERNMENT

1. As the common agent of the people and public, Government has borne the full brunt of the reactions released by War on a global scale.
2. The physical and financial requirements, first of a "hot" War and then of a

"cold," or mixed military and civilian, economy, has spread Government control to production, technology, personal liberty, finance, and trade; all to permit marshalling Force on a world-wide scope.

3. Resultant extraordinarily high tax rates have drastically changed all normal economic relationships and bases for planning and decisions.

4. The progressive drawing of issues between Systems of Compulsion, Force and Materialism and Systems of Liberty, Reason and Religion, has brought public interest and participation in Government to an entirely new degree.

5. As issues and forces became more complex and technical, at a progressively less comprehensible pace, Governments have been drawn in to protect and advance the social gains of individuals; and to achieve some rough balance among powerful big forces and institutions in the political, economic and social structure of a wholly new kind of Industrial Society.

6. Consequently, Government has outstripped—both nationally and internationally—available Principles of Administration; which were never formulated for application to derive Order and hold off Chaos in such large-scale political, social and economic activities.

III. SCIENCE AND TECHNOLOGY

1. The requirements both of War and of the Industrial Society have terrifically multiplied Research and Technology.

2. The resultant scientific discoveries have increasingly been found to be inter-locked with each other; from Physics and Mechanics, to Electricity and Electronics, to Chemistry and Metallurgy, to Nucleonics, Cybernetics and Relativity.

3. Development of Fuels and of Power has proceeded at a rapidly accelerating rate; where power is now replacing not only manual but also many classes of mental workers; with resultant new problems of unemployment and of use of leisure time.

4. Resultant advances have produced the fully Automatic Factory and Office for many processes; and have made it possible to make materials, machines and even energy itself from sources never before available for use by Man.

5. Parallel astounding advances have come in medicine, in foods, and in Health; as Science derived such new machines and mechanical products.

6. Such scientific impacts have crystallized far-reaching changes in Man's ideas of material value—of labor, of finance, of land and crops and minerals, of trade, of government and even of morality.

IV. BUSINESS ORGANIZATION AND MANAGEMENT

1. The whole scale of Business organizations and problems has multiplied proportionately to the impacts of global War, of colossal Governments and of ever-ramifying Science.

2. Vast increases have resulted—and required Management—in mechanization, in productivity and in volume of output of goods and services; despite higher wages, a shorter work-week and a much larger proportion of women in the work force.

3. The super-position of global military requirements on an expanding civilian economy in a new Industrial Society has brought advances in the physical Distribution of goods; but lagging application of the principles of engineering to the needs of mass Distribution with a free Market, which can have deeply serious effects if the out-size Military requirements shrink suddenly.

4. The resultant enhanced importance and power of Industrial Managers—operating chiefly in large enterprises whose basic ownership is dispersed widely, whereas their Management is concentrated in non-owner hands—has stimulated very rapid improvisation of counter-forces to prevent monopolistic or tyrannical use of Management's power. Some such counter-forces center in Unions; some in Scientists with capacity to obsolete whole industries; some in large, closely managed pools of intermediate capital such as insurance companies and mutual funds. But the latter in turn are countered by the ability of Business to finance its prodigious expansion increasingly by either retained earnings or Government contracts.

5. There has been a net lag in the development of a Science of Management competent to bring patterns of Order and Organization into increasingly Big Enterprises; not only in business, but also in Unions, in Educational Institutions and in Government Operations, both civil and military.

6. The picture has been further confused by the growing requirement of Managers to give heed to more and more factors external to the enterprise, as well as to its internal operations, in setting objectives and in making decisions.

V. HOME AND THE INDIVIDUAL

1. The home, while still the basic social unit, has been weakened in this capacity; and has broadly lost its status as the major Social Center of the economy and society.

2. Improved facilities for transportation—both public and personal, both on the ground and through the air—have brought a sudden, enormous mobility of people—and with it a corresponding instability of individuals, moving freely and rapidly from house to house, from area to area, from industry to industry, even from hemisphere to hemisphere.

3. Growing standards of income and of expenditure, of savings and of security insurance, and of living standards and of culture have resulted at a speedy rate; with increased home ownership despite all the mobility and despite increasing number of both men and women in the working forces of trade and industry. While there has been some trend of people away from agriculture,

both farm productivity and living standards have been enhanced by electrification and mechanization.

4. Demands have grown for more and deeper formal education; as the specialization of work brings parallel frustration and leisure.

5. Improved health, physical stature and chance of reasonable individual longevity has resulted, with lessened risks of premature death from disease and with changing causes of death, but not a major advance in normal maximum dying age.

6. The impact of all such confusing and multiplying forces has brought parallel disintegration and revival of basic spiritual values during the decade; especially as technology through better communication and transportation has brought multiplied awareness of materialistic potentials on the one hand, but multiplied fears of lethal weapons, forces and actual or prospective destruction on the other hand.

Such are the changes with which Managers—both as individuals and as leaders of public and private institutions—must increasingly cope. Such are the challenges of the last decade of the first Fifty Years of the Scientific Management Movement from 1952 to 1962.

COMMENTS
Robert T. Livingston

1. I doubt whether it is necessary for me to attempt to sell this meeting upon the importance of the management function. Nor shall I attempt to rigidly define the function. I think that you will all agree with me that two aspects can be seen: Organization—the design function and administration; the function of operation. I refuse to argue about their relative importance, but I will claim that as the economic tempo increases, as communication possibility becomes more rapid, as the penalty for bad decisions improperly implemented becomes more important, Organization becomes more important. Organization becomes of greater importance than heretofore. So, too, with our Administration. The day of off-the-cuff decisions enforced by bribe, fear or drive is gone. If our society and way of life is to persist, we must apply 1952 Thinking to 1952 Problems.

2. The past ten years have seen the birth of understanding about atomic fission and atomic fusion, and the potential inherent for the good of man is as great as the potential available for his destruction. But I venture to say that the potential which the physicist has offered will sink into relative insignificance when we realize the potential which is available due to the release of the creative impulses of mankind. This, my friends, is our duty: to discover how to release creatively these impulses whereby men working together will solve the problems of tomorrow. It is not in the field of nucleonics, or cybernetics, or automation that the great progress of the next fifty years is to come. Not at all—it is in the field of *understanding* man.

3. Production can be thought of as the combination of four basic elements in goal-directed projects. These four basic elements are: materials; machines and/or processes; memory-specification, communication, call it what you will, it is stored information; and man. With these four basic elements we can create a matrix of inter-actions which is worthwhile exploring. I will leave it to one of you to pursue the subject—obviously there are fifteen classes of interactions which must be comprehended. But I would like to call your attention to the simple concepts that flow from a consideration of this matrix.

4. Today we can call on the synthetic chemist or the metallurgist, and he will give us a material with almost any given set of characteristics—it may be very expensive, but the possibility is there. Our Mechanical, Civil, and Electrical Engineers, among them, can design a machine of most amazing complexity, in which can be incorporated potential response to almost any stimuli and which can remember (if you will) a log table, steam tables, an inspection and control process, or what have you.

5. Thus we, Man, have almost complete control over material, machine and memory (and a machine can be designed which won't make mistakes)—all that remains is man. Man to whose service the engineer, by definition, is dedicated. Man for whom the machines produce and change material. Man who in the materialistic philosophy is the *Alpha Cum Omega* of the social and economic system, and yet it is man who is least effectively used in our modern social and economic system.

I submit to you:

(1) That the potential gains due to understanding man are terrific;
(2) That we engineers, as engineers, are derelict in our duty as engineers if we don't apply to the study of man those abilities, skills and techniques that we have applied to materials, methods and memory.

It is the idea that I am bringing to you today. Now let us explore what I mean and what we must, I feel, do.

6. And I say to you that it is my belief that we must develop a Theory of Management, a Theory of Management in operationally verifiable terms, a Theory of Management whereby we can predict, where we can take actions and measure the probability of the occurrence of events in light of that action. I'd like to outline to you the way I think we have, in the past, been operating. As I look back over the technique of management, and I shan't repeat what I have written in my paper, it seems to me that we have concerned ourselves with the knowledge of the how to solve individual problems. This is art. We gradually moved into a period of solving classes of problems, and I like to characterize this as the period of "know-what." The problems to be solved were related to a process, or a material, or a product—here was the skilled artisan. Next, we moved to the period of "know-how"; problems became more general, but there was still a restriction of area of application, and what was well known in one area often was, and is, unknown in another. Now we are moving from the "know-how" to the "know-why" and process and methodology, rather than application, become

important. Of course, there will always be a direct feed forward from *know-what* to *know-how* and similarly to *know-why,* and an equally important feedback both directly and indirectly, from know-why to know-how and to know-who.

7. The manager, and especially the engineer, occupies an important mid-position between the "Commercial" and the "Research." This does not mean that he is unaware of either one or the other, but it does mean that he is more concerned with this big middle group, concerned with translating the dreams of the researcher into the practical problems of the man concerned with commercial application. As a matter of fact, the engineer-manager is quite apt to invade either field when he finds the practitioners in those fields cannot give him the information he needs to solve the problems that he faces.

8. How about a Theory of Management—that I feel confident must and will evolve. It must be consonant with, and a part of, a still greater theory—the Theory of Man which will include the above Theory of Management, and to think in terms of hierarchy:

> A Theory of Cultures;
> A Theory of Social Institutions;

and below the Theory of Management:

> A Theory of Groups;
> A Theory of Individual Behavior.

You will, I am sure, recognize that each of these theories is the interest of several disciplines and at present, there is no completely agreed-upon theory in any case. But in spite of the competition which exists among the psychologists, for example, as to the theory of Individual Behavior, there is, I venture to say, far more basic agreement than you would realize when you hear two psychologists in discussion.

9. Along this line I have found that we engineers of management have had to venture into strange fields. At first I found it difficult to justify, for example, my own study of psychology, sociology and applied anthropology, but then when I looked upon the management engineer as a catalyzer, I found most of my brothers evaporated. We need not claim authority in these fields, but what we must assume is understanding. It is, I think, our job to bring these diverse disciplines together and to direct their abilities to the solution of this important problem. We, it is, I am convinced, who can act as interpreter; and I am increasingly convinced that the solutions of the problems of tomorrow lie in the hands of the people who can bring all the diverse disciplines to bear their power on the solution of the problem, and I submit to you that the discipline which can provide the means whereby these powerful concepts can be brought to bear on this problem of immediacy is an important discipline and need not worry about status in the future.

10. You may dismiss what I have said and what I am saying as the ivory-towered dreaming of an academician. I assure you that this is not the case. It is not the case

practically, and it is not the case theoretically. Practically, in my own consulting practice, I have not hesitated to bring psychologists, and indeed in one case a philosopher and a methodologist, in to help me solve the very practical problems. Give them the consulting fee, put their noses to the grindstone, give them the problem and the facts, and they can save you a lot of trouble. So, too, with their theories. We are only just starting to synthesize their work, but as I say previously, I think we know a whole lot more than we realize we know. BUT, it has got to be coordinated.

11. Finally, may I say a word for fundamental research. People are apt to dismiss the "long-hair" as impractical. Actually, when viewed in long to perspective, fundamental research may be more practical than developmental. For it is fundamental research which will help to keep us from going down blind alleys; and I submit to you that today there is no field more promising, no field of research in which the potential of profit is greater, than this field in which I urge the need for fundamental research and the development of an operationally verifiable theory of management.

AMERICA'S PRODUCTION AND ITS INFLUENCE IN THE INTERNATIONAL SITUATION

Harold Coes

Before discussing the contribution American Industry may make to the industrial development of backward countries, let us consider the principle factors that have enabled the U.S. to out-produce all other industrial nations.

1. The Free Enterprise System;
2. The philosophy of low costs, high wages and low prices;
3. Competition; no cartels;
4. Incentives for labor, capital, management and stockholders;
5. Our flexible, resilient economy, and the interdependence of its component parts;
6. Scientific Management;
7. Research and development and the rapid adaptation of the findings in all fields;
8. Acceptance of a high obsolescence factor in techniques, methods, and capital plant and equipment;
9. Reinvestment of earnings in the enterprise;
10. The spirit and power of America.

Now bear in mind that many, I could almost say most, of our foreign friends do not accept all of these factors. Certainly not items 1, 2, 3, 4, 5, and 8. (Then read again those items.) They say our system is too rough on the individual enterprise. Hence, the cartel system that preserves the least efficient.

Next, let us broadly consider the economic background that generally prevails in most of the backward countries. Primarily, the economy is based on agriculture and the export of raw materials. It is true that no country has obtained a high standard of living or risen to be a first class power on just this background.

But to industrialize, you have to have markets, both domestic and export. Before you can have a domestic market for industrial products, you have to greatly increase production by improving agricultural methods and thereby returns. Production in these countries is, per acre, less than one-half of ours. Similarly, the extraction of raw materials has to be greatly improved and costs lowered. Yet many of these countries do not understand this and certainly do not understand how it is accomplished.

Let me cite an incident of my own experience in India. I was visited in Calcutta by a couple of Indian capitalists, brothers, known to be exceedingly wealthy. They had been educated in England, traveled widely in Europe and the U.S. They wanted to discuss with me the manufacture of automobiles in India. I thought that by manufacture they meant to assemble component parts manufactured abroad. But no, they wanted to manufacture the engines, transmissions, differentials, frames, bodies, etc. I asked them how many automobiles and trucks exclusive of military vehicles were assembled or imported in a year. They said 18,000 to 20,000, which was correct. I told them, "Well you have been in Detroit and in England. You should know that to produce 20,000 vehicles is only a day's work in the U.S. for the automobile industry, and perhaps only several days' work in England. Furthermore, the capital investment per car to be produced as you plan would be of the order of $————. How do you propose to compete with that?" They answered, "Look how many people we have." "Yes," I said, "but 95 to 98 per cent of them have no purchasing power. Who are going to purchase your production?"

I encountered similar situations in Mexico.

If by the use of Point IV and MSA technical assistance applied at the grass roots in a single village in India, for example, it is demonstrated to the farmers how they can very materially increase their production, their quality, lower their costs and raise their earnings, and thus proceed to work out all over India, then you have laid the foundation for industrialization by raising the purchasing power, the basis of a market for industrial products.

Similarly, if by improved methods, the same thing is done in the extraction of raw materials, again a basis for an industrial products market is laid. In the case of raw materials, a next step could be taken by partly refining the raw materials so as to reduce the bulk and the cost of freight on bulk that has to be thrown away.

The U.S. can help in all these cases. But the applications must be made at the grass roots. This is a slow process, but once the isolated demonstrations have been made and the word gets around as to what has been accomplished, acceptance will be rapid and the pace greatly accelerated.

Once the foregoing tasks have been accomplished and the purchasing power in the country is rising, plans for industrialization can be made. It is wise to start with the simplest products that are now imported in sufficient quantity to warrant their manufacture in the country. Here again, the U.S. can assist with its know-how and the exportation to the country of its capital goods and its experts to train the workers in the use of the machinery, etc.

If the backward countries will then create the proper climate for the investment of private foreign capital, then U.S. capital could, and probably would, flow to the under-developed countries. Then a country could see for itself what can be accomplished when an American company sets up shop and how it is done. Some of this is going on now, but not enough.

By raising the standard of living in a backward country, or rather assisting in the operation, the U.S. would benefit two ways. First, the country would be more stable economically and politically and be less vulnerable to communist propaganda. Second, a market would be provided, and a growing market at that, for not only our machinery, etc., but for many of our products that are not manufactured in that country but for which there will be a demand as purchasing power rises.

It all gets down to this: that the backward countries must develop basic plans and programs along the lines sketchily blocked out in broad terms. Here is stated how we in this country can assist.

Many consulting management engineering firms and engineering contractors are assisting in this work now all over the world, in some cases, working with agencies of the U.S. government of the under-developed country.

This is, as I see it, from my experience in working with ECA and also directly with the government of one or more of these countries, a way to develop world commerce.

But I want to warn that there is no royal, short-cut way to do the job. It involves a lot of work, of thinking, planning, frustration, and patience. The ability to develop the plans and programs that best suit the conditions in the country. Do not for a minute think you can take our techniques, methods and industrial and economic philosophies and cram them down the throats of the country, because you can't.

CHANGING PRESSURES UPON THE EXECUTIVE

Erwin H. Schell

Introductory

Industrial establishments in America can no longer be viewed solely as economic, wealth-producing organizations, although this may properly continue to be their primary purpose. Today, the typical manufacturing plant must also accept its challenges and shoulder its responsibilities as a social institution, as a political nucleus, as a governmental resource, as a military garrison, and as a vital element in international trade.

447

The New Administrative Multiplex

These differing lights in which industry is now viewed necessarily make multiplex the outlook of the top executive. His observation of the world about him must be through a mosaic of lenses, each differing markedly from the others.

In these varied executive roles, the top executive wears a wardrobe of caps. Depending upon circumstance and situation, the president is called upon to play the part of leader, of trustee, of super-citizen, of statesman, of patriot and of internationalist.

Again, as he views the pattern of his responsibilities, he finds that he must be concerned with the welfare not only of all parties at immediate interest, such as the employees, the stockholders, the consumers and the vendors, but he must further serve the needs of his community, of his industry or trade, of his government, of the military arm, and of growing international affiliations.

Current pressures are heavy upon him. He is called upon to be interested in and to support all new internal developments. How often we hear it said of an industrial innovation, "If we can sell the idea to the president and gain his support, it is bound to succeed."

Again, there is pressure upon him to represent his establishment in its many external or so-called social relations. The president's day is no longer restricted to a given sector of the clock face. His out-of-hours activities in extra-industrial affairs are of great significance to the welfare of his business, no less than those tasks which he shoulders during his regular hours.

He is pressed upon to serve local, state and national governmental bodies. He is at times impressed to coöperate actively with military agencies in the production of essential wartime products. And increasingly, stress may be put upon him to adjust his business and its operations to the intensified competition of free international trade.

The New Executive Dilemma

As we view this multiplex of roles, responsibilities and necessities which impact upon top management, we cannot but realize the extraordinary dilemma in which our business leaders now find themselves. Yesterday's administrative problems, while often concerning, could frequently benefit by the admixture of time and delay. Today's issues call for prompt solution and immediate and definite decision. More than this, the current climate of accelerative change in which executives live and move and have their being is steadily increasing the frequency with which far-reaching decisions must be made.

To an increasing degree, these decisions are no longer unilateral, but rest upon pre-agreements with other influential and powerful groups requiring highly developed skills in topmost areas of negotiation and persuasion.

As the tasks of the chief executive are multiplying, are becoming more complex and more demanding, the incumbent of this high position finds that he may not increase his natural talents commensurately. He is, at best, the product of the slow evolution of centuries, whereas the problems which abound about him are products of today's onrushing creativeness.

Finally, the extraordinary profusion of completely new concepts which pour out from the cornucopias of scientific research and development urge, and indeed demand, executive leadership into new and unexplored fields of manufacturing, where the pioneer must proceed without benefit of standards or even of previous custom or convention.

We can begin to understand the validity of a question said to have been put by the Queen of Holland, which runs:

> Why is it that the men who are governing the world must be characteristically on the verge of nervous breakdown?

I should not infer that this problem has not been recognized. I only maintain that it has not been solved. During the last decade, we have seen an extraordinary delegation of decisions downward. Decentralization has been one medium of effecting this devolution of authority and responsibility.

Again, we are reminded by Colonel Urwick, distinguished British authority, that for many years the military organization has dealt with this problem by the establishment of a general staff composed not of specialists, but of true generalists to whom general issues may be assigned for consideration and recommendation.

Finally, we are seeing a mighty upsurge in the use of mechanical and electronic equipment, revealing patterns of simple design deep in the abstruse complexities which result from industry's constant aggregation of new and related knowledge.

Yet nowhere do we find complete satisfaction with the devices now at hand. Perhaps we are on the verge of some new discovery in organization or communication which may lift us out of the morasses of complexity now threatening to engulf our leaders. If so, the vision of just what these saving graces may be is not now clear.

Conclusion

My purpose here is not to bury our industrial Caesars nor to praise them. My purpose is rather to reveal what a real fix they are in, with the hope that ensuing discussion may point some ways in which relief may be afforded.

ERWIN H. SCHELL

Industrial Continuum and the Nature of Man*

1952-1962

The preceding papers in these Volumes have dealt with what were—and are—present-day problems in the Science of Managing.

In this selection, Professor Schell looks into the future at mid-point in the 1952–1962 decade. His thesis: though man himself is accustomed to continuum (repetitive or flow-activities)—and can make rapid adjustment to sudden changes—in his natural environment, the pressures of dynamic and revolutionary advances in science and industry pose a great problem in accelerating our industrial continuum.

More challenges and responsibilities for Managerial proficiency, for new awareness of institutional social consciousness, for ever-widening delegation of judgment and action— all are forcing Managers to discover just what should be the precise objectives of their enterprise; how these objectives may be quantitatively evaluated; and how these evaluations may be put to immediate and preventive use.

* "Industrial Continuum and the Nature of Man," an Address delivered before the Society for the Advancement of Management, New York City, November 3, 1955. Permission to reprint by courtesy of the author.

INDUSTRIAL CONTINUUM AND THE NATURE OF MAN

Erwin H. Schell

I. *Introduction*

TECHNICAL PROGRESS HAS A WAY of enforcing social change. Often we are not immediately aware of its influence.

We have seen machinery replace man's brawn, man's skills, man's susceptibility to error—and now man's judgment—in the operation of productive processes; and we have seen other dynamic corrections and adjustments, such as the elimination of undue variances in work in process and the compensation for tool wear.

More and more, industrial facilities are making possible those repetitive or flow-activities which have a quality of continuum or, as Webster put it, "That which is continuous and selfsame; that of which no distinction of content can be affirmed except by reference to something else."

Industrial continuum has recently received impetus from one aspect of servo-mechanisms which has been nicknamed "feed-back," enabling corrections for undue variations to be automatically made in the process itself.

Growing interest in these evaluative devices has overflowed into the executive and service areas and raised pertinent questions concerning other evaluative devices for the accomplishments of administrators, line officials, purchasing agents, personnel directors, chief inspectors, storekeepers and, indeed, the entire gamut of the managerial hierarchy. Hence this conference.

I should now like to discuss with you some basic aspects of this growth in industrial continuum and evaluation, as it relates to the nature of man himself.

II. *Industrial Continuum and Man's Environment*

The effect of industrial continuum upon man's environment may prove to be profound. Manufacturing procedures have long had as their objectives the improving and insuring of a high quality of continuum in hand or machine operations. Stabilization of output has been earnestly sought by both organized labor and management. To this end it has been generally affirmed that evenness in repetitive procedures throughout the daily work-period and throughout the year was a highly desirable attainment.

Yet this entire concept is at direct odds with man's natural environment. The slope of the earth's axis brings the rhythm of the seasons and with them the constant pattern of climatic change throughout the year. As a result, we have for many millions of years been accustomed to "annual living," and this influence continues to dominate the interims in our lives over which we exert control. We enjoy one Christmas, one Easter, one Thanksgiving Day each year; but we would not desire two of each.

With the farmer, each day of the year is in some degree unique in its activities which are comparable only with those of identical days of preceding years.

Such variations are not found in modern industrial work patterns; and, with the oncoming of automation, only now do we begin to glimpse a future day when non-evolutional repetitive activities of all sorts may be relegated to machines and other automatia.

It would appear that Nature abhors nonevolutional repetitions even as she abhors a vacuum; for wherever they are essential to human life, as in breathing, digestion or circulation, she contrives to have them take place without conscious volition.

Likewise, we discover that there are many things we may do—such as driving a car, knitting, or shaving—which we may learn to carry on without conscious attention. Indeed, it is in this area that many repetitive hand operations fall which, once mastered, permit the operator to enjoy a kind of restricted social intercourse at the work place with a lessened sense of monotony or tedium.

It is an interesting fact that there is no place in the world where the so-called factory system has been inaugurated without some degree of tension, not to say antagonism, arising between managers and employees. Such phenomena may have their base in a subconscious revolt of the working group against the unnatural bonds of repetitive activities which have not been so rigidly required of the managing or technical group. Certainly there are many examples of loyalty and devotion to military leaders where such extreme repetition does not prevail.

III. *Industrial Continuum and Man's Creativeness*

Industrial continuum is being heavily affected by cross-currents arising from man's incorrigible creativeness. Sweeping with ever-increasing velocity across the plains of progress, where industry is methodically striving for continuing gains from intensive analyses and steady improvement in areas of cost, quality and service, are the cross-winds of deeper and more radical change, springing from research and development. A whole new enginery of ingenuity and creativeness may abruptly engulf and transform older days and ways, as a result of the outpourings from the cornucopia of science and the arts in the form of generically new products, processes, organizations, facilities and relationships.

Here again, it would appear that man's creative nature once more overwhelms any concept that limits human effort, however productive or efficient, to repetitions that do not incorporate variety, flexibility and versatility, and above all, growth.

It may be argued that progress in those extensive and revolutional areas should take the form of a series of occasions or quanta, where forward creative surges are followed by less active periods when gains are consolidated and the rewards of intensive analysis are enjoyed. The annual model is one example of such rhythmic advance.

How may we construct our industrial continuum, with its high initial investment, so that our facilities no less than our viewpoint may be sufficiently flexible to harmonize with, and indeed to maintain a leading position in, the ever-more-rapid advances in the industry? The nature of man includes an ever-present quality of ingenuity and a desire for growth that industrial continuum may not disregard.

IV. *Industrial Continuum and Tomorrow's Leadership*

Industrial continuum bids fair to produce new challenges for the industrial executive. As we look across the industrial stage, with its ever-changing back-drop, its evolving prologue, discourse and epilogue, and its coming and going of human personalities, we find ourselves becoming less concerned about operating management. After all, we say, the administration of the machine, even with its modern complexities, is far less intricate than the administration of human beings, and therefore should be simpler to perform.

Here the record is against us. The weight of responsibility for these aggregations of machinery, mechanization, instrumentation and inter-relation, with their gargantuan appetites and energies, brings tension and concern to the best adjusted personality. As one such manager remarked to me: "This is a wonderful set-up when everything is working right, but it can pile up misery at a terrific rate when it gets off the track."

Again, many of our advanced processing installations are not yet old enough to pose what might be called normal maintenance problems, the exact nature of which is often still a matter of conjecture.

As I looked at one such vast installation of automation, I asked my guide: "Have you been able to establish a beginning and an end to your maintenance problem?"

And he replied: "We are only sure of this. Every part in this great machine has a life, just as do people. Until we have determined just what these life-spans are, we will not feel that we are approaching the solution of our problem."

To me the most serious aspect of industrial continuum in relation to the operating executive lies elsewhere.

These new aggregations, with their tremendous investment, their extraordinarily sensitive coordinations and their great speed of output, are inevitably incorporating additional and incessant responsibilities that refuse to be laid aside or delegated.

No longer can we permit of a kind of management that depends solely upon periodic reports on executive results; for too heavy penalties may attend a lack of immediate awareness during the interim of such measurements. Operating errors in the conduct of productive procedures can quickly become lethal in character.

Little by little, the noose of evaluative control over the executive function appears to be tightening. Already, executives in operating areas are having increasing difficulty in remaining away from the job for any but brief periods.

The deeper significance of this conference on measurement of management is now apparent. Industrial continuum is forcing us to discover just what should be the precise objectives of operating management; just how these objectives may be quantitatively evaluated; and just how these evaluations may be immediately put to constructive and preventive use. When these questions have been resolved, we shall see a fundamental change in the nature and parameter of the executive task.

Are we to allow our production executives to become enclosed within managerial routines as rapidly as repetitions are removed from the operators? If not, how are the hour-to-hour responsibilities for the new industrial behemoth to be properly shouldered?

Perhaps the bark of this possibility is worse than its bite. For many years the paper industry has operated with huge machines containing many self-corrective devices and costing as much as a million dollars each. Yet no great reverberations in executive conduct have been felt. Again, there is certainly nothing new in top management's attempt to judge of the effectiveness of the production-management group. But the rapid growth in consolidations no less than in automation, and the ensuing necessities for ever closer centralized awareness of operating conditions in each decentralized unit, will surely deepen the need for more sensitive and immediate methods of calipering the work and influence of those in whose hands the operating responsibilities rest.

The effect of growth in industrial continuum upon the leader himself promises to be profound. More than any other member of the organization, he will be ready and eager to learn; for leadership to be earned and maintained demands a forward position in the competitive procession. Such a place can rest only upon ever-advancing knowledge of the frontiers of the industrial and managerial arts.

The president of tomorrow's industry will become acutely aware of the significance of his enterprise as a social institution. Stability in operation and consistency in policy, as they relate to those new automated engineries, will have great influence upon the community in which his plants are situated and upon the trade with which he deals. The machines need take no cognizance of the seasons, nor of variety as such.

The president will increasingly be forced to rely upon others for counsel and advice regarding the multiplex of specialized responsibilities which surround him. To an increasing degree he will delegate decisions no less than actions. To an increasing degree he will employ machinery to promote immediate factual information. To an increasing degree he, too, will measure himself against quantitative standards of accomplishment.

Most important of all, he will find it necessary to accustom himself to new and greater scales of operating magnitude. As his areas of influence enlarge in accordance with the economic growth contours of the nation, his own status will advance commensurately.

V. *Industrial Continuum and Man's Insecurity*

There is a final aspect to industrial continuum that I would stress. In today's onrushing world we may not evade the fact that an attendant function to that of increasing velocity is that of increasing uncertainty. This manifestation is becoming more evident as the days pass. For example, the query regarding "where I will be five years from now" appears to be increasing.

Unquestionably, industrial continuum will continue to bring marked changes in organization and in responsibility. No top-management may gainsay this in view of the evident nature of tomorrow's competition.

The solution is not to be found in the elimination of change. Rather we shall look to sources of support and confidence that are not affected by change. Employee goodwill and trustfulness are, in reality, reserves which are precious accumulations in any business. They are not built in a day; they are the products of time and of unvarying character. They are in the nature of resources amassed over many years of fair and square dealings.

The new problem is this. Only too frequently this trust, this confidence, this goodwill, are symbolized by a top-official who has epitomized these ideals. With his passing, uncertainty, concern and fear arise.

Somehow we must find a way whereby the high character of an industrial institution may be carried steadily and safely forward. In this day of flux, tradition is not enough. Established policies are not enough. Some new form of organization may be necessary, to insure this end.

Somehow, some way, the members of the enterprise need to be assured that, come *what* may, and come *who* may, their interests will continue to be protected by the application of the high principles upon which the business has rested.

With the expansion of our industries and the growth in continuum, we can say with assurance that any going enterprise of normal status and competence must anticipate existence which will endure long after every person now on the payroll has passed on.

VI. *Conclusion*

As we try to assess the future of industry, we see dimly the new forms which it will assume under the tidal onrush of industrial continuum.

We see a decline of unnatural monotony, tedium and repetition from their past domination over the lives of many of our industrial workers.

We see the counter-flow of responsibility turning to operating management with an attendant demand for closer and more immediate evaluation of executive proficiency.

We see the powerful cross-currents of progress affecting the normal evolution of our enterprise, the merging of slow *intensive* improvement with the impact of rapid and *extensive* advance of a more fundamental nature.

We see challenges laid before leadership which call for rapid learning ability, for new manifestations of social consciousness and for ever-widening delegation of judgment and action.

We sense the need in our fluid world for testaments of honor and of character that are not the symbol of any one man, but reflect the "undying soul of the institution."

We feel the thrill of membership in a great procession moving inexorably forward into a better world.

We are certain—we are sure—that civilization is on the quick-step, marching to the ever-advancing tempo of scientific research and bowing its head in humility before the truth that shall keep us free!

HAROLD F. SMIDDY
and
LIONEL NAUM

Evolution of a "Science of Managing"
in America*

1912-1956

More than a simple chronology of dates and names, the authors of this paper have sought out the philosophical drives which both stimulated and limited the progress of a scientific approach to the rational conception and performance of Managerial work: securing results through the organized efforts of others.

It is an outline of the gradual historical development of the search for the basic principles of the Science of Managing rather than a simple recounting of experiment, methodology, or significant writings in that field. The paper, therefore, aptly "summarizes the summaries" for each of the organized "Management Movement" decades reviewed in the earlier reports in this Volume.

* Smiddy, Harold F., and Lionel Naum, "Evolution of a 'Science of Managing' in America," *Management Science*, Vol. I, October 1954. Permission to reprint by courtesy of the Institute of Management Science.

EVOLUTION OF A "SCIENCE OF MANAGING" IN AMERICA

Harold F. Smiddy and Lionel Naum

Management Consultation Services, General Electric Company

I

WHEREVER PEOPLE HAVE GATHERED to pursue a common and desired end, there has been an inevitable necessity to organize minds, hands, materials, and the use of time for efficient and contributive work. Man has learned that individual and personal rewards derive largely from an harmonious combination of individual work and teamwork in a soundly organized frame of reference, and thus the core of the history of "Scientific Management" is formed from his search for the techniques of joint but voluntary participation while still preserving individual initiative, creative imagination, and increasingly productive output.

Any historical survey, to be of more than passing interest, and to be more than a simple chronology of dates and names, needs to seek out the philosophical drives which both stimulated and limited the progress of such a scientific approach to more rational conception and performance of managerial work, that is, of securing results through the organized efforts of others.

While it is important to know when things happened, this knowledge only becomes significant and useable when it is understood *why* things happened. This paper, therefore, is intended to outline the gradual historical development of the search for the basic principles of a "Science of Managing," and thus of Scientific Management, rather than to be a simple recounting of experiment, methodology, or significant writings in that field.

II

The philosophical sciences, and that dealing with the work of Managing is one of them, deal with concepts and abstractions not *easily* tested or proved quantitatively, especially on a current basis, and not *readily* subject to exact delineation, definition, standardization, or measurement. The ability to observe, to classify, to synthesize, and to act, are at least partially inhibited by the relationship and reciprocal impact of the observer and his environment.

The observer deals with the classic study of man, and he deals with one of its most complex branches, the seeking of orderly process out of divergent wills, unclear or even contradictory objectives, and transient and often unmeasurable forces. Because each observer is an integral factor in his own study, complete objectivity is impossible, and he is often faced with the conflict of that which reason tells him must be so and that which emotion tells him should be so.

But, by acceptance of the limitations in method, rather than rejection because of the difficulties, cumulative progress has been consistently sought and progressively achieved. As a result, a "Management Movement," which lived only in the hopes of a relatively few dedicated volunteers as recently as only three decades ago, has, as of today, grown irresistibly to an organized and intensifying world-wide drive and to an increasingly international educational force.

Despite such visible and accelerating progress in so short an historical era, the Science of Managing, when compared to the physical sciences, may still seem slow in evolution and uncertain in direction. Yet, fairly judged, it is neither.

The apparent slowness has only reflected the normal systemic inertia encountered wherever tradition and prejudice guide men's actions and wherever there is deliberate observation of cause and effect. Uncertainty and delay in such progress has really been the result neither of any lack of a true goal nor of unwillingness to follow a just direction, but is, rather, the result of a need to consider every avenue of possible study and, by the very nature of things, to reject far more than can be accepted.

What is being sought? Certainly not the solution of isolated problems or the rectification of each pressing business or social exigency. That would be in the nature of art. Certainly not merely the kind of "progress" determined by ability to answer the simple questions: "Will it work?" "Can you get by with it?"

What has been, and still is, sought in all these recurring efforts to define and develop a true "Science of Managing" are, rather, those kinds of fundamental principles which are the essential scientific foundation of all generalization based on classified observations and which give meaning, accuracy, and dependability to formulation of rules of action or policies, that, given a particular set of conditions, can be used or applied as guides with confidence in their effectiveness.

In other words, the search of the organized Management Movement and of the growing thousands of individual participants, both scholars and practitioners, is for principles, distilled out of what is now increasingly widely recorded experience in the social sciences, which can be applied to any and all situations involving the demands of Leadership by reason and persuasion rather than merely by rank or dictation.

To consider the shop, the office, or even the total business as something apart and unique from the more general problem of *organizing for accomplishment*, is, therefore, to take the short and unproductive view. The stubborn refusal of disciples of scientific management to fall into that kind of mental trap is itself one of the firm reasons for the growing understanding and acceptance—locally, nationally, and internationally—that management principles can be applied to guidance of all kinds of organized efforts and can be a base for Management Education which leads to professional rather than whimsical managerial responsibility.

How is this "search" being conducted? Essentially, it has gone forward on two levels. First, there has been the elemental, "action" group whose members will always be necessary to avoid crises, but who rarely have time for rigorous thought. They have been putting out fires rather than developing methods of fire prevention. At best, they keep the work of the day from lagging, and they provide data for the file of experience.

Second, and most important, are those who, by time and circumstance, are determined to find and follow carefully measured paths, distinct though not remote from immediate demands.

Fortunately, this latter group is increasing both in size and influence, and in recent years their work has been credited with growth from deep roots and not merely from a knowing wave of the hand. It is because such men, and women, have boldly and persuasively demonstrated that there are basic truths which underlie the study of the relationships of men in common effort, and have shown that these truths can be demonstrated, applied, and measured, that acceptance of the needed fundamental study to develop an accepted "Science of Managing" is being won.

There are still many who regard the idea and concept of a "Science of Managing" as a scholarly diversion, a type of *post hoc* rationalization that is created and dies in the confines of the lecture hall. But, especially in the United States, while there have been, to be sure, the theorists and while their contributions have been indispensable, there have also been the practical men, and more often than not, both theoretical concepts and practical applications have found common spokesmen. In the complex organization of modern technological society, there has been a necessary division of thought and labor, and yet the carefully balanced alloy of the philosopher and the practitioner has been the metal for forging the characteristic Industrial Society of today.

Although, as Dr. Albert Einstein has pointed out, "We now realize, with special clarity, how much in error are those theorists who believe that theory comes inductively from experience," [1] the immutable demands of science are such that new concepts inevitably bear at least the subjective imprint of past experience, and that, inevitably, there must be a commingling of theory and practice.

In sum, the object and method of the search are clear. They are to establish a true Science of Managing based upon a valid, moral, and ethically acceptable philosophy of management by the impartial observation of social components as discrete entities within and related to a total common purpose. The search, especially in busi-

---

[1] Dr. Albert Einstein, *Out of My Later Years.* New York: Philosophical Library, Inc., 1950, p. 72.

ness and little less in government, has been, and will continue to be, conducted in a climate of reality for:

> Life cannot wait until the sciences may have explained the universe scientifically. We cannot put off living until we are ready. The most salient characteristic of life is its coerciveness: it is always urgent "here and now," without any possible post-ponement . . .[2]

III

There have been many definitions of "Scientific Management," or as we prefer to phrase it, of a specific "Science of Managing." Mostly, they have been reflections of their time and frequently have served the needs of brevity more than of understanding. Yet awareness of the need for managing skills dates back, of course, beyond the beginning of recorded history. There are three phases, however, which, at the risk of rather obvious over-simplification, can be divided in time.

Before the nineteenth century, industry and business as we know it today were basically craft, individual, or, at best, guild matters. Dominating other aspects and counting above other endeavor usually was the organization and pursuit of territorial conquest. The energy of creative leadership was devoted in large part to the expansion of geographic horizons and the consequent need to discover, to take over, and to govern new territories.

Thus, there is evidence of "management" in military structures as in the conduct of civilian public affairs, but it was a type of management in which thought over and above the satisfaction of immediate requirements was usually of minimum proportions or impact. This era was perhaps the clearest example of management as an art; that is, the application of knowledge without systemization, and ordinarily on a definitely personalized basis.

The second period, on this scale of classification, began in the early part of the nineteenth century, following closely upon the heels of the introduction of the power loom and the steam engine. Here the first clearly definitive movement toward understanding the managerial, and even the broader social, implications of rapid technological progress was made, although nearly always in the light of just adequate and immediate solutions.

The information necessary to establish a true "Science of Managing" was still not at hand. The implications of constructive and successful steps taken in the direction of sound and rational organization were largely overlooked. Controlled experiment, accurate observation, and statistical correlation of human processes sometimes fell far short of more than lip service. Those who had created the industrial revolution, however, were concerned with the changing world they had brought into being, and the writings indicate at least a growing realization of a serious, impending human problem.

[2] Ortega y Gasset, from *Mission of the University*, London: Kegan Paul, 1946, p. 146.

In the last half of the nineteenth century, therefore, they talked hopefully of a "science of management." But, because they dealt only with specific fragments of a complex problem, the principles they accepted are seen by the broader view of hindsight to have been overly narrow and superficial; and the science they established was, by today's dimensions at least, only a quasi-science.

A more serious danger inherent in the limited understanding of the nineteenth century mechanists has been pointed out by A. N. Whitehead:

> A factory with its machinery, its community of operatives, its social service to the general population, its dependence upon organizing and designing genius, its potentialities as a source of wealth to the holders of its stock is an organism exhibiting a variety of vivid values. What we want to train is the habit of apprehending such an organism in its completeness. It is very arguable that the science of political economy, as studied in its first period after the death of Adam Smith (1790), did more harm than good. It destroyed many economic fallacies, and taught how to think about the economic revolution then in progress. But, it riveted on men a certain set of abstractions which were disastrous in their influence on modern mentality. It dehumanized industry.[3]

Many historians mark the first decade of the present, or twentieth, century as the beginning of the work of investigating the principles of management along lines which provide statistical validity; although even casual analysis, especially of papers on cost accounting and on work analyses before such bodies as the American Society of Mechanical Engineers, shows clearly that the foundation studies for such investigation had been developing for at least twenty years previously.

The examination of work skills in terms of output, which had thus received growing attention in the last quarter of the preceding century, was progressively restudied and carried forward with remarkable diligence and with increasingly startling results.

Resources in men and materials were expended in a great surge of discovery, but, unfortunately, the comparative abundance of the things man needed to make, to build, and to expand was in effect an embarrassment of riches. In the haste to make mightily, men fell too often into ways of leadership by command and by compulsion. The latent power of the people, which Gustave LeBon termed the "psychological law of the mental unity of crowds," [4] was accordingly marshalled in a pattern of social revolt, directed at such industrial methods because, while they did produce mightily, they tended to distribute inequitably and to make advances with inadequate regard for human developments.

Students of social status, customs, and trends became concerned with the creation, maintenance, and growth of the business, and specifically of the industrial enterprise as perhaps the most significant of current social phenomena. They realized, at last, that the total equation of civilization was heavily, perhaps even dominantly, affected by its business and industrial factors.

[3] A. N. Whitehead, *Science and the Modern World*, Macmillan Co., 1925.
[4] Gustave LeBon, *The Crowd*. London: Ernest Benn Ltd., 1952, p. 24.

It is within the last forty years, in consequence, that we have at last turned our primary, rather than our incidental, attention from *the* man, *the* machine, *the* product, to total enterprise, and even to Industrial Society, as an entity.

Those concerned with the Science of Managing are going back, now, over the accumulated knowledge and experience of centuries with new attitudes to discover the basic principles and patterns "which, like the great religions of the world, have the power to arouse the faith and hold the support of the great body of individual men and women throughout the ages."

IV

The birth of the organized movement in search of a rational and cohesive science of management is generally credited to Frederick Winslow Taylor.[5] His book, *The Principles of Scientific Management,* published in 1911, and synthesizing and advancing the theses developed in his earlier experiments and writings from around 1880 to that time, seriously upset many traditional concepts of management.

It is interesting to study Taylor's development as, in the course of a long and productive life, both as a practitioner and engineer in and as a writer on the work of Managing, his attention and emphasis shifted from the exploration of discrete facets of industrial processes to a search for underlying principles which governed the operation of those processes. It is, in a sense, the condensed pattern of the development of a real management science.

Taylor was born in 1856 and, after a rather cursory education, became apprenticed to the Enterprise Hydraulic Works in Philadelphia in 1874. He became concerned with the serious gap between the potential output and the actual output of shop workers and when he became a foreman, he determined to study the means of increasing productivity.

His early attempts were penetrating studies of the machine as a unit of productivity. Carefully controlled experiments were made on metal cutting techniques at Bethlehem Steel, at first alone and later with the aid of such associates as Carl Barth, Henry Gantt, and William Sellers. Every conceivable variation in speed, feed, depth of cut, and kind of tool was made and an empirical understanding of optimum combinations was established. In parallel with these empirical advances, it is significant that Taylor also sought the aid of able mathematicians of the day to find theoretical explanations and formulas from the abundant data with its complex and baffling variables, which their work amassed.

[5] References in this paper to individual practitioners and writers on Scientific Management are made solely to indicate by example the *progression of ideas* that developed with changing times. This paper is not an attempt to mention systematically even the outstanding pioneers of the "Management Movement." For a systematic listing of such pioneers, and for a comprehensive presentation of their contributions, see the forthcoming *Golden Book of Management,* prepared by CIOS, the Comité International de l'Organisation Scientifique, with headquarters at Geneva, Switzerland, which now represents the organized management societies of some twenty-four free nations at the international level. Any attempt to list even the leading current authorities in the field would simply require another large book in itself.

Encouraged by the success of the metal cutting work, Taylor made many other studies which dealt with the techniques of production. His work, during this period, was characterized primarily by his concern with end results, yet also by significant parallel attempts to deduce basic meanings. However, just as the metal cutting experiments dealt with what was happening more than why it happened, he failed, for the moment, to perceive the full general implications of his studies as an example of one of the elemental processes of scientific management.

Paralleling Taylor's and other early explorations, Frank and Lillian Gilbreth undertook a remarkable series of studies, which were distinguished by the fact that they definitely recognized and recorded with persuasive clarity that the basic unit of productivity had to include the worker as well as the machine and on a quantitative and specific basis. In 1909, for example, they published a work entitled *A Bricklaying System* and, in 1911, followed it with the more comprehensive *Motion Study*.

Their work, while of tremendous importance in creating an understanding of motion economy, of the techniques of increasing output by reducing incremental effort, and of the tools of measurement, is of deeper and more lasting importance in that it showed the significance of integrated thinking. They found and preached for all to know that it was the optimum combination of worker skills and machine operation, rather than the best of either alone, that could narrow the gap between potential and realized production.

The full import of the contribution of the industrial psychologist was not at first recognized. In reviewing the history of the American management movement, Colonel Lyndall F. Urwick gave this warm evaluation of the Gilbreth team:

> If they (the ASME) had not been (aware of human problems involved)—and Taylor either failed to encounter, or to recognize the significance of, the early work in industrial psychology contributed by Walter Dill Scott, Hugo Munsterberg, and others—there was the amazing fact that one of them, Frank Bunker Gilbreth, happened to fall in love with a girl who was a psychologist by education, a teacher by profession, and a mother by vocation. I know of no occurrence in the whole history of human thought more worthy of the epithet "providential" than that fact. Here were three engineers—Taylor, Gantt, and Gilbreth—struggling to realize the wider implications of their technique, in travail with a "mental revolution," their great danger that they might not appreciate the difference between applying scientific thinking to material things and to human beings, and one of them married Lillian Moller, a woman who by training, by instinct, and by experience was deeply aware of human beings, the perfect mental complement in the work to which they had set their hands.[6]

As such work and that of many other pioneers progressed steadily, it is significant that Taylor, too, increasingly appreciated the fuller meanings of his work, and out of such developing awareness he offered this concept of "the manager" in *The Principles of Scientific Management*:

[6] Lyndall F. Urwick, *Management's Debt to the Engineers*. The ASME Calvin W. Rice Lecture.

These *new* duties of the manager are grouped under four heads:

1. They develop a science for each element of man's work, which replaces the old rule-of-thumb method.
2. They scientifically select and then train, teach, and develop the workman, whereas in the past he chose his own work and trained himself the best he could.
3. They heartily cooperate with the men so as to insure all the work being done in accordance with the principles of the science which have been developed.
4. There is an almost equal division of the work between the management and the workmen. The management takes over all work for which it is better fitted than the workmen, while in the past almost all of the work and the greater part of the responsibility were thrown upon the men.

And, in that same treatise, he ably summarized the powerful concepts which he had evolved and clarified in his more than thirty-five years of resourceful, persistent, and classified studies in these memorable words:

The writer is one of those who believes that more and more will the third party (the whole people), as it becomes acquainted with the true facts, insist that justice shall be done to all three parties (employer, employee, public). It will demand the largest efficiency from both employers and employees. It will no longer tolerate the type of employer who has his eye on dividends alone, who refuses to do his full share of the work and who merely cracks the whip over the heads of his workmen and attempts to drive them into harder work for low pay. No more will it tolerate tyranny on the part of labor which demands one increase after another in pay and shorter hours, while at the same time it becomes less, instead of more, efficient.

And the means which the writer firmly believes will be adopted to bring about, first, efficiency both in employer and employee, and then an equitable division of the profits of their joint efforts, will be scientific management, which has for its sole aim the attainment of justice for all three parties through impartial scientific investigation of all the elements of the problem. For a time both sides will rebel against this advance. The workers will resent any interference with their old rule-of-thumb methods, and the management will resent being asked to take on new duties and burdens; but in the end the people, through enlightened public opinion, will force the new order of things upon both employer and employee.

. . . Scientific management does not necessarily involve any great invention, nor the discovery of new or startling facts. It does, however, involve a certain *combination* of elements which have not existed in the past, namely, old knowledge so collected, analyzed, grouped and classified into laws and rules that it constitutes a science; accompanied by complete change in the mental attitude of the working men as well as of those on the side of management, toward each other, and toward their respective duties and responsibilities. Also a new division of the duties between the two sides and intimate, friendly cooperation to an extent that is impossible under the philosophy of the old management . . .

It is no single element, but rather this whole combination, that constitutes scientific management, which may be summarized as:

Science, not rule-of-thumb
Harmony, not discord
Cooperation, not individualism

Maximum output, in place of restricted output
The development of each man to his greatest efficiency and prosperity

467

The time is fast going by for the great personal or individual achievement of any one man standing alone and without the help of those around him. And the time is coming when all great things will be done by that type of cooperation in which each man performs the function for which he is best suited, each man preserves his own individuality and is supreme in his particular function, and each man at the same time loses none of his originality and proper personal initiative, and yet is controlled by and must work harmoniously with many other men.

Both Taylor and the Gilbreths had thus restated, and indeed proved, two basic concepts which set the pattern of the industrial revolution over a hundred years before. Adam Smith in *Wealth of Nations,* 1776, suggested the principle of the division of labor:

> This great increase of the quantity of work which, in consequence of the division of labor, the same number of people are capable of performing, is owing to three different circumstances; first, to the increase of dexterity in every particular workman; second, to the saving of the time which is commonly lost in passing from one species of work to another; and lastly, to the invention of a great number of machines which facilitate and abridge labor, and enable one man to do the work of many.

This, of course, was the historical precedent of the work in the early 1900's which was concerned with the organization of production skills and which has since been extended and enlarged by the contributions of Engstrom, Maynard, Segur, and many others in this country and by fellow scholars and practitioners in these fields abroad.

Charles Babbage, British mathematician and scholar, provided the second governing concept of *transference of skill* in his *Economy of Machinery and Manufacture,* published in 1832:

> That the master manufacturer, by dividing the work to be executed into different processes, each requiring different degrees of skill and force, can purchase exactly that precise quantity of both which is necessary for each process; whereas, if the whole work were executed by one workman, that person must possess sufficient skill to perform the most difficult, and sufficient strength to execute the most laborious, of the operations into which the art is divided.

It is interesting to compare the statements of Babbage and Taylor. Superficially, they seem to say much of the same; actually, Taylor's four principles of managing introduced the means by which Babbage's "transference of skill" *might be accomplished.* While many still think of Taylor as a seeker of cold efficiency, the true scope of his work is more accurately envisioned in this prefatory summation from his 1911 book:

> The principal object of management should be to secure the maximum prosperity for the employer, coupled with the maximum prosperity for each employee.
> The words "maximum prosperity" are used, in their broad sense, to mean not only large dividends for the company or owner, but the development of every branch of the business to its highest state of excellence, so that the prosperity may be permanent.

In the same way maximum prosperity for each employee means not only high wages than are usually received by men of his class, but, of more importance still, it also means the development of each man to his state of maximum efficiency, so that he may be able to do, generally speaking, the highest grade of work for which his natural abilities fit him, and it further means giving him, when possible, this class of work to do . . .

The majority of these men (employers and employees) believe that the fundamental interests of employees and employers are necessarily antagonistic. Scientific management, on the contrary, has for its very foundation the firm conviction that the true interests of the two are one and the same; that prosperity for the employer cannot exist through a long term of years unless it is accompanied by prosperity for the employee, and *vice versa;* and that it is possible to give the workman what he wants—a low labor cost—for his manufactures.[7]

Another milestone of considerable stimulative value was passed in connection with the testimony of Harrington Emerson and other engineers before the Interstate Commerce Commission. In October of 1910, Louis D. Brandeis and Henry L. Gantt brought together a group of engineers to choose the most suitable designation for the new philosophy of management.

Mr. Brandeis was the principal attorney of freight shippers who were fighting the imposition of railroad rate increases. The essence of his strategy was to prove by competent testimony that a method existed whereby the railroads could not only reduce rates but could, at the same time, reduce costs and increase wages. He realized that the case would be strengthened if all his witnesses called the same things by the same names and would agree on a single name to designate the system of management they represented.

Mr. Emerson pointed out, under careful questioning by Mr. Brandeis, that the railroads of America could save at least a million dollars a day by the application of scientific principles to the operation of their business. Sudden realization among business leaders everywhere that the then proudest industrial achievement, the system of railroads, was actually something less than the flawless gem of American enterprise, brought at last the needed widespread attention and support the management movement had lacked and gave the newly chosen name, Scientific Management, an official introduction.

A conference of some three hundred businessmen, consultants, and educators was called in 1912 at Tuck School at Dartmouth to discuss the possible courses of action uncovered by such new avenues of management thinking. The deliberation of these historic sessions, powerfully preserved by Harlow Persons, are considered by many scholars to mark the "Charter" of an *organized* "Management Movement" in this country within which to progress and cumulate individual contributions in a meaningful way.

Almost overnight, "Scientific Management" became a matter of public concern and open debate. As so often happens, however, enthusiasm outran understanding.

[7] Frederick W. Taylor, *The Principles of Scientific Management,* 1911, p. 9-10.

Although resistance to excesses was prompt, the "efficiency expert" became the apostle of exploitation in the eyes of the great body of labor, rather than a leader for mutual progress and agreement.

Among management people themselves there was still a further dissimilarity of enthusiasm, reflecting that human nature is the common characteristic of both the managerial and the individual worker. Traditionalists regarded the work of the management investigators as so much pap and set out on an active de-bunking movement, rooted in an attempt to maintain the only ways of work they could or wanted to understand. Progressives refused the challenge of a pointless battle and began to re-evaluate their responsibilities as managers.

Contrast these two answers to a survey conducted by the American Society of Mechanical Engineers and quoted in the first of that Association's *Ten Year Progress in Management Reports*, published in 1912, which from 1912 to 1932 were under the distinguished guidance of L. P. Alford. In response to a request for a definition of the new element in the art of management, the traditionalist viewpoint held:

> I am not aware that a *new* element in the art of management has been discovered . . .
>
> There have been no new discoveries in scientific management of industrial institutions. Common-sense men have used common-sense methods always. The term "scientific management" is a catch-word which assumes that industrial institutions have not been scientifically managed—which is not the case. My experience and the experience of my friends has been that there has been no new element injected into the art of management.
>
> In the writer's opinion there is very little that is new about it (the art of management). There is hardly any part of it that has not been practised by managers for the past 100 years. The trouble is there are not enough managers with sufficient initiative to set the system moving properly.
>
> . . . the problem presented is not the adoption of something entirely new; but rather the extension to every detail of our work of something which we have already tried.

This was the classic pattern of the resistance. The writer made categorical admission of two basic hazards in the path of industrial development—the lack of adequately trained and inspired managers and the need for the extension of scientific method to the over-all enterprise. He offered neither solution nor alternative and apparently was willing to believe that the changing nature of management was a fictitious academic dream.

The ASME Committee, with J. M. Dodge as Chairman and Alford, himself, as Secretary, rejected this concept of "impossibility" and selected from among the many favorable responses one which seemed best to convey the nature of the then so-new "science":

> The best designation of the new element I believe to be "scientific management." This term already has been adopted quite generally and although frequently misused, carries with it the fundamental idea that the management of labor is a proc-

ess requiring thorough analytical treatment and involving scientific as opposed to "rule-of-thumb" methods.

The writer ventures to define the new element briefly, but broadly, as: The critical observation, accurate description, analysis, and classification of all industrial and business phenomena of a recurring nature, including all forms of cooperative human effort and the systematic application of the resulting records to secure the most economical and efficient production and regulation of future phenomena.

Stripped of technicalities the method of the modern efficiency engineer is simply this: First, to analyze and study each piece of work before it is performed; second, to decide how it can be done with a minimum of wasted motion and energy; third, to instruct the workman so that he may do the work in the manner selected as most efficient.

The Taylor System is not a method of pay, a specific ruling of account books, not the use of high-speed steel. It is simply an honest, intelligent effort to arrive at the absolute control in every department; to let tabulated and unimpeachable fact take the place of individual opinion; to develop "team play" to its highest possibility.

As we conceive it, scientific management consists in the conscious application of the laws inherent in the practise of successful managers and in the laws of science in general. It has been called management engineering, which seems more fully to cover its general scope than a science.

The 1912 (ASME) Progress Report continues in reference to this second letter:

These quotations convey the ideas of a conscious effort to ascertain and study facts and systematically to apply them in instructing the workmen and in controlling every department of industry. Setting these against the underlying principle of the transference of skill, we conceive the prominent element in present-day industrial management to be: *The mental attitude that consciously applies the transference of skill to all the activities of industry.*

The work of the committee, advanced and comprehensive though it then was, of course still fell short of a full appreciation of the basic nature of scientific management. They rejected as inaccurate and muddled a suggested approach to a specific means of putting into practice the "attitude that consciously applies the transference of skill." In the light of present theory and practice, however, this statement by an unnamed correspondent of the Committee is neither fatally inaccurate nor particularly muddled in conceptual understanding, even though the "functional foreman" concept which was advocated to permit specialization in skills, has since been found to be less desirable than the single foreman backed and aided by functional staff specialists:

The regulative principles of management along scientific lines include four important elements:
a. Planning of the processes and operations in detail by a special department organized for this purpose.
b. Functional organization by which each man superintending the workman is responsible for a single line of effort. This is distinctly opposed to the older type of military organization, where every man in the management is given a combination of executive, legislative, and judicial functions.

    c. Training the worker so as to require him to do each job in what has been found to be the best method of operation.

    d. Equable payment of the workers based on quantity and quality of output of each individual. This involves scientific analysis of each operation to determine the proper time that should be required for its accomplishment and also high payment for the worker who obtains the object sought.

As a result of the interest in the railroad rate cases, of the Dartmouth meeting, and of the generally increased attention of engineers and the public, 1912 and 1913 saw the formation of many new associations. Most of them, at the time, were essentially either splinter groups broken off from the basic ASME body or else newly organized as a result of somewhat different objectives or the desire of specialists to emphasize special facets of the movement.

One of the most important of these new societies was also one of the most short lived. It was important because it numbered among its members of record that kind of mixture of outstanding industrial executives and business managers, as well as management scholars, theorists, educators, economists, and publicists, which has allowed theory and practice to crossfertilize each other as the American Industrial Society has evolved. Its name, the Efficiency Society, was unfortunate since the word "efficiency" had begun to have a rather caustic effect on the public. Its reasons for failure were, however, somewhat more fundamental. Charles Buxton Going, in outlining the purposes and objectives of the Society, wrote:

> The essence of the Efficiency Movement is insistence upon a determination of standards of achievement—equitable and reasonable standards by which the ratio of useful result secured to the effort expended, or the expense incurred in any given case, may be compared with the ratio that should exist in a normal utilization of the agencies at hand. Efficiency does not demand nor even encourage strenuousness. It does not impose nor even countenance parsimony. It merely demands equivalence, equivalence between power supplied and work performed; equivalence between natural resources utilized and products obtained; equivalence between vital opportunity and individual or national health; equivalence between attainable degrees of security and the actual proportion of casualties; equivalence between production capacity and finished product.[8]

One can hardly take issue with the "insistence" or the "demands." Certainly they are only objectives which are approachable and beneficial to society.

Yet, there is an air of coldness and of compulsion about this statement which could hardly be expected to win understanding or reduce antagonism. What seemed to be essentially lacking was an adequate awareness that the man at the machine might value and protect his own conception of his own dignity—that in the last analysis any hope for a more efficient world would necessarily have to depend on

---

[8] Charles Buxton Going, "The Efficiency Movement. An Outline." *Transactions*, Efficiency Society, Inc., 1912, Vol. 1, p. 13.

making the worker aware and voluntarily appreciative of the fact that although his objectives and those of the enterprise might normally be different, both sets of objectives could only be achieved together; that is, that their desires were not mutually exclusive, merely different.

Requoting Taylor on this point: "Scientific Management, on the contrary, has for its very foundation the firm conviction that the true interests of the two are one and the same . . ." [9] Although, of course, Taylor generalized—the "true interest" often being overshadowed by the *apparent* interest—he clearly appreciated the nature and magnitude of the human problem.

So, also, did others. A. Hamilton Church and L. P. Alford, for example, wrote:

> Some of the conditions of personal effectiveness are these: The individual must feel leadership; have adequate encouragement and reward; be physically fit and under good physical conditions; and receive a definite allotment of responsibility.
>
> These conditions apply not only to the operative force but to all grades of employees. In fact, some of them apply with greater urgency to the man "higher-up" than to the actual worker.
>
> The truth is, of course, that no single element of a system, or even a combination of half a dozen of such elements . . . more than touch the fringe of the questions. Highly organized systems may coexist with fine *esprit de corps* but the latter is not dependent on any form of system or organization.
>
> Of all the conditions controlling a fine working atmosphere, leadership probably plays the most important part . . . The weakness of one prominent school of management doctrine is that it pretends that it has superseded leadership by substituting therefor elaborate mechanism. Such a contention betrays a complete misapprehension of how men are constituted and of what the true functions of elaborate mechanisms really are. All such mechanism is but a collection of mechanical tentacles or feelers to enable the controlling mind and spirit of the management to be in several places at once. If personality behind these tentacles is a feeble one, the mechanism will not supplement its deficiencies in the slightest degree. [10]

This was the visionary concept which, in the hands of those who were to carry on the work, has been embellished and amplified as one of the basic tenets of the "Science of Managing."

It found expression in the formation of such associations as The Society to Promote the Science of Management and the National Association of Corporation Schools, the later group devoted primarily to the problems of training in industry. Somewhat later, in 1917, the growing interest in connection with war work led to the formation of the Society of Industrial Engineers.

Soundly conceived, these organizations grew in prestige over the years. The first and third eventually became the present Society for the Advancement of Management, and the second, also after mergers with others, became the present American Management Association.

[9] Taylor, *op. cit.*, p. 9.
[10] A. Hamilton Church and L. P. Alford, "The Principles of Management." *American Machinist*, May 30, 1912.

In reviewing the rise and fall of various management organizations, a possible key to their success or failure may be found in the answers to Professor Dwight Waldo's questions:

> Are students of administration trying to solve the problem of human cooperation on too low a plane? Have they, by the double process of regarding more and more formal data over a wider and wider field of human organization, lost insight, penetration? Is formal analysis of organizations without regard to the purposes that inspire them but a tedious elaboration of the insignificant? [11]

Where the sights have been properly set, and the objectives honestly derived from the inherent obligations imposed on the work by the needs of society in general, and of individual human beings in particular, management associations have flourished. They are accepted now as a necessary and desirable professional component of our technological industrial society and are progressively expanding their contributions based on their sound foundation.

V

The years between 1912 and 1922, the date of Alford's second ASME Progress Report, were years of international unrest and of world-wide war. Demands on current material and human resources had required almost the total attention of management thinking, and the theoretical aspects of the report were, therefore, very nearly restatements of the 1912 Report. *Practically*, however, it was an era of great advances, since the unprecedented demands of the war effort required the *application* of every organizational and functional skill at hand.

One of the characteristics of a science, the alternate play and shifting dominance of theory and practice as demanded by necessity, then became evident in the Science of Managing.

If it is possible to assess against one man the stimulation for making the theoretics of management into working realities during World War I, such appraisal would undoubtedly point to Bernard Baruch. Both in the specific structure of his War Industries Board, as it was finally constituted in 1918, and in substituting centralized and authoritative governmental planning for the free market and the law of supply and demand which in effect enforced efficient managerial attitudes by such devices as rigid priorities, fixed prices, and absolute schedules, he gave industry little choice but to streamline and clean house or to fail. Heavy production schedules and severely limited profits thus practically forced these industry leaders, who had not done so through foresight and conviction, to turn to scientific management as a means of survival.

Baruch seemed peculiarly gifted in his ability to look at the mobilization effort as essentially an economic proposition. He demanded, and finally received, authority

[11] Dwight Waldo, *The Administrative State*. The Ronald Press Co., p. 211.

to make decisions and enforce them over the total field of supply and demand of not only the materials of war itself, but over the total economy. Most importantly, however, he substantially avoided the inherent dictatorial dangers of such a concentration of power by delegating his authority to subordinates in order to put decision-making in the hands of experienced economic and industrial experts who were close to the scene of action.

Out of the chaos of the 1914–1917 period, a time when the President's Advisory Commission was in the untenable position of being asked to make decisions but prevented by charter from enforcing the decisions, the United States thus finally achieved the integration of its aims and its capabilities, aided, of course, by that terrible but effective commonness of purpose and spirit which the fires of war so rapidly forged. How it was done is summed up by James Tyson in these words:

> The great principle followed throughout the Board's dealing with industry was that of voluntary cooperation with the big stick in the closet. The biggest problem was to increase production so as to raise the output of industry up somewhere nearer the tremendous demands of the government. For this reason it was necessary to give business every encouragement, by allowing a margin of profit and also by attempting to arrive at an agreement with each trade before imposing conservation or other regulations . . . From the time of his early attempts to bring producers together . . . he (Baruch) followed this policy of close alliance rather than one of arbitrary control.
>
> Perhaps no better appraisal of the final forms of this cooperating could be found than the observation of Paul Von Hindenburg in his memoirs, when he said of American Industry: "Her brilliant, if pitiless, war industry had entered the service of patriotism and had not failed it. Under the compulsion of military necessity a ruthless autocracy was at work and rightly, even in this land at the portals of which the Statue of Liberty flashes its blinding light across the sea. They understood war!" [12]

The principles of leadership include of necessity an understanding of the limitations of those who are led.

Whether these limitations are the result of tradition, of prejudice, or of apathy, they exist and have to be dealt with in an atmosphere of reality. That not every man wants to be or is capable of being captain of his own ship was demonstrated in the attempts of Edward and Lincoln Filene, who were both early theorists and early practitioners of scientific management, to put their famous Boston department store on a cooperative basis.

Edward Filene, described by one of his associates as an "ingenuous and ingenious idealist" embarked on a program in 1912 which, in the cold light of hindsight, was as noted for its impracticality as it was for its humanity. He and his brother tried desperately to encourage the interest and active participation of the workers in the enterprise by establishing a Cooperative Association together with plans for the eventual

[12] James L. Tyson, "The War Industries Board, 1917–18." Supplement to *Fortune*, September, 1940, p. 16.

transfer of all stock to employees. Indifference toward the exercise of power and resistance toward assuming responsibility for their own corporate destiny on the part of the workers was so startlingly apparent that Lincoln Steffens facetiously suggested that Filene might have to hire some agitators to put his program across.

The effort to put the enterprise in the hands of the workers continued unsuccessfully for more than ten years. It failed, not because of basic violations of ethical standards or of public and employee interests, but because of the failure of the Filenes to establish a system of communication with their employees which would allow them to determine the employees' concept of the manager's and worker's common interests.

The failure, a personal disaster for Edward Filene, made nevertheless two significant contributions to the business community. It showed that managing is a mantle of responsibility not willingly accepted by all people. Moreover, it demonstrated the fundamental need for thorough and undistorted study of all the facets of a problem. Thus, it highlighted, for management theorists and practitioners, the importances of these three elements of business managerial thinking: Thinking ahead, thinking through, and thinking whole.

VI

The awakening of the true nature of the modern American leadership process came about in the period following World War I. Now, at last, acute realization of the closely geared relationship of the business enterprise as an integral part of, and at the same time as a significant contributor to a general pattern of social development, was broadly achieved.

The story of this awakening in industry is, in large part, vividly reported in the gifted observations and writings of Mary Parker Follett. Her papers and lectures covering some thirty years of uniquely contributive observation are remarkable both for their breadth of application and for the penetrating understanding of motive and need.

She realized that the true quality of modern business Leadership stems from the appreciation of the basic needs and aspirations and of the mutual dependence of men in a complex social organism. Throughout her long career Miss Follett was fortunate in having the friendship and advice of the many industry and business leaders, including especially many in the management of the New England Telephone and Telegraph Company, who shared with her the benefit of their experience, and for whom she was able to express the meaning and import of their work. Her relationships with the telephone system were especially fortunate because the gifted early managerial work of Theodore Vail, president of the parent company in the Bell System, had provided an environment of management by well-defined and far-seeing policies within a clearly-designed functional organization structure that has in essence survived to this day and that was peculiarly appropriate for her perceptive observation and advice.

Mary Follett received her formal education at Radcliffe College. Her work there and her subsequent contributions earned her a place among the College's fifty most distinguished graduates. Metcalf and Urwick, in their collection of her papers, *Dynamic Administration,* attempted to define the special quality of her attitudes which gave her work such significance. It is repeated here because it is, in a way, the definition of a rare managerial trait:

> Mary Follett's outstanding characteristic was a facility for winning the confidence and esteem of those with whom she came in contact; she established a deeply-rooted understanding and friendship with a wide circle of eminent men and women on both sides of the Atlantic. The root of this social gift was her vivid interest in life. Every individual's experience, his relations with others and with the social groups—large or small—of which he was a part, were the food for her thought. She listened with alert and kindly attention; she discussed problems in a temper which drew the best out of the individual with whom she was talking. The strength of the personal associations she thus built up were remarkable.

Miss Follett progressed from community activities to social work, and from there to vocational guidance and finally to business and industrial organization. In the latter work she drew heavily upon her experience in practical psychology, and her lectures and papers were strongly woven with the threads of understanding and sympathy. Her philosophy was, of course, the synthesis of the studies of many people concerned with the theory of organization.

In the meantime, Mrs. Gilbreth, like many others prominent in the history of the management movement, continued her analysis of industrial problems, delineating specific worker and manager attributes which contributed to the balance of the business economy. At the same time comprehensive full-length books began to supplement the shorter conference-type papers as the building blocks of the literature of Management. Thus, such volumes as Mooney and Reiley's *Onward Industry,* and later their *The Principles of Organization,* Fayol's *Industrial and General Administration,* Barnard's *Functions of the Executive,* and Brown's *Industrial Organization* typify the magnitude and scope of the source material to which Miss Follett added her own observation and imagination. It is noteworthy also that these writers were practicing industrialists, two from General Motors, one from the mining industry, one from the Bell Telephone System, and the last from the Johns-Manville Corporation.

Such writings and those of many other leading industrialists, consultants, and educators afforded a firm base for the present comprehensive literature in this field. Thus, the following brief quotations from the Follett papers are, in fact, representative of the creative outpouring of an era rather than of a single person:

On conflict:

> As conflict—difference—is here in the world, as we cannot avoid it, we should, I think, use it. Instead of condemning it, we should set it to work for us . . . There are three main ways of dealing with conflict: domination, compromise, and integration. Domination, obviously, is a victory of one side over the other. This is the easiest

way of dealing with conflict, the easiest for the moment but not usually successful in the long run.

The second way of dealing with conflict, that of compromise, we understand well, for it is the way we settle most of our controversies . . . Yet no one really wants to compromise, because that means a giving up of something. Is there then any other method of ending conflict? There is a way beginning now to be recognized at least, and occasionally followed: when two desires are *integrated*, that means that a solution has been found in which both desires have found a place, that neither side has to sacrifice anything.

On Business as an integrative unity:

It seems to me that the first test of business administration, of industrial organization, should be whether you have a business with all its parts so coordinated, so moving together in their closely knit and adjusted activities, so linking, interlocking, interrelating, that they make a work unit—that is, not a congeries of separate pieces, but what I have called a functionwhole or integrative unity.

On the nature of Power:

So far as my observation has gone, it seems to me that whereas power usually means power-over, the power of some person or group over some other person or group, it is possible to develop the conception of power-with, a jointly developed power, a co-active, not a coercive power.

On the Psychology of consent and participation:

Many people are now getting beyond the consent-of-the-governed stage in their thinking, yet there are political scientists who are still advocating it. And, indeed, it is much better to have the consent of the governed than not to have it . . . but we are also recognizing today that it is only a first step; that not consent but participation is the right basis for all social relations.

The literature of management during the period between the two World Wars shows how completely Miss Follett's views gave expression to the framework which had become a fundamental part of the thinking of industry.

Although it would be impossible in this limited treatise to give even an indication of the wealth of writing done during this period, no paper on the history of management concepts would be possible without at least a partial mention of the many contributions made here and abroad. It is interesting to note the significant degree to which many of these fundamental books were the work of men whose professional careers had been directly concerned with business operations. Few of them were "writers," and it is almost by incidental and fortunate circumstances that their work is so readable, not discounting, of course, that clarity of conviction and of purpose are themselves no mean aids to such clarity of presentation.

Dr. Harry Arthur Hopf, whose own work will be discussed at a later point, listed twelve indispensable books, chiefly of this general period, and his reviews on five are so indicative of the form which the evolving "science of managing" was assuming that they deserve to be quoted here in part: [13]

[13] Appendix A.

The Philosophy of Management, by Oliver Sheldon (of Great Britain), was "written from a broad perspective; it stresses the importance of scientific and ethical principles, gives an excellent exposition of the social and industrial background, and deals in an authoritative manner with fundamentals of management."

Industrial and General Administration by Henri Fayol (a leading French manager of mining and industrial firms). "His masterly analysis of the essential functions of a business enterprise, his selection among them of administration for special treatment leading to a statement of five underlying principles, and his advocacy of the latter in the form of the Administrative Doctrine, combined to lay the foundation for a new school of thought known as 'Fayolism.'"

Top-Management Organization and Control, by Holden, Fish, and Smith (with combined experience in educational and industrial circles in California), "deals with a field which has hitherto been little explored . . . On the strength of their research study of the management policies and practices of thirty-one leading American industrial corporations, the authors have performed the signally valuable service of bringing together, in admirably organized form, a great amount of factual and interpretive material bearing upon some of the most important and complex management problems with which large-scale industrial organization is confronted."

The Principles of Organization by Mooney and Reiley (of the General Motors organization) is a scholarly work dominated to a large extent by the historic approach. It covers the history of the management effort as it has applied to the organization of the state, the church, the army, and industry. "This is not a work which may be readily mastered. Its careful study will, however, supply the reader with a sound framework of principles which will serve excellently the purpose of orientation."

Lectures on Organization by Russell Robb is a collection of the lectures delivered in the course on industrial organization at Harvard University. "The author, a distinguished engineer (connected with the Stone & Webster engineering, financing, and management organization) who died in 1927, brought admirably to expression in these lectures a varied experience distilled into a philosophy which, taken as a whole, constitutes perhaps the single most authoritative and appealing exposition stemming from an American to be found in the literature of organization."

Other indispensable books listed by Dr. Hopf were *The Design of Manufacturing Enterprises* by Walter Rautenstrauch, *Industrial Organization and Management* by Ralph Davis, *Industrial Management* by Lansburgh and Spriegel, *Budgetary Control* by James McKinsey, *Personnel Management* by Scott, Clothier, Mathewson, and Spriegel, *Functions of the Executive* by Chester Barnard, and *The Art of Leadership* by Ordway Tead. The role of these authors is also interesting, showing how such universities as Columbia, Ohio State, and Northwestern, as well as industrial firms, were centers of thought of the steadily evolving "science of managing."

In reading these books, the difference in emphasis in fundamental thinking during the 'twenties and 'thirties compared to that of the first two decades of the century is apparent. The essence of a deeper *philosophy* of Scientific Management was gradually being distilled and assembled out of the diverse objectives which had been the goals of early investigators. Over-all planning and measurement were replacing the patchwork approach, and though detailed studies of particular situations were necessarily continued, they were increasingly referenced to the framework of the total social scene.

The basic developments of the period were those of bringing into closer blend a proper mixture of the workers' and managers' individual emotional needs and the requirements of an industrial enterprise constituted for the rigors of competitive life in an increasingly complex technological environment. The Science of Managing thus began to appreciate and encompass the techniques of multiplying human skills as well as mechanical power.

VII

When the final review of the history of management during this half-century is written, perhaps it may seek a representative of the movement who, in his work and in his writing, symbolizes the search for the basic and irrefutable principles of the science. They will need to look no further than Dr. Harry Arthur Hopf. Except by an extensive first-hand study of his writings, which unfortunately consist of many separate talks and articles rather than bound volumes, it is impossible to gauge even closely the remarkable gifts he left as a legacy to the student and practitioner of today.

Dr. Hopf, of English birth, came to America in 1898. His first job as a foreign language stenographer for an insurance company was an education in the unending frustration that was the normally accepted part of the non-management employee in business and industry of the time. He observed the disorganization of enterprises devoted solely to the demands of day-to-day problems, the dissatisfactions that came from indecisive or arbitrarily decisive management, the absence of rewards and compensation related even vaguely to effort and contribution at every level.

Writing in *Net Results*, a regular publication of the Institute of Management he later established, Dr. Hopf said:

> With courage (or was it foolhardiness?) and vigor I attacked several situations literally crying for improvement. It was then that I learned for the first time that the way of the reformer is hard, for it required years of the most arduous effort to win a sympathetic hearing for any suggestions. And with the advent of the new life insurance laws in New York State in 1907, my company, in common with other similar institutions, apparently surrendered itself to a case of paralysis of management which was destined to persist for some years ...

Arduous effort was the normal way of life for Dr. Hopf. His activity as an industrial and business advisor, his participation as founder and pilot of expanded management society activities, his work as a government consultant during both major wars, his seemingly endless capacity to study, to understand, and to offer solutions for the basic problems of the management science paint a picture of nearly legendary proportions.

Out of his many and varied contributions, two, perhaps more than any others, have earned him an enduring place in the annals of the management movement. Dr. Hopf, in his studies of the life insurance business was concerned, of course, with the problem of net efficiency. He noted that the criteria of success were universally related to size, and that these criteria were both wrong and potentially disastrous. Investigations into other industries revealed that this universality was not confined to the insurance business, but that nearly everyone engaged in industry just assumed that the bigger they were, the better, the more efficient, and the more secure they were.

At the Sixth International Congress for Scientific Management, held in London in 1935, he suggested that the time was ripe for the strengthening of the science of management and its transformation to the more inclusive one: optimology—the science of the optimum. In this talk Dr. Hopf said:

> Among the most profound problems with which society must concern itself under present-day conditions is that relating to the determination, achievement, and maintenance of optimal conditions in all types of organized human enterprise. The overwhelming economic disaster, from the effects of which the world is still suffering, halted with ruthless force an era of unparalleled expansion which, in the United States of America at least, assumed proportions indicative of a belief in the feasibility of unlimited growth and unchecked size.
>
> As we falteringly proceed upon the road to recovery, we are faced with new political, social, and economic trends and doctrines which are evidently destined to bring into being forms of organization and control without precedent in our experience, and to call for qualities of cooperation and joint action on the part of businessmen, engineers, social scientists, government officials, labour representatives, and others, far beyond any need of the past. Having, then, narrowly escaped complete destruction upon the rock of Scylla, are we now being drawn with increasing force into the whirlpool of Charybdis?

Dr. Hopf defined the optimum—for government as well as business—as that state of development of an enterprise which, when reached and maintained, tends to perpetuate an equilibrium among the factors of size, cost, and human capacity which would provide ideal realization of the organizational objectives, and he pointed out that the optimum size was at this state of equilibrium rather than connected, in any way, with bigness alone.

Although Dr. Hopf placed no arbitrary limitations on size, he demonstrated that perpetuation of a growing enterprise depended upon the concomitant upward shifting of the equilibrium point. He emphasized that the natural economic barriers to growth are rarely reached, but that the limiting barriers were, most generally, organizational in nature.

In concluding his paper, Dr. Hopf restated a conception of a method of for-

481

mulating a technique to determine optimal size and relationships which he had originally presented at a meeting of the Taylor Society in 1930. They have become almost a working code of the mid-century science of management:

1. Establish the objectives of the business in comprehensive terms;
2. Define those general policies which should be followed regardless of operating conditions or results;
3. Define the task of management in human terms;
4. Staff the executive group with members who are competent to perform successfully the tasks assigned to them;
5. Furnish the executive group with standards of accomplishment by which performance can be accurately measured;
6. Study operating results and establish trends of accomplishment;
7. Adjust the rate of replacement of members of the executive group in line with requirements for maintaining the standards set;
8. Consider particularly the factor of age in its relation to productive capacity of executives;
9. Analyze all dynamic elements so as to discern the possible operation of the law of diminishing returns with respect to any element, substituting measurement for judgement, wherever possible;
10. Establish the optimal size of organization at the level at which the most favourable operating results can be secured, within the limits of the predetermined objectives and policies and without causing an executive overload at any point in the organization.

Dr. Hopf argued vigorously throughout his life for new perspectives in management. He believed that managing, as such, had to become a special and professional activity. In speaking before the Society of Industrial Engineers in 1933, he quoted Dennison and Willitts' [14] classic definition of a profession:

1. A profession is an occupation which requires intellectual training as contrasted with mechanical skill;
2. A profession employs the fruits of science, uses the scientific method, and maintains an experimental attitude toward information;
3. The professed knowledge is used by its applicant to the service of others, usually in a manner governed by a code of ethics;
4. The amount of financial return is not the chief measure of success;
5. The professions are given public and often legal recognition.

Dr. Hopf examined the work of managing in the light of these criteria, seeking to establish a system of methods which would allow the professional manager to apply the first three as operational techniques. He suggested four basic divisions of the work as forming the dynamics of management: planning, organizing, coordinating, and controlling, a significant and penetrating pioneer attempt to divide the over-all work of the professional manager into primary constituent elements.

In describing the meaning of these four key words, Dr. Hopf continued:

[14] Henry S. Dennison, of the Dennison Manufacturing Company, and Joseph H. Willitts of the University of Pennsylvania.

The first of these (planning) involves subdivision of activities to a point where they are within the compass of performance by persons of moderate ability. Failure to observe the requirement is bound to result in the creation of undue supervisory burdens and in obstructions to the smooth flow of operating routines.

The second requirement (organizing) calls for proper relative evaluation of operating units and their grouping along related lines. When the maintenance of arbitrary lines of demarcation among departments, bureaus, divisions, sections, branches, units, etc., comes to be regarded as of greater importance than preservation of the integrity of operating procedures, only disorganization and consequent lack of coordination ensues . . .

The third requirement (coordinating) is the establishment of clear lines of authority, responsibility, and reporting relationships . . . Maintenance of clear lines of authority, responsibility, and reporting relationships under this type of control hinges to a large extent upon integration of the often divergent concepts held by the administrators of the manner in which their relationships to one another shall be composed and of the character of personal supervision over the organization which each shall exercise.

The fourth requirement (controlling) goes right to the root of the problem of administrative coordination. It involves the separation of planning from performance, a *sine qua non* of effective organization. Progress in undertaking such separation is often attended by conflicts between the points of view of the staff, which is responsible for planning, and the line, which is charged with the accomplishment of satisfactory operating results. Unless conflicts can be resolved in favor of cooperative action, sound conditions of administrative coordination are impossible.

Like other great concepts in the philosophies, this one is deceptive in its simplicity. Its value as a working thesis, however, is unquestioned, for, with relatively evolutionary changes, it points yet to most of the basic keys to successful and professional managing.

The range of Dr. Hopf's work encompassed practically all areas of business thinking in both its current and its historical and in both its national and its international aspects. He was at once the theoretician and the practical man, the dreamer and the doer, the pragmatic statistician and the adventurous explorer. These words of Woodrow Wilson on the nature of leadership, written many years before Dr. Hopf's death, well describe this "first universal man of management": [15]

That the leader of men must have such sympathetic insight as shall enable him to know quite unerringly the motives which move other men in the mass is of course self-evident; but this insight which he must have is not the Shakespearean insight. It need not pierce the particular secrets of individual men: it need only know what it is that lies waiting to be stirred in the minds and purposes of groups and masses of men.[16]

[15] As he was called, *in memoriam,* in *Net Results* for October, 1949. Alvin E. Dodd, Executive Vice-Chairman, U.S. Council of the International Chamber of Commerce and President *Emeritus,* American Management Association, and many other business and industrial leaders paid a final tribute to Dr. Hopf through the medium of this little magazine which he and Mrs. Hopf had written for so many years.

[16] Woodrow Wilson, *Leaders of Men.* Princeton University Press, Princeton, N. J., 1952.

VIII

The modern "Science of Managing" in its evolving full dimensions has come from this historical background, but it is none the less a true product of our own current day.

It is the application of ethical principles by qualified professional managers to the problems of creating and maintaining a complex pattern of order which serves, in optimum fashion, the common interests of the people—that is, of the customers and the public as well as the owners, the executives, and the employees—and of the enterprise itself as a key and characteristic element of today's Industrial Society.

Inherent in the acceptance of such a statement is the responsibility to determine the ethical principles which govern a situation, the qualifications of a professional manager, the pattern of order, and the common interests.

The ethical principles can be briefed simply. To have meaning and to generate faith, a genuine "Science of Managing" can only exist in a climate of liberty, of reason, of morality, and of religion. Outside it—in an air of compulsion, force, materialism, and atheism—it is reduced to impotence and cannot exist any more than the civilization of which it is a part can continue under such circumstances.

Deeply grounded in the understanding of our position is the acceptance of the natural rights of the individual as a natural person and that these, coming to him as a person in his own right, transcend in importance these other rights of society as an organized grouping of such individuals where functions come from them to be exercised for them. The individual creates his society not by self-abrogation of these rights, but by his voluntary modification of his liberties derived from them. This is the common interest. This makes possible those kinds of common purpose which justify joint teamwork in organized activities.

Dr. Einstein describes the temperament of the individual as an essentially independent being who willingly becomes a part of and accepts the obligations of a social environment:

> Man is, at one and the same time, a solitary being and a social being. As a solitary being, he attempts to protect his own existence and that of those who are closest to him, to satisfy his personal desires, and to develop his innate abilities. As a social being, he seeks to gain the recognition and affection of his fellow human beings, to share in their pleasures, to comfort them in their sorrows, and to improve their conditions of life . . . The abstract concept "society" means to the individual human being the sum total of his direct and indirect relations to his contemporaries and to all people of earlier generations. The individual is able to think, feel, strive, and work by himself; but he depends so much upon society—in his physical, intellectual, and emotional existence—that it is impossible to think of him, or to understand him, outside the framework of society.[17]

In order to join his personal aspirations understandingly and satisfyingly with those of the Society of which he is a part, it has become more and more necessary for

[17] Einstein, *op. cit.*, p. 126. It is significant that in still later writings, Dr. Einstein—now clearly established as one of the foremost scientists of the ages—goes on to reject the concept of a purely random and patternless universe, in the striking phrase, "I cannot believe that God plays dice with the cosmos."

man to seek for a rational pattern within which to guide and govern his actions. The patterns of order which constitute the goals of this elemental search of all people are achieved by the integration of the results of observation into generalized laws which can be applied with measurably successful results.

Writing of *Management and the American Future*,[18] Lawrence H. Appley, now President of the American Management Association, characterized the professional manager as ". . . an individual who, because of his training, experience, and competence, is employed to develop and expand the assets and realizations of owners." His horizons might well have been widened to include every conceivable area of human effort where Leadership is a necessity.

The concept of professional managing as Leadership by persuasion rather than by command, and the codification of the Professional Manager's distinct and unique work into the four sub-functional elements of planning, organizing, integrating, and measuring, is another of the hard-won milestones in the development of a true Science of Managing.[19]

Speaking of the emphasis placed on developing professional managers by General Electric Company, President Ralph J. Cordiner has said:

> In such an approach is plainly found one deep source of our basic business climate which has made possible the productivity and the better living standards for more and more people which have literally thrust our country into its present position of world-wide leadership and responsibility. But this in turn brings new need to seek how to do a better and more professional job of management.

J. Wilson Newman, President of Dun and Bradstreet, added further understanding of the significance of the Professional Manager concept when he said:

> Free enterprise brings up the subject of free will and decisions. In our country a man can risk his money, time, and skill in business without restraint. That is the way it should be, but as suppliers we are morally obligated to help him with all the friendly guidance we can offer. There is increasing evidence, too, that the new generation of entrepreneurs are better equipped in experience and understanding than were their fathers or grandfathers, although the hazards they face today are certainly greater and more complex . . .
>
> Yet the basic problem is human and emotional rather than statistical. All the fixed operating data can be offset by the intangibles of human nature. The impulse

[18] *Management at Mid-Century,* General Management Series No. 169, American Management Association, New York, 1954, p. 5.

[19] The modification of Dr. Hopf's earlier concept of "planning, organizing, coordinating and controlling," and the rejection of such incomplete classifications as "planning, organizing, and commanding," is apparent. Coordinating is the bringing together of actions; integrating implies unifying to form a complete whole. Control, Dr. Hopf's word, involves the exercise of guiding or restraining power, but such action inherently denies the substance of other sub-functions. Measuring is the process of reviewing performance against predetermined standards for the predicted results of planning, of making such measurements known, and thus of providing a corrective feed-back to the process, so that re-planning, re-organizing, and re-integrating may proceed; thus recognizing the need in organized efforts both for objectives, policies and clear structure on the one hand and for dynamic and vital progress on the other hand.

to business risk isn't generated in statistics. It finds life in the eye of the individual who sees an opportunity and measures the risk to achieve it. The quality of his judgment is tested by his ability to overcome obstacles.[20]

IX

During the years of World War II, a new understanding of the problems born of organizations came into being. As in the time of the first World War, the demands of survival speeded the acceptance of the theories of the Science of Managing. Again, practice caught up with theory, but this time a new technology brought time for new horizons.

Again, spurred by the fires of War, the managers of American business, together with the scientists as their partners, and with the spirit of both workers and soldiers to turn ideas and plans to reality, rose to new heights. Global logistics set the demands; the competitive enterprise system, modified once more by governmental Production direction, met the challenge.

But this time the scientific sweat of the ensuing decades provided a lubricant that allowed a multiplication of output almost fantastic in retrospect. The *principles* of managing enterprises of wide span and great diversity proved flexible enough to meet the test; and to allow the approach of Leadership by persuasion once again to vanquish the totalitarian, or command, bid for supremacy.

A most significant factor in this period was that the principle of "division of labor" was successfully applied to the work of Managing, itself, to entirely new degrees. The whole philosophy of Decentralization developed to new dimensions, not merely decentralization to new geographic areas and to new plants, or even decentralization to separate "product businesses" within a common corporate framework, but actually as Mr. Cordiner said in a memorable address to the American Management Association in 1945, "the decentralization of decision making itself," so that the authority actually to *decide* was as close as possible to the work or action specifically calling for decisions.

Once more Dr. Hopf was chosen to summarize these trends. In an article called "Evolution in Organization During the Past Decade," presented at the first post-war International Management Congress of CIOS at Stockholm in 1947, he listed the following outstanding managerial trends and advances since the seventh CIOS Congress in Washington in 1939:

1. Development of the personnel function;
2. Decentralization of management and operation;
3. Increased recognition and application of general principles of organization;
4. Creation of new units of organization to meet increasing economic and social responsibilities;
5. Improvement of techniques for policy formulation and execution.

[20] *Op. cit.*, American Management Association, New York, 1954, p. 21.

It is also important to note at this point that the United States Management Societies were active contributors to the war effort, satisfying the insistent pleas of industry for technical aid, and, at the same time, following a process of continual measuring, tempering, and re-application of organizational and operating principles.

Such ability to handle problems—of overwhelming magnitude compared to those of the first war—and to simultaneously continue to advance the Science of Managing was due, in no small part, to the newly developing techniques of organizational communications. The engineer proved once again that the essential nature of managing was a derivative of the scientific method and that his place in guiding the affairs of men was essential to the vitality of the movement, not mere accident or prior right.

Scientists and engineers who had worked to establish a factual basis on which communications systems could be predicated, came to realize the general resemblance of large social patterns to those of specific electrical or mechanical networks. Dr. Norbert Wiener, who is widely credited with leading the study and with coining the name "Cybernetics" from the Greek word meaning the art of the pilot or steersman, said:

> One of the most interesting aspects of the world is that it may be considered to be made up of patterns. A pattern is essentially an arrangement. It is characterized by the order of the elements of which it is made, rather than by the intrinsic nature of these elements.[21]

He went on further to point out that a pattern can be used to convey information and will usually convey more information than the statement of isolated facts since it also conveys interrelations.

Dr. Wiener made the penetrating observation that there is implied in the adoption of automation as an outgrowth of Cybernetics a transcending problem, for economic and for political and social statesmen alike, in "Handling the social-political responsibility to see that some way of handling their (the permanently displaced workers) leisure is provided, to make them fit into a society that is a going concern—since, in the face of radical changes, the statesmanship of management cannot stop at the edge of the individual firm.[22]

Dr. Claude Shannon of the Bell Telephone Laboratories and others carried Wiener's structural concept into fields which provided the management scientist with working theories which would allow him to apply and measure the principles of professional management in rigorous fashion.

In the first place, they established the importance of effective communications as the key to proper operation of any system involving more than a single element. What was true of the electrical network was true in even larger measure of the corporate enterprise.

Thus, Wiener, Shannon, and their associates and contemporaries believed that

[21] Norbert Wiener, *The Human Use of Human Beings*. Houghton Mifflin Company.
[22] Meeting of New York Chapter of the Society for Advancement of Management, 1950.

"one of the lessons of Cybernetics is that any organism is held together by the possession of means for the acquisition, use, retention, and transmission of information" and that "communication of information is a problem in statistics . . . and that the theory, of course, does more than express a philosophy of communication, it provides universal measures." [23]

The ability to transmit directive information to implement change and the ability to feed back the results of the change was shown to be a function of the use of optimum channels through the minimum number of transfer or recording points. In terms of the enterprise, as an organic whole, they showed that effective operation can be only achieved when directive information, the result of decision making, is created and applied as close as possible to the point of action, and when the channels of information, transmission, and performance feed-back are soundly conceived. Thus, they further affirmed the soundness of the widespread decentralization of managerial authority and responsibility, so characteristic of this period, which has to an astounding extent allowed customer and public benefits from the combined social acceptability of the relatively small decentralized business and the technological and other resources of the larger modern corporation.

In the second place, the Cyberneticists showed the possibilities of mathematical analysis in problems of business organization. Dr. Zay Jeffries, scientist and retired Vice-President of the General Electric Company, said in 1951:

> Our progress depends to a considerable extent on seeing to it that simplification processes move forward in approximate balance with the complicating processes. If this can be accomplished, then individuals with given ability can expect to go forward indefinitely without becoming casualties of their own complexity.

The simplification processes for scientific management are many, but are greatly multiplied today by the rapid emergence of essentially statistical, mathematical, and logical method. These latter kinds of developments are divorced from traditional actuarial methods by the special attitudes of mind that bring them into play. Three essential steps form the basic technique which distinguish the work:

1. Thorough exploration and precise, understandable documentation of facts concerned in an operation will reveal broad principles and affective parameters, or governing factors and variables.
2. The discovered principles and parameters may, in most instances, be defined quantitatively and manipulated with predictable results, so long as the system of which they are a part is essentially stable, as the fairly mature business characteristically tends to be.
3. The disclosure of principles and the studied manipulation of affecting parameters will provide optimum procedures and processes, measurable work simplification, great precision of guidance, and better management.

[23] Francis Bello, "The Information Theory," *Fortune*, December, 1953.

This is the technique of what is now coming to be called "Operations Research & Synthesis." Thus, the mathematician provided the professional manager not only with applicable theories, but he has also provided him with an important working tool.

The general use of computers in speeding the analysis and interpretation of the operations research process is growing rapidly and is facilitating the managerial approach based on "Thinking Through" to an ever more useful degree; which incidentally but re-affirms the perceptive foresight of Taylor in taking his steel plant data, and his speeds and feeds formulas, to the mathematicians for solution even before the turn of the twentieth century.

Such use of today's modern electronics computers, moreover, progressively allows the pre-testing of an almost unlimited number of variables to determine their interrelation and their individual effect on alternative end objectives. Scientific management has thus, in effect, been handed the priceless technique of telescoping the time required in analyzing its course to an entirely new degree.

X

This "history" of the evolution of the management movement in America has, by definition, concerned itself only casually and but little with the great and important contributions of the many theorists and experimenters in the field in Europe and other parts of the World. The development of basic principles has in no sense, of course, been a purely American effort, so, in fairness, it must be pointed out that the "history" written here is thus only one American expression of what has, in fact, been a worldwide search.

CIOS, the International Committee for Scientific Management, has acted in behalf of some twenty or more member-organizations of the free world. Since its foundation in 1926, it has been a potent force in sustaining international amity through trying economic and political times. The Gold Medal of CIOS is thus widely recognized as a symbol of the highest achievement in the management field.

Another omission, necessary since this paper has dealt with the concepts of the Science of Managing, has been the catalytic activities of our own government, except when government direction has superseded normal economic interplay under the stress of global-scale War. However, the national government, representing the interests of all the people, has had the responsibility of maintaining balance among all these interests and consequently has influenced sharply, by both positive and negative stimulation, the creation of a distinctly American form of capitalism which is now enjoined by its very nature from being monopolistic.

The resultant competitive atmosphere, inherent in this philosophy of capitalism, has been one of the significant spurring forces which has helped to move Scientific Management out of the library or classroom and into the shop.

Despite all the natural forces of both politics and bureaucracy, starting with the introduction of cost cards in the Frankford Arsenal in the 1880's by Henry Metcalf and continuing through to the present day, various departments of the government have made active use of the techniques of scientific management in their own operations.

Particularly notable are, of course, the long and constructive contributions of Mr. Herbert Hoover, who, as Secretary of Commerce in the mid-twenties, made significant steps in the elimination of waste in industry and in the standardization of products; and who, with the great first President Masaryk of the then new republic of Czechoslovakia, was co-sponsor of the first International Management Congress at Prague in 1924. As President, Mr. Hoover later began a program for the improvement of governmental bureaus, and, as Chairman of the Committee on Organization of the Executive Branch of the Government, he continued this work years later during 1948 and 1949, and again in 1953 and 1954.

XI

What, then, is the present status of the Science of Managing? Is it, in the words of Mr. A. M. Lederer, the "Fifth Force," equal to and as necessary as the forces for labor, owners, government and consumers?[24]

It would seem, in practice today, impossible to deny the importance of management without denying simultaneously the factual nature and complexity of our current technological culture. In accepting the inevitable pattern which lies ahead, the place of such a Fifth Force is thus evident, and the character and quality of the Professional Manager who will both guide and discipline this "force" is of lasting moment.

In a paper written in 1951, "Notes on a Theory of Advice," Lyman Bryson of Columbia University emphasized the important obligation of the Professional Manager with respect to the integration of knowledge and authority which are essential counterparts of the managing function:

> The function of advice is one of the oldest in human affairs and certain abstract generalizations about it that could have been made in paleolithic times are still true.
>
> Most of these generalizations, however, have not been made and, as far as can be discovered, no standard treatise in this field has ever been written.
>
> There are mountain piles of books on salesmanship, which is not disinterested advice, and a molehill of books on leadership, but nothing on the technique and difficulties of trying to put knowledge at the service of power.
>
> The right relation of knowledge and power is, however, one of the big problems of our age.
>
> We need to give the closest scrutiny to the processes whereby decisions are made, and the effect on those decisions of rational information, if we are to master the difficulties of freedom in a time when power is so developed and knowledge is so dispersed.

[24] Mr. Lederer, partner in the consulting firm of Morris and VanWormer, is President of the Council for International Progress in Management (U.S.A.) and Deputy President of CIOS.

The function of advice is one of the crucial points in that relation and on that account may well be studied first.

Peter Drucker, in the face of such conditions, well describes the threefold job of the Manager in connection with today's business enterprise. By substituting country, institution, family, or any of the collective nouns which represent group entities for the word "company" and "enterprise," the universal nature of the "manager's" job, in this sense, is readily made apparent. As Mr. Drucker puts it:

It is management's first responsibility to decide what economic factors and trends are likely to affect the company's future welfare.

The second function of management is the organization and efficient utilization of the enterprise's human resources. In the industrial enterprise it is not individuals who produce, but a human organization.

The third major function of management is to provide a functioning management. This means that management has to provide for its own succession. . . . It is tomorrow's management that will determine whether the enterprise will prosper ten years hence and indeed whether it will survive . . . today's management can at least make sure that there will be available to make tomorrow's decisions men who are fully qualified, fully trained, and fully tested in actual performance.[25]

Similar growing awareness of the necessity and almost universal applicability of the managerial functions in all areas of society has become truly international in scope. For instance, Mr. Lederer in mid-1953 described to members of the Council for International Progress in Management (U.S.A.) a renaissance of European industry which "finds its expression in a European Management Movement eager to catch up with a comparable management movement in the United States, which has its roots in the same philosophical belief and which has translated that belief into practical applications to an Industrial Society."[26]

The enduring place of the Scientific Management Movement, therefore, seems assured. To those who have made a professional life of its study or practice, these further words of Lawrence Appley may serve as both encouragement and credo:

The future of America is dependent upon the caliber of management to be found in the ranks of business and industry. It is management that sets the pace and motivates labor to do its job. It is the combination of a courageous, competent management and a high-moraled, highly productive labor force that makes more things available for more people, and therefore, increases the standard of living.

This management competency which is able to motivate labor to greater productivity requires sensitivity to certain moral obligations to the community. It must be understood by such management that our present form of society can be preserved only when those on the receiving end of leadership experience that for which democracy stands. If people are to know what a democracy really is, then they must enjoy its benefits in their work, as well as in their play. They must really

[25] Peter F. Drucker, *The New Society*. Harper & Bros., 1949, p. 204. See also Drucker's earlier books on *The End of Economic Man, The Future of Industrial Man, Concept of the Corporation,* and *The Practice of Management.*

[26] President's Report for First Six Months, CIPM, 1953.

feel and believe that their bosses are interested in them as individuals and in their development to the fullest potential of character, personality, and individual productivity.

The greatest doctors, teachers, lawyers, and engineers are those who have some sense of the human values involved in their work. So it is and will continue to be with managers. The price of leadership is criticism, but its more-than-compensating reward is sense of attainment.[27]

In a hundred and fifty years we have come from narrow and dimly perceived horizons into a world of limitless possibilities and new scientific, as well as human, frontiers. The Science of Managing is, like all true sciences, creating an expanding universe of concepts and principles. Because it has come to recognize its problems as a part of, and a party to, the nature of our culture, it will continue as an unabating challenge to thought and ingenuity so long as free men continue to join in common effort to achieve desired ends.

[27] Lawrence A. Appley, *Management and the American Future.* Number 169, American Management Association General Management Series, p. 13.

HARRY ARTHUR HOPF

Soundings in the Literature
*of Management**

1945

To supplement these volumes of selected papers on the Science of Managing, "Soundings" seemed an excellent choice. With its wealth of information, it is the logical place from which an interested student or reader can complement his desire for more knowledge to enrich his self-development.

* Hopf, Harry Arthur, "Soundings in the Literature of Management: Fifty Books the Educated Practitioner Should Know," Publication No. 6, Hopf Institute of Management, Inc., Ossining, New York, 1945. Permission to reprint by courtesy of Mrs. Harry A. Hopf. (*Note:* The Hopf Institute of Management, Inc. is now called the Harry Arthur Hopf Memorial Management Library. It is located at Crotonville, New York, as part of the Management Research and Development Institute.)

SOUNDINGS IN THE LITERATURE OF MANAGEMENT

Harry Arthur Hopf

Foreword

WHEN THE PAN-AMERICAN COMMITTEE of the New York Chapter of the Society for the Advancement of Management was organized, it sought a simple and direct program. The committee wanted to avoid duplication of the work for Latin America carried on by so many agencies. It wanted to direct its efforts to the field of management.

At a luncheon meeting of representatives of management in Washington, it was stated that the Office of the Coordinator of Inter-American Affairs would be interested in sending to Latin America sets of books that would present the basic principles of the art and science of management. It was essential that the list be short but that the scope be wide. The question was where to get such a list, for it was recognized that it could be prepared only by someone grounded in the divers philosophies and techniques of management in this country and abroad. These considerations led to the unanimous selection of Harry Arthur Hopf.

Dr. Hopf gladly cooperated and took time from his busy life to prepare the desired list. His knowledge, experience, broad reading and critical faculty, aided by the extensive library of the Hopf Institute, provided the foundation for compiling such a condensed list. The product of his labors, slightly amplified, as stated by him, and supplied with illuminating annotations not included in the original list, appears in the following pages. Due to the limitations imposed, many good books have necessarily been omitted; doubtless, too, there will not be universal agreement regarding the value of all the books selected.

It is a significant fact, nevertheless, that whenever the list is mentioned, someone wants to see it; every time it is read, out comes a pencil to note the names of books someone is impelled to read, knowing that they must be important. The value of the list lies in the authoritative knowledge which has entered into its preparation. Now that it is to be made generally available in the English-speaking countries of the world, students everywhere will unquestionably benefit greatly from the sound guidance furnished by one of our foremost scholars in management.

R. OAKLEY KENNEDY
Chairman, Pan-American Committee,
Society for the Advancement of Management

New York, May 15, 1945.

FIFTY BOOKS THE EDUCATED PRACTITIONER SHOULD KNOW

During the course of his service on the bench, a well-known American judge sustained an impressive but undeserved reputation for wisdom by the simple expedient of keeping lawyers and litigants in the dark concerning the reasons underlying his decisions. One day, however, in an unguarded moment, he launched into a long and detailed explanation of the basis for a judgment rendered by him. It proved so unconvincing that his intellectual prestige suffered a blow from which it failed to recover.

This story should perhaps be regarded as an admonition when undertaking to explain the basis of preparation of a list of books on management. It would, of course, be relatively easy for any qualified student of the field to bring together a list of pertinent works and, without supporting comment, put it into circulation as the product of his thought and judgment. To follow such a course would, however, it seems to me, vitiate much of the value that might otherwise be extracted from a project of this character. The usefulness of such a list to students of the field cannot but be enhanced if, first of all, the points of departure adhered to in preparing it are carefully explained, and then each book is annotated in sufficient detail to convey a clear and objective characterization of its scope and quality.

Apart from the foregoing considerations, it appeals to me as essential to place a definite limit upon the number of books that the list should contain. Naturally, any limit that may be set is exposed to the criticism of being arbitrary; but, from a practical viewpoint, it has the virtue of compelling the exercise of keen discrimination in the process of selection and the precise balancing of a number of factors calling for objective judgment.

Perhaps a brief explanation of the genesis of the list published in these pages will be of interest. Some months ago, a group of prominent men in Washington extended to me an invitation to prepare a list of books on management, to be circulated in Latin American countries by the Office of the Coordinator of Inter-American Relations. R. Oakley Kennedy, who wrote me in behalf of the group, stated that it was desired to confine the list to twelve "must" books and twenty "recommended" books.

Much as I was in sympathy with the proposed limitations, I realized at once that the problem of classification presented certain difficulties. This was especially because works dealing with various aspects of "scientific management" could not be ignored, despite the fact that they belong to a period which is today to a large extent of historic interest only. Therefore, I came to the conclusion that it would be best not to attempt to include such works in either of the two categories indicated, but to list them separately. It seemed to me that proper weight would thus be accorded to pioneers such as Taylor, Gantt, Emerson and Gilbreth and their followers.

Another difficulty derived from the manner in which works by authors writing in languages other than English should be treated. Many important contributions to the literature of management have originated in foreign sources. Unfortunately, however, they have not, save in a few rare instances, been translated into English and are consequently inaccessible to students whose linguistic abilities are confined to that language. It appeared to me as advisable, therefore, to restrict the list to works in English, especially as under present conditions it is practically impossible to obtain publications from Continental Europe.

Reference should also be made to publications by management associations and societies. Practically all of these are in the form of journals, proceedings and monographs. They represent in the aggregate a rich collection of material of great value to students of management. They do not, however—so it seems to me at least—belong in a restricted list of books. This observation applies also to the several handbooks in the fields of administration, management, production, sales, etc., that are available to American readers.

With respect to the books finally entering into the composition of my list, which originally consisted of forty-four references (including twelve on scientific management) and for present purposes has been expanded to a round fifty in number, the following comments will prove helpful in judging the validity of the selections made:

1. The general pattern is definitely restricted to works of broadly inclusive character dealing with fundamentals and not bearing heavily on techniques;
2. The attempt has been made to consider special phases of management only in a limited fashion. This will account for the paucity, or even absence, of reference to works on psychology, distribution, finance, accounting, advertising, etc.;
3. Where several works on the same subject appear, they have been chosen because of the diverse treatment employed by the respective authors;
4. Most of the authors included in the list are authorities on the subjects they write about. I have not hesitated, however, to feature the writings of some men who are known more for their ability to bring together existing knowledge in a logical, cohesive and interpretive manner leading to correct synthesis, than for what they may have contributed to the advancement of management by original discoveries based upon research and practical experience;
5. Because of the great changes that have occurred in the past three decades, I have endeavored to list mainly such books as are of recent origin. Nevertheless, I could not overlook those of the older books which are in effect timeless, because their authors were endowed with degrees of knowledge and experience sufficiently great to enable them to produce works of permanent value.

I should like, finally, to say that in making the selections featured in the list I have tried to reduce to a minimum any bias of which I may be possessed. Perhaps the most acceptable assurance of the value of the list lies in the fact that whenever I consult any of the works it contains, I invariably add to my knowledge of management. It is my earnest hope that publication of the list may assist in opening up to students of management opportunities for equipping themselves, through study of the works in question, to deal more effectively with the complex problems of our troubled times.

I. Readings in Scientific Management

Because of their historic importance, works on scientific management are accorded priority of reference and comment. The fourteen works presented constitute a limited selection from among the greater number of publications available. In the preparation of the list, the attempt has been made to accomplish three objectives: to acquaint the present-day reader with the substance and evolution of scientific management, to give proper emphasis to certain specific works relating to this field, and to feature definitive appraisals of the lives and activities of the most distinguished of the leaders, *e.g.*, Taylor and Gantt.

The *Dartmouth Scientific Management Conference*,[1] * the first of its kind to be held, served to bring into focus the major aspects of the new doctrine as described by its chief exponents, many of whom took active parts in the proceedings. The conference owed its inception to the initiative of H. S. Person (then a member of the Tuck School faculty), a fact for which this foremost interpreter of Taylorian principles has never received adequate recognition.

Drury's *Scientific Management—A History and Criticism*,[2] prepared at a time still too soon after the event to permit of permanently valuable interpretation, nevertheless offers to students an opportunity for orientation, as well as somewhat intimate portraits of the leading figures. This work still has value for those who wish to become familiar with the origins and early development of scientific management.

Hunt's *Scientific Management Since Taylor* [3] presents, on the other hand, an evaluation which is authoritative, first of all, because it stems from men who were progenitors, catalysts or practitioners of various phases of the movement and, secondly, because it was sufficiently removed in point of time from its inception to warrant the conclusion that the perspectives employed are sound. Moreover, the work has the benefit of the labors of a sympathetic, understanding and capable editor.

Person's *Scientific Management in American Industry* [4] represents the most ambitious, and also the most successful, attempt at synthesis undertaken. It is a comprehensive treatise, based upon contributions by some twenty-six authors, and the single most authoritative source of information and interpretation with respect to scientific management at the disposal of the student. It is doubtful whether this work would have been possible without the expert guidance provided by its editor, H. S. Person, whose long years of study of the underlying philosophy are reflected admirably in the contributions of which he is the author.

The works listed as Nos. 5 to 11, inclusive, are hardly in need of specific reference. They are among the classics associated with scientific management; the names of their authors are familiar to every student of the field. Taken as a group, and de-

* NOTE: The numerals in this text refer to the list beginning on page 498.

spite the dissimilarity of their individual approaches to the broad problems they sought to solve, these pioneers laid the foundations for a new school of thought, a new philosophy, which has left its impress upon later generations.

Copley's biography of Taylor [12] and Alford's of Gantt [13] constitute adequate and able appraisals of these great leaders. It is to be hoped that before too long a time elapses similar studies of other leaders in the field of scientific management will become available. Clark's *The Gantt Chart*,[14] written by a close associate of Gantt, describes a technique originated by the latter for relating work planned and work performed to each other and to the time element. This little book has been translated into many languages and is of permanent value.

Selected List of Books on Scientific Management

1. SCIENTIFIC MANAGEMENT. *Addresses and Discussions at the Conference on Scientific Management held October 12-13-14, 1911.* Amos Tuck School of Administration and Finance, Dartmouth College, Hanover, New Hampshire, 1912. Pp. 388

2. SCIENTIFIC MANAGEMENT: *A History and Criticism.* By HORACE BOOKWALTER DRURY, Columbia University, New York, 1915. Pp. 222

3. SCIENTIFIC MANAGEMENT SINCE TAYLOR. *A Collection of Authoritative Papers. Edited by* EDWARD EYRE HUNT. McGraw-Hill Book Company, New York and London, 1924. Pp. xv + 263

4. SCIENTIFIC MANAGEMENT IN AMERICAN INDUSTRY. *By the* Taylor Society, HARLOW S. PERSON, *Editor.* Harper & Brothers, New York and London, 1929. Pp. xix + 479

5. THE PRINCIPLES OF SCIENTIFIC MANAGEMENT. By FREDERICK WINSLOW TAYLOR. Harper & Brothers, New York and London (1911) 1923. Pp. 144

6. SHOP MANAGEMENT. *By* FREDERICK WINSLOW TAYLOR. Harper & Brothers, New York and London, (1903) 1911. Pp. 207

7. INDUSTRIAL LEADERSHIP. *By* HENRY LAURENCE GANTT. Yale University Press, New Haven, Connecticut, 1916. Pp. xii + 128

8. WORK, WAGES AND PROFITS. *By* HENRY LAURENCE GANTT. Second Edition, The Engineering Magazine Company, New York (1910) 1919. Pp. 312

9. TWELVE PRINCIPLES OF EFFICIENCY. *By* HARRINGTON EMERSON. Fifth Edition, Engineering Magazine Company, New York (1911) 1919. Pp. xviii + 423

10. PRIMER OF SCIENTIFIC MANAGEMENT. *By* FRANK B. GILBRETH. Second Edition, D. Van Nostrand Company, New York, (1911) 1914. Pp. viii + 108

11. APPLIED MOTION STUDY. *By* FRANK B. *and* LILLIAN M. GILBRETH. Sturgis & Walton Company, New York, 1917. Pp. xviii + 220

12. FREDERICK W. TAYLOR, FATHER OF SCIENTIFIC MANAGEMENT. *By* FRANK BARKLEY COPLEY. Taylor Society, New York, 1923. Vol. I-Pp. xxviii + 467; Vol. II-Pp. vii + 472

13. HENRY LAURENCE GANTT, LEADER IN INDUSTRY. *By* LEON P. ALFORD. American Society of Mechanical Engineers, New York, 1934. Pp. xiii + 315

14. THE GANTT CHART. *By* WALLACE CLARK. The Ronald Press Company, New York, 1922. Pp. xii + 157

NOTE: *Figures shown in parentheses denote year of first publication.*

II. TWELVE INDISPENSABLE WORKS

The second part of the list deals with what I regard as indispensable works in the field of management. I submit it with suitable comments appended to each work chosen and with the candid admission that its preparation has constituted a labor of love, as well as an expression of my lasting intellectual obligation to the several authors represented.

1. THE PHILOSOPHY OF MANAGEMENT. *By* OLIVER SHELDON. Sir Isaac Pitman & Sons, Ltd., New York and London, 1923. Pp. xvi + 296

Since its publication over twenty years ago, this work has become a recognized classic. Written from a broad perspective, it stresses the importance of scientific and ethical principles, gives an excellent exposition of the social and industrial background, and deals in an authoritative manner with fundamentals of management. The author, an Oxford graduate and British industrialist, naturally reflects British viewpoints and practices; he writes with considerable charm of expression, and his exposition is at all times readily understandable. His treatment throughout is scholarly and intellectually stimulating.

2. INDUSTRIAL AND GENERAL ADMINISTRATION. *By* HENRI FAYOL. English Translation—Sir Isaac Pitman & Sons, Ltd., New York and London, 1930. Pp. 84. French Publisher—Dunod—Paris—1920. Pp. 174

A famous work by a great French engineer who died in 1925. His masterly analysis of the essential functions of a business enterprise, his selection among them of administration for special treatment leading to a statement of five underlying principles, and his advocacy of the latter in the form of the Administrative Doctrine, combined to lay the foundation for a new school of thought known as "Fayolism." With characteristic logic, Fayol expounded his theories over a long period of years, did not hesitate to defend them vigorously when they appeared to clash with the principles advocated by Taylor, and had the satisfaction before his death at an advanced age to see his contributions to the science of administration widely recognized and accepted.

3. TOP-MANAGEMENT ORGANIZATION AND CONTROL. *By* PAUL E. HOLDEN, LOUNSBURY S. FISH *and* HUBERT L. SMITH. Stanford University

Press, Stanford University, California, 1941. Pp. xvii + 239. London: Humphrey Milford—Oxford University Press

This work deals with a field which has hitherto been little explored. Instead of being the product of unverifiable personal experience, however, it belongs in the category of a scientific contribution to the sum total of knowledge in the field indicated. On the strength of their research study of the management policies and practices of thirty-one leading American industrial corporations, the authors have performed the signally valuable service of bringing together, in admirably organized form, a great amount of factual and interpretive material bearing upon some of the most important and complex management problems with which large-scale industrial organization is confronted.

4. THE PRINCIPLES OF ORGANIZATION. *By* James D. Mooney *and* Alan C. Reiley. Harper & Brothers, New York and London, 1939. Pp. x + 223

This is a scholarly treatment of the subject dominated to a large extent by the historic viewpoint. Recognizing the universality of organization, the authors devote the initial chapters of their work to an exposition of the coordinative, scalar and functional principles of organization and the staff phase of functionalism. The body of their treatise deals on a broad scale with principles of organization underlying such institutions as state, church, army and industry, and considerable space is devoted to a discussion of their evolution through various great epochs into which human progress may be divided. The final seven chapters concern themselves altogether with modern industrial organization and the present challenge to leadership. This is not a work which may be readily mastered. Its careful study will, however, supply the reader with a sound framework of principles which will serve excellently the purpose of orientation.

5. LECTURES ON ORGANIZATION. *By* Russell Robb. Delivered in the course on industrial organization at the Graduate School of Business Administration of Harvard University. Privately printed, 1910; pp. 68. Inquiries may be addressed to the Harry Arthur Hopf Memorial Management Library, Crotonville, New York.

This little work, consisting of three lectures is and has long been an American classic. The author, a distinguished engineer who died in 1927, brought admirably to expression in these lectures a varied experience distilled into a philosophy which, taken as a whole, constitutes perhaps the single most authoritative and appealing exposition stemming from an American to be found in the literature of organization. In the order given, the lectures deal with organization as affected by purpose and conditions, the limits of organization, and the organization of administration. Their study and mastery are essential to the attainment of a comprehensive understanding of the force of organization.

6. THE DESIGN OF MANUFACTURING ENTERPRISES. *By* WALTER RAUTENSTRAUCH. Pitman Publishing Corporation, New York and Chicago, 1941. Pp. x + 298.

For the successful conduct of any industrial enterprise, whether large or small, it is essential that an effective economic design be provided. This is the thesis advanced by the author, a noted authority in the field of industrial engineering and head of the Department of Industrial Engineering of Columbia University. Dr. Rautenstrauch devotes his work to a concise and illuminating exposition of all the major factors that must be considered in connection with attainment of the objective stated, dealing first with business as a whole and then considering a number of selected problems. Principles and methods supported by the author's wide and varied experience are fully presented and discussed, with a clarity of statement that makes for ready understanding and assimilation by the student.

7. INDUSTRIAL ORGANIZATION AND MANAGEMENT. *By* RALPH C. DAVIS. Harper & Brothers, New York and London, 1940. Pp. xxii + 636.

Among the general works on the subject, this book takes high rank. It is an exhaustive examination of problems of industrial organization and management introduced by a half-dozen chapters which comprise a thorough and singularly enlightening statement and discussion of basic material dealing with philosophy and principles. The author is well grounded in the literature of his field, facile in the interpretation of theory and practice, and reveals mastery of his subject by the competent and discriminating manner in which he has organized the presentation of his material. The book is of permanent value to both the practitioner and the student.

8. INDUSTRIAL MANAGEMENT. *By* RICHARD H. LANSBURGH and WILLIAM R. SPRIEGEL. Third Edition, John Wiley & Sons, Inc., New York, 1940. Pp. xi + 666.

This is the third edition of a well-known work by the late Richard H. Lansburgh, which was published over twenty years ago and in the intervening time has become a standard text on the subject. The current revision of the work was prepared by the authors with the principal aim in view of presenting a sound philosophy of management. Policies and principles are considered in the light of their successful application, and throughout the work a conscious effort has been made to induce development of a scientific state of mind toward business problems. The material presented is excellently organized and balanced as to relative importance; a valuable bibliography, arranged by subject, has been appended.

9. BUDGETARY CONTROL. *By* JAMES O. McKINSEY. Ronald Press Company, New York, 1922. Pp. viii + 474.

Although this work was published in 1922, and a great deal has been written on the subject of budgeting in the past twenty years, Prof. McKinsey's text has lost none of its value with the passage of time; it must still be regarded as an outstanding contribution. The author, whose untimely death in 1937 terminated a brilliant career as teacher, professional consultant and business executive, was noted for the penetrating character of his thinking and the lasting quality of his contributions to the solution of business problems. He was particularly gifted in the art of exposition, a fact of which there is abundant evidence in his writings.

10. PERSONNEL MANAGEMENT. *By* WALTER DILL SCOTT, ROBERT C. CLOTHIER, STANLEY B. MATHEWSON and WILLIAM R. SPRIEGEL. Third Edition, McGraw-Hill Book Company, New York and London, 1941. Pp. xii + 589.

Now in its third edition, this work is a text of recognized value in the field it aims to cover. Two distinguished pioneers in the scientific exploration of personnel problems, Dr. Scott and Dr. Clothier, who later became the chief administrators of well-known universities, were responsible for preparation of the original text, published in 1923. The second edition was brought out by Stanley B. Mathewson, and the current one has had the benefit of the collaboration of Dr. Scott and Dr. Spriegel. In connection with the latest revision, surveys of the practices of some 231 companies were undertaken and the results employed in guiding the conclusions of the authors. Students will find this work rich in background material, stimulating in the presentation of principles and practices, and pervaded by a thoroughly constructive attitude regarding the vitally important problems discussed.

11. FUNCTIONS OF THE EXECUTIVE. *By* CHESTER I. BARNARD. Harvard University Press, Cambridge, Massachusetts, 1938. Pp. xvi + 334.

To study and master this work constitutes an intellectual challenge. Originally prepared for a series of lectures at Lowell Institute in Boston, the material was later revised and expanded to the definitive form in which it was finally published. The author, a leading public utility executive with many years of experience in observing and dealing with problems of organization, has brought to bear upon his subject unusual powers of synthesis and the ability to harmonize effectively its theoretical and practical aspects. The breadth of perspective possessed by the author has enabled him to bring within the range of consideration a formidable array of fields of knowledge which serve to fortify the orientation he provides.

12. THE ART OF LEADERSHIP. *By* ORDWAY TEAD. McGraw-Hill Book Company, New York and London, 1935. Pp. xi + 308.

Addressing itself to examination of a "relatively unexplored art," this work, by a distinguished educator, author and interpreter of management, is of quite as much significance and value today as it was when published ten years ago. Leadership continues to be perhaps our single, most urgent problem in industry no less than in other walks of life. Here we have a contribution to an understanding of its meaning and methods written with a perspective and with convictions derived from deep study and broad experience. No reader can lay down this book without a feeling that he has become enriched by absorbing the products of its incisive and wise analysis of foremost imponderables in management.

III. Twenty-Four Recommended Works

The third part of the list embraces a total of twenty-four works, each of which is recommended to the reader as an able and illuminating discussion of the field it is designed to cover. In a few instances, these works are of so impressive a quality that it proved a difficult matter to draw lines of demarcation between them and the twelve works characterized as indispensable. Taken as a whole, the twenty-four works provide a thoroughly adequate foundation for the acquisition of a comprehensive knowledge of the substance of management.

1. SCIENCE AND PRACTICE OF MANAGEMENT. *By* A. Hamilton Church. The Engineering Magazine Company, New York, 1914. Pp. xviii + 535.

Because the author recognized that the "application of disconnected ideas, however valuable in their special place these may be, does not make a science," he sought to substitute for the disconnected ideas initially represented by the elements of scientific management, an approach to the reduction of the "regulative principles of management to their simplest terms." Thus he aimed "to provide a basic classification for administrative activity on which a detailed structure could subsequently be built up." The resulting study is in every sense of the word a pioneering effort of fundamental importance and value. Unfortunately, Church's contribution, due perhaps to lack of aggressive publicity, did not succeed in attracting lasting attention; before many years had elapsed, references to it began to pass from the pages of newer books. It is a privilege to rescue this work from the neglect it has suffered and to urge students to become familiar with the remarkable synthesis of management it presents.

2. HIGHER CONTROL IN MANAGEMENT. *By* T. G. Rose. Fourth Edition, Sir Isaac Pitman & Sons, Ltd., London, 1944. Pp. xvi + 279.

Since the time of publication of the first edition, in 1934, this work by an able English consultant in the field of management has won constantly increasing acceptance at the hands of the British public. It is written wholly from the viewpoint of supplying the type of information needed by a managing director to exercise effective control over the progress of the enterprise for whose success he is responsible. While the material used for illustrative purposes is drawn from British practice, American readers will obtain from it a clear insight into techniques which could with profit be applied to fostering more effective control of our own enterprises.

3. THE TECHNIQUE OF EXECUTIVE CONTROL. *By* ERWIN HASKELL SCHELL. Second Edition, McGraw-Hill Book Company, New York and London, 1934. Pp. x + 133.

When this little work appeared, in 1924, a reviewer of the New York Times expressed the opinion that the author had done a good and wise thing by publishing it. This opinion has stood the test of time, for there is as much to be gained from an appreciation of Prof. Schell's philosophy today as there was in the less informed but simpler period of twenty years ago. The author, one of our most distinguished educators in the field of business administration, brings to expression in his treatise sound, tolerant and constructive viewpoints whose appeal to executives of all types is undeniable. His contribution to an understanding of what must always remain a difficult art is of permanent value.

4. DYNAMIC ADMINISTRATION. *The Collected Papers of Mary Parker Follett. Edited by* HENRY C. METCALF *and* LYNDALL URWICK. Management Publications Trust, Ltd., New York and London, 1941. Pp. 320.

Described by the editors in their introduction to this work as a political and business philosopher of the first rank, Mary Parker Follett was a singularly gifted woman who devoted an exceedingly active life, which came to an end in 1933, to the study of broad political, social and industrial problems, with special emphasis on organization and administration. This collection of her papers, edited by two men who, apart from possessing unique qualifications for the task by reason of their respective backgrounds, had the inestimable advantage of personal association with her (the one in America and the other in England), brings to expression a profound philosophy whose teachings should become common knowledge among business administrators in all fields of enterprise.

5. THE ELEMENTS OF ADMINISTRATION. *By* LYNDALL URWICK. Harper & Brothers, New York, 1944. Pp. 132.

Administration is one of the most frequently misunderstood and, therefore, misapplied terms in the vocabulary of the business executive. Because problems of administration have steadily become more and more complicated, there has long existed a need for supplementing the meager literature of the subject with an authoritative exposition of its fundamentals. This task was undertaken by Col. Urwick, a noted English writer on administration and cognate subjects; the outcome represents a contribution of distinct value which is rapidly winning the approval of informed students of the field. Familiarity with the contents of this volume is bound to stimulate thinking along many collateral lines not suggested by its title.

6. ADMINISTRATIVE PROCEDURE. *By* COMSTOCK GLASER. American Council on Public Affairs, Washington, D.C., 1941. Pp. 207.

This work, which deals altogether with the business of government, contains on its title page the statement that it is a practical handbook for the administrative analyst. Dr. Glaser is too modest in thus describing the character of his treatise, for in it he not alone probes deeply into the "processes of administration and the anatomy of administrative organizations," but also enunciates a philosophy concerning administration in general which is one of its most stimulating and valuable features. The author is thoroughly familiar with the literature of the field, has been at great pains carefully to define the more important terms used in the text, and has succeeded in producing a work which is thoroughly readable and interesting. Students of administration, whether connected with government or industry, will find knowledge of this treatise essential to a better understanding of administration.

7. ADMINISTRATIVE PROFICIENCY IN BUSINESS. *By* ERWIN HASKELL SCHELL. McGraw-Hill Book Company, New York and London, 1936. Pp. x + 292.

It is the judgment of the author that in an industrial nation there is no more significant group of men than the business administrators. Prof. Schell has spent many years in preparing men for the ultimate acceptance of high responsibilities in the field of administration. From this long and varied experience he has distilled a certain philosophy, cultivated a way of reasoning, an outlook upon life, which are reflected in what he has written. The aim of this book is to analyze and delineate "those attainable qualities of personality and character that underlie proficiency." It is addressed not alone to men who are already versed in the technique of executive management, but also to "those younger businessmen of promise, who have early determined to prepare themselves, in point of education, training, and experience for future industrial positions of large responsibility." To both groups the author brings a message which cannot fail to impress by its authoritative character, its warmth of utterance, and the challenge to action by which it is animated. The work is admirably conceived and endowed with great potentialities for helpfulness.

8. FUNDAMENTALS OF BUSINESS ORGANIZATION. *By* WEBSTER ROBINSON. McGraw-Hill Book Company, New York and London, 1925. Pp. ix + 230.

This work constitutes one of the earlier attempts to formulate a synthesis in the field of organization. In it Dr. Robinson advanced the view (not at all generally accepted twenty years ago) that "regardless of the size or character of a business there are certain basic factors and relationships which are essential to its effective organization." The work is devoted to presentation and discussion of eight fundamentals of organization; these were so clearly perceived by the author that they remain valid despite the enormous changes in economic, social and political conditions which have occurred in the intervening time. In the light of accumulated knowledge and experience, a restatement of fundamentals undertaken now would doubtless result in a shift in emphasis and the inclusion of additional factors. The book is relatively small in compass and very well written; it should prove extremely helpful for purposes of general orientation.

9. PRINCIPLES OF ORGANIZATION. *By* HENRY P. DUTTON. McGraw-Hill Book Company, New York and London, 1931. Pp. x + 315.

In every respect a modern treatment of the subject, this work is distinguished by a scientific approach to the consideration of organization which embraces factors not usually brought within the range of discussion by other writers. In the first five chapters, the author presents a clear and convincing statement of fundamental principles entering into the general problem of organization. The next four chapters relate to the more concrete ground occupied by standardization, planning, division of duties, and the line organization. The following four chapters cover some of the psychological aspects of organization as expressed in the individual and his purposes, the individual and his group, group decision and group thinking. Of the final four chapters, three are devoted to consideration of the practical problems involved in selection and training, incentive, and discipline, and the last to the organization and its outside relations. The author is thoroughly steeped in his subject, his references to source material are discriminating and reflect a wide range of selection, and his style is such as to create sustained interest.

10. PRINCIPLES OF INDUSTRIAL ORGANIZATION. *By* DEXTER S. KIMBALL and DEXTER S. KIMBALL, JR. Fifth Edition, revised. McGraw-Hill Book Company, New York and London, 1939. Pp. xix + 478.

Originally published in 1913, this book has gone through five editions in the past thirty years and is still in demand as a standard work in the field it covers. In the preparation of the fourth and fifth editions, Dr. Kimball, Dean *Emeritus* of the College of Engineering, Cornell University, had the collaboration of his son, Dexter S. Kimball, Jr., also a teacher and practitioner of industrial engineering. The product of their labors extends beyond a discussion of principles of industrial organization, and includes consideration of the evolution of industry, the economic and social effects of inventions, the growth of industrial enterprises and of other industrial tendencies. The body of the work contains a wealth of material on major phases of organization; among the concluding chapters, those on cost finding, compensation of labor, measures of management and industrial relations should be singled out for special emphasis of their quality and value. Students will find this work a mine of information, presented in authoritative and readable manner.

11. BUSINESS ORGANIZATION AND MANAGEMENT. *By* ELMORE PETERSEN and E. GROSVENOR PLOWMAN. Richard D. Irwin, Inc., Chicago, 1941. Pp. xv + 691.

From the fact that this work runs to approximately six hundred pages, with almost another hundred devoted to presentation of supplemental material for teaching purposes, an excellent bibliography and a very well constructed index, one may conclude that the authors have labored long and earnestly in its preparation. They have labored to good purpose, for although their treatment is not exactly inspired—indeed, in some respects is rather pedestrian—the product constitutes a soundly conceived, well integrated and exhaustive discussion of basic theory and principles. This work is especially designed for use as a college textbook, but the seasoned practitioner will discover in it much that will prove helpful in clarifying his perceptions of the field covered. The numerous diagrams, charts and other illustrations, most of which stem from the authors, are one of its praiseworthy features.

12. ORGANIZATION ENGINEERING. *By* HENRY DENNISON. McGraw-Hill Book Company, New York and London, 1931. Pp. viii + 204.

Between the covers of this little book, the author has compressed into an admirable statement a distillation of much that he has learned about organization in a lifetime of activity as a business executive and a leader devoted to the cause of science and the humanities. Mr. Dennison prefaces his text with the statement that it is intended to be suggestive rather than comprehensive and that "a special effort is made to offer an ordering of the whole subject matter which will help a further systematic development of the science and art of organization engineering, and increase the amount of research devoted to it." The significance of the work derives from the authority with which Mr. Dennison speaks; its value is enhanced by his ripe philosophy and the simplicity and directness of statement so effectively employed.

13. PRINCIPLES OF INDUSTRIAL MANAGEMENT FOR ENGINEERS. *By* LEON P. ALFORD. The Ronald Press Company, New York, 1940. Pp. xxii + 531.

Completed by the author within less than two years of his untimely death, in 1942, this work may be characterized as a synthesis of the results of his long-continued labors and researches in the field of management. By reason of his intimate connection with all stages of evolution in this field from the inception of the scientific management movement, as well as of his contributions as a scientist and interpreter of principles, Dr. Alford was in a unique position to prepare a comprehensive text that would present in definitive form the principles and methods of industrial administration and management. This he accomplished with great success; moreover, guided by his engineering training and habits of thought, he made adequate use of mathematical analysis in furnishing quantitative answers to specific management problems. While this work was written primarily as a college text, it qualifies also as a valuable reference book for operating executives.

14. THE SCIENCE OF PRODUCTION ORGANIZATION. *By* E. H. ANDERSON and G. T. SCHWENNING. John Wiley & Sons, Inc., New York, 1938. Pp. x + 282.

Two scholars engaged in the teaching of business administration at the University of North Carolina combined forces to produce this work. They recognized the need for publication of a book that would appraise and integrate the thoughts of numerous writers on the various aspects of organization. From perhaps as wide a range of examination of the pertinent literature as is disclosed in the writings of any other author in the field, Drs. Anderson and Schwenning have prepared a text which constitutes a scientific approach to the study of organization. The authors take the position that there is a science of organization and that it is the product of evolution rather than of a single theory. One does not have to agree with all of their conclusions to acknowledge that they have made a scholarly contribution to a better understanding of problems that are among the greatest confronting industry and society today. This is a text of finished form and content which, if only for the wealth of definitions it contains, should be a welcome addition to any management library.

15. PERSONNEL ADMINISTRATION: ITS PRINCIPLES AND PRACTICE. *By* ORDWAY TEAD and HENRY C. METCALF. Third Edition, McGraw-Hill Book Company, New York and London, 1933. Pp. xiv + 519.

Published originally in 1920, this work is among the earliest dealing comprehensively with the field of human relations in industry. During the twenty-five years it has been available to the public, sweeping changes in economic and social conditions have occurred; these have naturally created the need for revising earlier concepts of the scope and objectives of personnel administration. Comparison of the first and third editions of this work demonstrates, however, that while the text of the latter has been amplified in some respects and shortened in others, the pattern of the original was constructed in so fundamental and penetrating a manner that it has required little modification. The authors, one of whom (Dr. Metcalf) died three years ago, have paralleled in their own development the most significant stages of evolution of the personnel movement; in fact, as pioneers in the field, they have contributed in no small measure to the increasing recognition of sound principles and enlightened practices.

16. PERSONNEL MANAGEMENT AND INDUSTRIAL RELATIONS. *By* DALE YODER. Prentice-Hall, Inc., New York, 1942. Pp. xxii + 848.

Based on an earlier work under a slightly different title, this volume, of encyclopædic character and proportions, presents a treatment of the subject complete enough to satisfy even the most exacting requirements. In its 848 pages (including the index), the author has carefully considered not only the various phases of personnel administration from selection to superannuation, but also the more dynamic aspects of industrial relations as they have developed during the past decade and a half. Dr. Yoder's background as an economist and his varied experience in important capacities in public service have equipped him to apply a broad perspective to the consideration of personnel problems and to give due weight to the essential function of scientific research in their solution. The extensive references to statistical methods and materials provide a rather unusual feature in a book of this character, justified no doubt by the increasing need for science to prevail in a field where uninformed and prejudiced opinion has often frustrated ascertainment of the truth.

17. PERSONNEL RELATIONS. *By* J. E. WALTERS. The Ronald Press Company, New York, 1945. Pp. xx + 547.

Written largely out of the broad and varied experience of its author, this work considers the problem of personnel relations as it may be interpreted in a setting of democracy. In contrast with approaches made by other writers, the author initiates his discussion by naming workers, management and the government as the principal determinants of personnel relations; in that order he proceeds to develop his subject. The reader comes to grips at once with the dynamics of labor unions; he is then introduced to organized concepts of personnel relations as they have gradually been accepted by management. Part Three, comprising twelve chapters, affords a clear and comprehensive view of the host of techniques that must be utilized in order to do justice to specific practical problems. The five chapters of Part Four are concerned with the impacts of governmental co-operation and regulation, and the last part presents the case for greater co-operation among the three principal determinants, with a summary of the ideals whose attainment should be sought. This is the latest work on the subject to appear; it is fundamental in approach, objective and informed in treatment, and stands as a scholarly contribution to the literature.

18. MANAGEMENT AND THE WORKER. *By* F. J. ROETHLISBERGER and W. J. DICKSON. Harvard University Press, Cambridge, Massachusetts, 1939. Pp. xxiv + 615.

This work is in the nature of a descriptive and analytical report on perhaps the most extended and sustained scientific investigation of human beings at work of which there is a record. The famous "Hawthorne Experiments," a series of inquiries into the human effect of work and working conditions, were initiated at the Hawthorne Works of the Western Electric Company, Chicago, in 1927 and continued until 1932. For a period of six or seven years thereafter, scientists connected with various phases of the investigation devoted themselves to the preparation and publication of findings, conclusions and other data derived from the investigation. F. J. Roethlisberger, Associate Professor of Industrial Research of the Harvard Graduate School of Business Administration, and W. J. Dickson, Chief of Employee Relations Research Department of the Western Electric Company, were continuously associated with the project; as authors of this volume they have rendered a signal service to students of management everywhere. It is much to be regretted that so few practitioners are familiar with its contents.

19. EXECUTIVE SALARIES AND BONUS PLANS. *By* JOHN CALHOUN BAKER. McGraw-Hill Book Company, New York and London, 1938. Pp. xxiv + 274.

Among the most difficult problems confronting business today are those relating to the compensation of executives. Comparatively little has been written on this subject, due probably to the fact that prior to a decade or so ago, facts concerning prevailing practices were not available, except in fugitive form. Save for the study by F. W. Taussig and W. S. Barker, published in the Quarterly Journal of Economics, November, 1925, this work is the first to deal analytically with the problem on the basis of extensive statistical data. The author, at the time of publication of his study Associate Director of Research of the Graduate School of Business Administration of Harvard University, obtained his source material from the Federal Trade Commission and the Securities and Exchange Commission. Although he makes no pretensions to having developed a theory or philosophy about executive payments, he has made available the results of research which, despite rapidly changing conditions and the lapse of time, are of current interest and should act as stimuli and guides to further investigations.

20. SALARY DETERMINATION. *By* JOHN W. RIEGEL. Bureau of Industrial Relations, University of Michigan, Ann Arbor, Michigan, 1940. Pp. 278.

Equitable salary determination is one of the most effective devices or tools which may be employed by management to motivate the attitudes of employees and lay a sound foundation for increased accomplishment. Dr. Riegel's study is based upon a survey made by him of common policies and selected practices in forty American corporations engaged in a variety of activities, including manufacturing, public utilities, retailing, banking, insurance, etc. To delimit the area of his investigation, he confined himself to the second and third of the following four groups: (1) wage earners, (2) routine workers on salary, (3) managers and technicians paid less than $10,000. per year, and (4) top executives. His primary purpose was to organize and clarify major considerations involved in salary determination. He has brought together a large amount of useful information on various aspects of salary administration and has presented it in logical sequence, with conciseness of statement. Familiarity with the contents of this book should prove helpful to all executives struggling with the intricacies of the problems discussed.

21. MOTION AND TIME STUDY. *By* RALPH M. BARNES. Second Edition, John Wiley & Sons, Inc., New York, 1940. Pp. xi + 390.

Motion and time analyses are among the best known and most spectacular techniques created and utilized by the pioneers in scientific management. Taylor originated time study in order to provide a basis for rate setting; the Gilbreths developed motion study in furtherance of their search for the principles and techniques underlying the "one best way" of performing a task. Dr. Barnes, a member of the faculty of the College of Engineering, University of Iowa, has long been noted for his deep scientific interest in the field of motion and time study and for the results which have attended the researches in which he and his associates are constantly engaged. The first edition of this work was published in 1937; the second edition, with certain features enlarged upon and more illustrative material included, appeared three years later. It has found wide approval as a *vade-mecum* for students and practitioners.

22. WAGE INCENTIVE METHODS. *By* CHARLES WALTER LYTLE. Revised Edition. The Ronald Press Company, New York, 1942. Pp. xix + 462.

Prof. Lytle's work, originally published in 1929, appeared thirteen years later in a revised and enlarged edition. As the author himself inferred on this occasion, the lapse of time occurring between the first and second editions had permitted the evolution of wage incentives to proceed to a point at which "the principles and techniques which can now be presented amount virtually to a science." This work is exhaustive in scope, authoritative in manner of treatment, and stimulating throughout to the reader who desires to inform himself concerning theory and practice in an important but highly technical field of management. As a thorough student and teacher, Prof. Lytle has not failed to provide his work with a great number of graphic illustrations and tables of immense practical aid to the reader. They are splendidly reproduced and constitute a tribute to the craftsmanship of the printer.

23. MIDDLE MANAGEMENT. *By* MARY CUSHING HOWARD NILES. Harper & Brothers, New York and London, 1941. Pp. xi + 270.

Middle management is the term—and it is a good one—that the author has chosen to apply to the occupants of those levels of the organizational structure located immediately below the zone of top management. The author describes them as "junior administrators" and classifies them as department heads, with responsibility for indirect supervision of a hundred or more, in many cases several hundred, persons. The book is devoted to consideration of the problems of the junior administrator; on the strength of diversified experience as a consultant, primarily to insurance companies, Mrs. Niles includes within its compass the products of keen analysis of environmental factors and human relationships, pervaded by a thorough understanding of the broader concerns of management. Written with simplicity, earnestness and a commendable quality of objectivity, this work should prove of practical value to junior administrators ambitious to make the most of their potentialities and opportunities.

24. TEXTBOOK OF OFFICE MANAGEMENT. *By* WILLIAM HENRY LEFFINGWELL and EDWIN MARSHALL ROBINSON. McGraw-Hill Book Company, New York and London, 1943. Pp. xiii + 469.

Despite the fact that the literature includes a number of volumes relating to the subject of office management, this work by the late William Henry Leffingwell, which originally appeared in 1932, must still be ranked as the leading text of its kind. The revision undertaken by Prof. Robinson has had the effect of giving greater coherence to the structure of the book and of strengthening it in other respects for teaching purposes. In all its essential aspects, including the statement of principles which Leffingwell so ably presented and expounded, the book has remained substantially unaltered.

It constitutes the product of long experience by a distinguished authority and should be read and digested by all office managers who wish to think and act in terms of fundamentals.

*　　　*　　　*

In bringing this omnibus review to a close, it may not be amiss to stress the fact that the guiding principle adhered to in doing justice to the problem of selection was to favor, wherever possible, works that would contribute to enlargement of the reader's intellectual horizon. While I fully recognize the important role played by specialization in the attainment of operating results, I have encountered its atrophying effects too often in management to rest content with any other course.

In management we need more educated men and fewer specialists. We need far more the capacity to think in terms of fundamentals than the ability to be facile in the use of instruments of precision. We need more philosophers with a spirit of inquiry dominated by broad perspective and fewer technicians whose customary approach only too often narrows down to a point. Above all, we need men whose intellectual equipment will enable them to accept and to act upon the implications of the optimum.

If as the result of reading the works included in the foregoing list broader perspectives and more lasting intellectual stimuli are provided to only a handful of students or practitioners of management, the labor involved in its preparation will not have been in vain.

DATE DUE

MR 19 '64			
AG 7 '90			
DE 11 90			
GAYLORD			PRINTED IN U.S.A.